The Stephen King Companion

Revised Edition

Other Andrews and McMeel books
by George Beahm

The Stephen King Story

War of Words: The Censorship Debate

Michael Jordan: A Shooting Star

The Stephen King Companion

Revised Edition

Edited by
GEORGE BEAHM

Andrews and McMeel
A Universal Press Syndicate Company
Kansas City

For information write: Andrews and McMeel,
a Universal Press Syndicate Company, 4900 Main Street,
Kansas City, Missouri 64112.

Library of Congress Cataloging-in-Publication Data

The Stephen King companion / edited by George W. Beahm. — Rev. ed.
    p. cm.
    Includes bibliographical references.
    ISBN 0-8362-0455-7
    1. King, Stephen, 1947–   —Criticism and interpretation.
    2. Horror tales, American—History and criticism. I. Beahm, George W.
PS3561.I483Z88   1995
813'.54—dc20   95-23170
                                          CIP

See page 309 for continuation of copyright notice.
Cover photography by Thomas Kristich.
Book design: Hillside Studio, Inc.
Composition: Connell Zeko Type and Graphics
First edition.

ATTENTION: SCHOOLS AND BUSINESSES

Andrews and McMeel books are available at quantity discounts
with bulk purchase for educational, business, or sales promotional
use. For information, write to: Special Sales Department, Andrews and
McMeel, 4900 Main Street, Kansas City, Missouri 64112.

for Mary

Stephen King in downtown Bangor.

Contents

Part 1
The Real World of Stephen King

Part 2
The Unreal World of Stephen King

Publishing

Writing

Part 3:
🕮 Chronological Look at the Books
by Michael R. Collings

Three-headed creature sits atop a corner of the fence fronting the King residence in Bangor.

**I think with the best writing you actually
feel the writer's joy, the writer's vision,
or something like that. God,
it's a strange way to make a living.
It's a child's activity, really.**

Stephen King, from "The Author Talks" (Recorded Books, 1987)

As Kierkegaard said so well, "The self is only that which it is
in the process of becoming." Art, same thing.

Chris Stevens, Cicely's philosopher/deejay on "Northern Exposure"

*

I first heard of George Beahm in the early eighties when I was working on my
second book, *The Complete Stephen King Encyclopedia.*

My publisher, Tom Schultheiss, told me that George had called and introduced himself and informed him that he too was working on a book about
Stephen King.

After Tom had a brief conversation with George, it became obvious to both
of us that George and I were traveling parallel literary paths, but in vastly different vehicles, and so we both went forward with our King tomes.

I finally got to speak to George a short time after that and, like the epi-
grammatic Chris Stevens on "Northern Exposure" who meets his long-lost
brother, George and I became immediate and devoted friends.

George's book, *The Stephen King Companion,* was published about the
same time as my *King Encyclopedia,* and now, several years later, George is publishing a revised and expanded edition of his book, just as I am beginning work
on an expanded edition of my own King volume.

Carl Jung, who developed the theory of synchronicity, believed that there was
no such thing as random coincidence. Ol' Carl was probably on to something.
George and I are about the same age, have similar tastes and interests, both
work in popular culture, and, perhaps most important, get each other's jokes.
And George Beahm is the only colleague with whom I am totally open about
my new book ideas. It's difficult to know whom to trust today, yet I trust George
Beahm. And even though you could technically describe us as rivals (since we
are both clamoring for that part of King's audience that also buys books *about*

Big Steve), there has never been a millisecond of competitive skirmishing between us.

I have always been impressed with George Beahm's fervent work ethic and forthright honesty. George is a man of staunch character who is the living embodiment of what it means to be a genuine writer. As I have said in the past, George has a writer's soul and is completely devoted to his art. And his craft.

Our respective books—*The Stephen King Companion* and *The Complete Stephen King Encyclopedia*—were both labors of love. George and I each wrote our King books because we believed they were necessary, and because we are both King fans of the first rank. We take King and his work seriously and it is our hope that the two of us have done our share toward neutralizing (and, I hope, refuting) any number of vitriolic reviews of King's work.

George and I both see Stephen King as an important American writer.

George brought a lot to the original *Companion*. He gave King's readers a place to go for more information about the novels, the short stories, the movies, and, yes, the man.

George has an accessible writing style, and when it comes to research, he has the admirable ability of being able to coalesce and lucidly deconstruct large amounts of information and make that information readable and, more important, usable.

Stephen King has not shown any indications of slowing down. *Insomnia* is a number-one hit; he's planning on completing the *Dark Tower* series within the next few years; several movies based on his stories are in the works; he completed a tour with his "band," the Rock Bottom Remainders (the gang-written book about the tour, *Mid-Life Confidential,* is hilarious); and he did a cross-country book-signing tour for *Insomnia* on his *motorcycle.*

His is a wide-ranging career, and he personally has an eclectic and catholic farrago of interests.

King's pervasive inquisitiveness (he apparently reads everything he can get his hands on) invests his work with a texture and depth that define the Stephen King "voice." And they also allow a naturally prolific writer like King to continue to stretch and grow as an artist. To quote Chris Stevens, "Repetition is the death of art," and King has been consciously and deliberately attempting to expand his narrative vision with every new story.

That, perhaps, is the single element most responsible for an inordinately successful career that, as of this writing, spans more than two decades.

King's prodigious output gives writers like George and myself a lot to work with. King's fans want to know more about King and his work and, thus, we have our work cut out for us. God *is* in the details, and it is the noble job of people like George Beahm to put King and his work under the magnifying glass and tell his fans what he sees. There is opinion, and then there is *informed* opinion. George Beahm, in his original *Stephen King Companion,* provided fans with insights and opinions about King's work that helped them better understand and, of course, enjoy the work of their favorite writer.

And this new and improved edition of *The Stephen King Companion* continues that tradition.

Once again, George Beahm has lovingly turned his attention to the works of King, and presented facts about that work in an informative, entertaining package that, if my intuition speaks the truth, will simply send King's fans out to the stores to pick up the tales which they haven't read, but which George Beahm describes so invitingly.

This expanded edition of *The Stephen King Companion* is a welcome addition to the libraries of books about King, and it is my honor to step in front of the closed curtain and be the one to announce, "Ladies and gentlemen … I give you George Beahm."

A spider-motif gate at the King residence in Bangor.

Editor's Preface to the New Edition

When Andrews and McMeel published the original edition of *The Stephen King Companion* in 1989, neither they nor I realized that we would popularize the companion-book format. My modest hope was that the book would earn back the advance, buy me some time to spend a few months off to write another book, and share my enthusiasm for King's work with fellow readers.

The book exceeded my wildest expectations. In fact, it inspired several other companion books: *The Woody Allen Companion, The Robert Ludlum Companion, The Louis L'Amour Companion, The Tom Clancy Companion*, et al.

How successful was the book? Successful enough to warrant a new edition, which is a polite way of saying it was a critical and financial success—and a happy proof of the durability of Stephen King's appeal. The only drawback was that, with each passing year, the book showed its age.

Recently, when it became obvious that the book's reference material was hopelessly out of date, as was a large portion of the main text, I knew that an expanded and revised edition was warranted.

As it turned out, the book is not simply an expanded and revised edition— the original intent. This book is, in the main, a new book. I've retained some articles from the original edition, but they are the exceptions.

To the readers who bought the original edition and came back for more: it's good to see you again. And if you are a new King reader: welcome aboard.

For the record, there are two major differences between this edition and the previous one: Part Three of the original edition was composed of an alphabetical book-by-book look at King's fiction, written by me; this time, the book-by-book look is written by Dr. Michael R. Collings, who shares a double distinction as the most highly regarded King critic and the most prolific King critic for output. The book is immeasurably better for it; or as my book editor, Donna Martin, put it: "I agree with you that his assessments are uniformly excellent. His writing gives a certain authority both to King and to himself. It was a terrific idea to have him assess the books."

The second major difference is that the appendices have been deleted, and for an obvious reason: they most quickly date themselves; after a few years, the brand-new coat begins to look threadbare. (In the case of the price guide, written with Barry R. Levin, the problem was compounded: a price guide is most useful when it's a "moving" document, updated constantly, instead of being fixed in stone between the pages of a book that has an extended shelf life.)

For those of you who want the updated information, it's available in my quarterly newsletter, *Phantasmagoria* (see page 108), which also updates the appendices annually.

George Beahm

Williamsburg, Virginia
April 1995

The Stephen King
Companion

Stephen King at a press conference in Washington, D.C., at the American Booksellers Association convention.

Introduction
Surviving the Ride
by Clive Barker

The tygers of wrath are wiser than the horses of instruction.

William Blake, *The Marriage of Heaven and Hell*

*

First, a confession: I have no thesis. I come to these pages without an overview to propound; only a substantial enthusiasm for the work of Stephen King and a potpourri of thoughts on fear, fiction, dreams, and geographies which may bear some tenuous relation to one another and to King's fiction.

Theoretical thinking was never a great passion of mine, but ghost-trains are. And it's with a ghost-train I begin.

It's called—ambitiously enough—*L'Apocalypse*. To judge from the size of the exterior, the ride it houses is an epic; the vast, three-tiered facade dwarfs the punters who mill around outside, staring up with a mixture of trepidation and appetite at the hoardings, and wondering if they have the nerve to step out of the heat of the sun and into the stale darkness that awaits them through the swinging doors.

Surely, they reassure themselves, no fun-fair can be as bad as the paintings that cover every inch of the building suggest: for the pictures record atrocities that would have turned de Sade's stomach.

They're not particularly good paintings; they're rather too crudely rendered, and the gaudy primaries the artists have chosen seem ill suited to the subject matter. But the eye flits back and forth over the horrors described here, unable to disengage itself. In one corner, a shackled man is having his head sliced off; it seems to leap out at us, propelled by a geyser of scarlet blood. A few yards from this, above a row of arches that are edged with canary-yellow lights, a man watches his bowels being drawn from his abdomen by a cardinal in an advanced state of decomposition. Beside the entrance booth, a crucified woman is being burned alive in a chamber lined with white-hot

1

Photo by Carroll Hall, courtesy of the *Bangor Daily News*

Stephen King in front of his home in Bangor.

swords. We might be tempted to laugh at such *grand guignol* excesses, but we cannot. They are, for all the roughness of their presentation, deeply disturbing.

I've never ridden *L'Apocalypse*. I know it only as a photograph, culled from a magazine some dozen years ago, and treasured since. The photograph still speaks loudly to me. Of the indisputable glamour of the horrible; of its power to enthrall and repulse simultaneously. And it also reminds me—with its sweaty-palmed punters queuing beneath a crystal blue sky for a chance at the dark—that nobody ever lost money offering a good ride to Hell.

Which brings us, inevitably, to the architect of the most popular ghost-train rides in the world: Mr. Stephen King.

It's perhaps redundant, in a book celebrating Stephen King's skills, for me to list his merits at too great a length. We, his readers and admirers, know them well. But it may be worth our considering exactly *what* he's selling us through the charm and accessibility of his prose, the persuasiveness of his characters, the ruthless drive of his narratives.

He's selling death. He's selling tales of blood-drinkers, flesh-eaters, and the decay of the soul; of the destruction of sanity, community, and faith. In his fiction, even love's power to outwit the darkness is uncertain; the monsters will devour that too, given half a chance. Nor is innocence much of a defense. Children go to the grave as readily as the adult of the species, and those few resurrections that circumstances grant are not likely to be the glory promised from the pulpit.

Not, one would have thought, a particularly commercial range of subjects. But in King's hands their salability can scarcely be in question. He has turned the horror genre—so long an underdog on the publishing scene—into a force to be reckoned with.

Many reasons have been put forward for King's popularity. A common element in most of the theories is his *plausibility* as a writer. In the novels—though rather less in the short stories—he describes the confrontation between the real and the fantastic elements so believably that the reader's rational sensibilities are seldom, if ever, outraged. The images of power, of loss, of transformation, of wild children and terrible hotels, of beasts mythological and beasts rabid and beasts human—all are dropped so cunningly into the texture of the world he conjures, morsel upon morsel, that by the time our mouths are full, we're perfectly willing to swallow.

The net effect is akin to taking that ride on *L'Apocalypse,* only finding that the dummies on either side of the track, enacting over and over their appalling death scenes, closely resemble people we know. The horror is intensified immeasurably. We are no longer simple voyeurs, watching some artificial atrocity unfold in front of our eyes. We are intimately involved with the sufferers. We share their traumas and their terrors. We share too their hatred of their tormentors.

This is by no means the only approach to writing dark fantasy, of course. Many authors choose to plunge their readers into the world of the subconscious (which is, surely, the territory such fiction charts) with scarcely a glance over their shoulders at the "reality" the reader occupies. In the geography of the *fantastique,* for instance, Prince Prospero's castle—sealed so inadequately against the Red Death—stands far deeper in the world of pure dream than does the Overlook Hotel, whose rooms, though no less haunted by violent death, are far more realistically evoked than Poe's baroque conceits.

There are, inevitably, losses and gains on both sides. Poe sacrifices a certain accessibility by his method; one has to embrace the fictional conventions he has employed before the story can be fully savored. He gains, however, a mythic resonance which is out of all proportion to the meager pages *The Masque of the Red Death* occupies. He has, apparently, effortlessly, written himself into the landscape of our dreams.

King's method—which requires the establishing of a far more elaborate fictional "reality"—wins out through our commitment *to* that reality, and to the characters who inhabit it. It also earns the power to subvert our sense of the real, by showing us a world we think we know, then revealing another view of it entirely. What I believe he loses in the trade-off is a certain *ambiguity*. This I'll return to later.

First, a couple of thoughts on subversion. It has been argued, and forcibly, that for all the paraphernalia of revolution contained in King's fiction—the weak discovering unlooked-for strength (or promise) of transformation; a sense barely hidden beneath the chatty surface of the prose, that mythic elements are being juggled here—that, despite all this apocalyptic stuff, the author's worldview is at heart a conservative one. Is he perhaps a sheep in wolf's clothing, distressing us to cling closer to the values that his monsters jeopardize?

I admit to having some sympathy with this argument, and I admire most those of his tales which seem to show the world irredeemably changed, with no hope of a return to the comfortable, joyless, death-in-life that seems to be the late twentieth-century ideal. But if there is evidence that gives weight to such argument, there is also much in King's work that is genuinely subversive: imagery that evokes states of mind and conditions of flesh which, besides exciting our anxieties, excite also our desires and our perversities.

Why, you may ask, do I put such a high value upon subversion?

There are many reasons. The most pertinent here is my belief that fantastic fiction offers the writer exceptional possibilities in that direction, and I strongly believe a piece of work (be it play, book, poem) should be judged according to how enthusiastically it seizes the opportunity to do what it can do *uniquely*. The literature of the fantastic—and the movies, and the paintings—can reproduce, at its best, the texture of experience more closely than any "naturalistic" work, because it can embrace the complexity of the world we live in.

Which is to say: our minds. That's where we live, after all. And our minds are extraordinary melting pots, in which sensory information, and the memory of same, and intellectual ruminations, and nightmares, and dreams, simmer in an ever-richer stew. Where else but in works called (often pejoratively) *fantasies* can such a mixture of elements be placed side by side?

And if we once embrace the vision offered in such works, if we once allow the metaphors a home in our psyches, the subversion is under way. We may for the first time see ourselves as a *totality*—valuing our appetite for the forbidden rather than suppressing it, comprehending that our taste for the strange, or the morbid, or the paradoxical, is contrary to what we're brought up to believe, a sign of our good health. So I say—*subvert*. And never apologize.

That's one of King's crowning achievements. From the beginning, he's never apologized, never been ashamed to be a horror author. He values the *genre,* and if horror fiction is in turn more valued now than it was ten or twenty years ago it is surely in no small degree his doing. After all, the most obsessive of rationalists must find it difficult to ignore the man's existence: he's read on buses and trains; in universities and hospitals; by the good, the bad, and the morally indifferent.

At this juncture it may be worth remembering that the dreams he is usually concerned to evoke are normally known not as dreams but as *nightmares.* This is in itself worthy of note. We have other classes of dreams which are as common as nightmares. Erotic dreams, for instance; dreams of humiliation. But it's only the dream of terror which has been graced with a special name, as though we recognize that this experience, of all those that come to us in sleep, carries some essential significance. Is it perhaps that in our waking lives we feel (rightly or wrongly) that we have control over all other responses but that of fear? Certainly we may use the word *nightmare* freely to describe waking experience ("the traffic was a nightmare," we casually remark), but seldom do our lives reach that pitch of terror—accompanied by the blood-chilling sense of inevitability—that informs the dream of dread.

In reading a good piece of horror fiction, we may dip into the dreaming state at will; we may even hope to interpret some of the signs and signals that nightmares deliver to us. If not that, at least there is some comfort in knowing that these images are *shared.*

(An aside. One of the pleasures of any fiction is comparing the intricacies of response with other readers, but this process takes on a wonderfully paradoxical quality when two horror enthusiasts are exchanging views on a favorite book or film. The gleeful detailing of the carnage, the shared delight, as the key moments of revulsion and anxiety are remembered: we smile, talking of how we sweated.)

There are many kinds of nightmare. Some have familiar, even domestic settings, in which commonplace particulars are charged up with uncanny and inexplicable power to intimidate. It is this kind of nightmare that King is most adept at evoking, and the kind with which he is probably most readily identified. It is in a way a natural progression from rooting outlandish horrors—*Carrie; 'Salem's Lot*—in settings so familiar we might occupy them, to making objects *from* those settings (a dog, a car) themselves the objects of anxiety. I must say I prefer the earlier books by quite a measure, but that's in part because the Apocalypses conjured seem so much more comprehensive, and I have a practically limitless appetite for tales of the world turned inside out.

The other kind of nightmare is a different experience entirely and it is not, at least in the conventional sense, about threat. I mean the kind of dream voyage that takes you out of any recognizable context, and into some other state entirely. The kind that lifts you up (perhaps literally; for me such nightmares often begin with falling that turns into flight) and whips you away to a place both familiar and utterly new, utterly strange. You have never been to this place in your waking life, of that your dreaming self is certain; but there are presences here familiar to you, and sights around every corner that you will recognize even as they astonish you.

What actually happens on these voyages will run from the banal to the Wagnerian, depending on the dreamer's sense of irony, but the way this second sort of nightmare operates upon your psyche is totally different from the first. For one thing, the fears dealt with in the first sort are likely to be susceptible to analysis. They are fears of authority figures, or terminal disease, or making love to mother. But the second kind is, I believe, rooted not in the specifics of the personality, but in something more primitive; something that belongs to our response as thought-haunted matter to the world we're born into. The images that come to overwhelm us in this region are not, therefore, projections of neurosis; they are things vast; contradictory; mythological.

King can conjure such stuff with the best of them; I only regret that his brilliance as a creator of domestic demons has claimed him from writing more of that other region. When he turns his hand to it, the effect is stunning. *The Mist*, for example, is a story that begins in familiar King territory, and moves through a variety of modes—including scenes which, in their mingling of the monstrous and the commonplace work as high, grim comedy—toward a world lost to humanity, a world that echoes in the imagination long after the book has been closed. In the final section of the story the survivors encounter a creature so vast it doesn't even notice the protagonists:

> Its skin was deeply wrinkled and grooved, and clinging to it were scores, hundreds, of those pinkish "bugs" with the stalk-eyes. I don't know how big it actually was, but it passed directly over us. . . . Mrs. Repper said later she could not see the underside of its body, although she craned her neck up to look. She saw only two Cyclopean legs going up and up into the mist like living towers until they were lost to sight.

There is much more of breathtaking imaginative scope in *The Stand*, and in a more intimate, though no less persuasive fashion, in *The Shining* and *'Salem's Lot*. Moments when the terror becomes something more than a fight for life with

A display of banned King novels in a bookstore in Williamsburg, Virginia, during Banned Books Week.

an unwelcome intruder; when the horror reveals itself, even in the moment of causing us to recoil, as a source of fascination and awe and self-comprehension.

This is the root of the ambiguity which I spoke of before, and to which I said I would return. *Wanting* an encounter with forces that will change our lives—that will deliver us once and for all into the regions of the gods ("I had a dream that I saw God walking across Harrison on the far side of the lake, a God so gigantic that above the waist He was lost in a clear blue sky"—The Mist)—yet fearful that we are negligible things and so far beneath the concern of such powers that any confrontation will simply kill us.

Charting that ambiguity is, I would suggest, a function that the fantasy genre can uniquely fulfill. It is perhaps the liability of King's virtues that such ambiguity is often forfeited in exchange for a straightforward identification with the forces of light. King's monsters (human, subhuman, and Cyclopean) may on occasion be *comprehensible* to us, but they seldom exercise any serious claim on our sympathies. They are moral degenerates, whose colors are plain from the outset. We watch them kick dogs to death and devour children, and we are reinforced in the questionable certainty that we are not like them; that *we* are on the side of the angels.

Now *that's* fiction. We are not. Darkness has a place in all of us; a substantial place that must, for our health's sake, be respected and investigated.

After all, one of the reasons we read tales of terror is surely that we have an *appetite* for viewing anguish, and death, and all the paraphernalia of the monstrous. That's not the condition of the angels.

It seems to me vital that in this age of the New Righteousness—when moral rectitude is again a rallying cry, and the old hypocrisies are gaining acolytes by the hour—we should strive to avoid feeding delusions of perfectibility and instead celebrate the complexities and contradictions that, as I've said, fantastic fiction is uniquely qualified to address. If we can, we may yet keep from drowning in a wave of simplifications that include such great fake dichotomies as good versus evil, dark versus light, reality versus fiction. But we must be prepared to wear our paradoxes on our sleeve.

In King's work, it is so often the child who carries that wisdom; the child who synthesizes "real" and "imagined" experience without question, who knows instinctively that imagination can tell the truth the way the senses never can. That lesson can never be taught too often. It stands in direct contradiction to the basic principles which we are suckled upon and are taught to make us strong in the world. Principles of verifiable evidence; and of the logic that will lead, given its head, to terrible, but faultlessly logical, insanities.

I return again to the list of goods that King is selling in his fiction, and find my summary deficient. Yes, there is death on the list; and much about the soul's decay. But there's also *vision*.

Not the kind laid claim to by politicians or manufacturers or men of the cloth. Not the vision of the *better* economy, the *better* combustion engine, the *better* Eden. Those visions are devised to bind us and blind us. If we look too long at them we no longer understand what our dreams are telling us; and without that knowledge we are weak.

No, King offers us another kind of vision; he shows us adults what the children in his fiction so often take for granted: that on the journey which he has so eloquently charted, where no terror shows its face but on a street that we have ourselves trodden, it is not, finally, the stale formulae and the trite metaphysics we're taught from birth that will get us to the end of the ride alive; it is our intimacy with our dark and dreaming selves.

Part 1
The Real World of Stephen King

Truth is stranger than fiction—so strange, at times, that if it were to be written *as* fiction, no editor would buy it, saying that it was too unbelievable.

Consider this: In 1991 Eric Keene of San Antonio, Texas, showed up unannounced at King's office and said he wanted King to help him write a book. According to the *Bangor Daily News*, "That's a fairly common request, but De-Filippo [a King staffer] said it appeared that Keene was agitated and angry. Keene wanted King to buy him a pair of contact lenses, house him for a couple of months and keep him supplied with cigarettes and beer."

Two days later, when Stephen King was out of town, attending a basketball game in Philadelphia with one of his sons, Keene made his move. He broke into King's house at 6:00 A.M., entering through a kitchen window. When King's wife, Tabitha, went to investigate, she saw Keene, who told her he had a bomb. As the *News* later explained, the "hand-held detonator unit" turned out to be some "cardboard and some electronic parts from a calculator."

Keene—"armed" with his "bomb"—headed upstairs. (He later explained to the *News* that "I wanted to get into that attic. I did exactly what I planned to do by going up to that room. I looked at it as compensation for all the effort I went to.")

A schizophrenic who later pleaded innocent by reason of insanity, Keene never planted the "bomb," but this "little episode of terror"—as King put it—made him realize that, even with a fence around the property, the security measures were far too lax.

Today, the King house, as well as the office complex, is wired for closed-circuit television, with auto-scan cameras; the wrought-iron fence gates are always secured; and a numeric keypad is the only entry point to the driveway.

King, like other celebrities, has become a prisoner of his own success, something he never imagined in his wildest nightmares when he sat in the furnace room of his rented trailer in Hermon, Maine, where he pounded away on Tabitha King's high school typewriter, writing short stories for *Cavalier* and working on *Carrie,* which would in time carry him far from the snow-swept fields of rural Maine to a palatial house in the historic district of Bangor.

A permanent resident on every best-seller list, an entertainment figure with clout on the movie and television fronts, a celebrity in his own right, and *the* person most Americans think of when they point to their favorite bogeyman, King has come a long way from that snow-capped hill on which his rented trailer perched in Hermon seemingly a million years ago.

Nearing the half-century mark, King, as a writer, has beaten the odds. Unlike other best-seller authors who have written themselves out, told all their tales, and begun repeating themselves, King continues to break new ground, delighting and amazing readers who eagerly await each new King novel.

This, then, is the real world of Stephen King: his life, his career, his recent rock and roll career, his *being* a writer instead of writing (touring instead of sitting in front of that word processor); and an inside look at the William Arnold house, the most famous residence in Bangor, Maine, which the Kings call home—a castle under siege, as tourists drive by in rental cars and gawk at the ornate black fence encircling the property, as closed-circuit television cameras scan the grounds, just in case someone decides to pay the Kings an unwanted call.

Welcome to the *real* world of Stephen King.

1
Chronology

1939
- A merchant mariner, Donald Edwin King marries Nellie Ruth Pillsbury.

1945
- Donald Edwin King returns to Croton-on-Hudson, New York, to be with his wife.
- Kings adopt David Victor King.

1947
- Kings take up residence in Scarborough, Maine.
- Stephen Edwin King born September 21 in Portland, at Maine General Hospital.

1949
- Father deserts family; no one ever hears from him again.

1949–58
- King family—Ruth, Stephen, and David—moves to Fort Wayne, Indiana, then to Stratford, Connecticut.

1958
- Kings move to Durham, Maine.

1959–60
- Stephen discovers a box of horror and science-fiction paperback books that belonged to his father, an aspiring writer.

1962–66
- Attends Lisbon Falls High School.
- Publishes "I Was a Teenage Grave Robber," his first short story, in a fanzine, *Comics Review,* edited by Marv Wolfman.

Photo courtesy of the *Bangor Daily News*

Stephen King's yearbook picture from high school.

1966–70

- Attends University of Maine at Orono, graduating with a B.S. in English, a minor in speech, and a side interest in drama.
- Meets wife to be, Tabitha Jane Spruce, a poet and short-story writer.

- Publishes "The Glass Floor" in *Startling Mystery Stories,* his first professional sale (1967).
- Works in commercial laundry in Bangor.

1971
- Marries Tabitha Spruce.

1971–73
- Teaches English at Hampden Academy in Hampden, Maine (near Bangor). Lives in a rented trailer in Hermon, Maine.
- Begins "Carrie" as a short story (1972).

1973
- Sells *Carrie* to William Thompson of Doubleday.
- Mother dies of cancer.
- Moves family to North Windham, Maine.

1974
- Moves family to Boulder, Colorado.
- *Carrie* published by Doubleday.

1975
- Moves back to Maine, to Bridgton, and purchases first house.
- *'Salem's Lot* published by Doubleday.

1976
- *Carrie* released as a movie.

1977
- Sells house, moves family to England for a one-year visit, but returns after three months, purchasing a house in Center Lovell, Maine.
- *The Shining* published by Doubleday.
- *Rage* published under pen name Richard Bachman by New American Library as a mass market paperback original.

1978
- Takes position as writer-in-residence at University of Maine at Orono.
- Rents home in Orrington, Maine, site of original "Pet Sematary."
- *Night Shift* published by Doubleday.
- *The Stand* [I] published by Doubleday.

1979

- Returns to Center Lovell after one-year teaching stint.
- Attends World Fantasy Convention (Providence, Rhode Island) as Guest of Honor.
- *'Salem's Lot* aired as a TV miniseries.
- *The Dead Zone* published by Viking Press.
- *The Long Walk* published under pen name Richard Bachman by New American Library as a mass market paperback original

1980

- Buys Victorian mansion in Bangor, Maine—his current residence.
- Receives a special World Fantasy Award.
- *Firestarter* published by Viking Press.
- *The Shining* released as a movie.

1981

- *Danse Macabre*—his only nonfiction book—published by Everest House.
- *Cujo* published by Viking.
- *Roadwork* (Richard Bachman) published by New American Library.
- Receives Career Alumni Award from University of Maine.

1982

- *The Dark Tower: The Gunslinger* published by Donald M. Grant, Publisher.
- *Different Seasons* published by Viking.
- *Creepshow* (an EC–style comic book collection) with artist Berni Wrightson published by NAL.
- *The Running Man* published by NAL.
- *Creepshow I* released as a movie.
- *Fear Itself,* first critical collection about King's works, published by Underwood–Miller.
- *Stephen King,* first single-book look at King, published by Starmont House.

1983

- *Christine* published by Viking.
- *Pet Sematary* published by Doubleday.
- *Cycle of the Werewolf* published by a small press, Land of Enchantment.
- *Christine* released as a movie.
- *The Dead Zone* released as a movie.
- *Cujo* released as a movie.
- Tabitha publishes her first book, *Small World.*

1984

- *The Talisman* with Peter Straub published as a joint project at Viking/G.P. Putnam's Sons.
- Self-publishes *The Eyes of the Dragon* at Philtrum Press.
- *Cat's Eye* [an original movie anthology] released as a movie.
- *Children of the Corn* released as a movie.
- *Firestarter* released as a movie.
- *Thinner* published under pen name Richard Bachman by NAL Books in hardback.
- *Stephen King: The Art of Darkness* by Douglas E. Winter, written with King's cooperation, is published by NAL.

1985

- Reluctantly admits publicly his pen name, Richard Bachman.
- Directs *Maximum Overdrive* in Wilmington, North Carolina.
- King's secretary and sister-in-law, Stephanie Leonard, publishes first issue of *Castle Rock,* the official King newsletter.
- *Skeleton Crew* published by Putnam.
- *The Bachman Books,* an omnibus edition, published by NAL.
- *Silver Bullet [Cycle of the Werewolf]* released as a movie.
- Two student films based on King's short stories ("The Bogeyman" and "The Woman in the Room") released in videotape.

1986

- *It* published by Viking.
- *Gramma* airs on TV.
- *Maximum Overdrive* released as a movie.
- *Stand by Me* released as a movie.

1987

- *Misery* published by Viking.
- *The Eyes of the Dragon* (revised edition) published by Viking.
- *The Tommyknockers* published by Putnam.
- *Creepshow II* released as a movie.
- *Return to 'Salem's Lot* [a sequel in name only] released as a videocassette original.
- "Sorry, Right Number" is aired on TV.
- *Silver Bullet* (see *Cycle of the Werewolf*) published by New American Library.
- *The Dark Tower II: The Drawing of the Three* published by Donald M. Grant, Publisher, Inc.

1988

- *The Running Man* is released as a movie.
- *Nightmares in the Sky* published by Viking.

1989

- Assistant coach of West Bangor's Little League team (son Owen is on the team).
- *The Dark Half* published by Viking.
- *Dolan's Cadillac* published by Lord John Press as a limited-edition book.
- *My Pretty Pony* published by the Whitney Museum as a limited-edition book.
- *Pet Sematary* released as a movie.

1990

- *The Stand* [II] (the complete and uncut edition) published by Doubleday.
- *Four Past Midnight* published by Viking.
- *Misery* released as a movie.
- *Stephen King's Graveyard Shift* released as a movie.
- *Tales from the Darkside: The Movie* [with "Cat from Hell" by King] released as a movie.
- *Stephen King's "It"* airs on TV.

1991

- *Needful Things* published by Viking.
- *The Dark Half* released as a movie.
- *Stephen King's "The Golden Years"* airs on TV.
- *Sometimes They Come Back* airs on TV.
- *The Dark Tower III: The Wastelands* published by Donald M. Grant, Publisher, Inc.

1992

- Builds the Shawn Trevor Mansfield Complex, a Little League ballpark, behind his house.
- Performs at American Booksellers Association convention in Anaheim, California, with rock band, the Rock Bottom Remainders.
- *Gerald's Game* published at Viking.

1993

- *Nightmares and Dreamscapes* published by Viking.
- *Dolores Claiborne* published by Viking.

- Performs at American Booksellers Association convention in Miami with the Rock Bottom Remainders.
- *Needful Things* released as a movie.

1994

- Performs at American Booksellers Association convention in Los Angeles with the Rock Bottom Remainders.
- *The Stand* airs as ABC-TV miniseries.
- *Insomnia* published as a limited edition by Mark Ziesing, and in a trade edition by Viking.
- Hits the road for coast-to-coast book tour in October to ten cities to support independent bookstores.
- *The Shawshank Redemption* released as a movie.

1995

- *The Mangler* released as a movie.
- *Dolores Claiborne* released as a movie.
- *The Langoliers* airs on ABC-TV as a miniseries.
- Publishes *Rose Madder* at Viking.

1996

- *Desperation* to be published at Viking.
- *Regulators* to be published at Viking.

1997

- *The Dark Tower IV: Wizard and Glass* to be published at Donald M. Grant, Publisher, Inc.

The infamous "King with shotgun" cover to *The Maine Campus.*

2
The Student King
The Master of Modern Horror at Maine
by Sanford Phippen (class of '64)

The university served King well, taking a rather shy but brilliant Maine boy and turning him into an outgoing, productive asset to the state, yet leaving intact his wit, character, and eye for observing the people around him.

David Bright ('70), in *Portland Monthly*

✳

Very little has been written about King's college days, but in Maine *magazine (fall 1989), published by the Alumni Office at the University of Maine at Orono, Sanford Phippen (class of '64) gives us a look at the collegiate King. (Like King, Phippen was a writer-in-residence at UMO, preceding King's stint.)*

✳

He is certainly the University of Maine's most famous graduate. (Can you name another who has made the cover of *Time*?) What F. Scott Fitzgerald is to Princeton, what Nathaniel Hawthorne is to Bowdoin, and what Thomas Wolfe is to Chapel Hill, Stephen King is to Maine.

People tend to fall in love with authors more than with engineering programs, forestry schools—maybe even athletic teams. Look at the people who come to the state because of E. B. White, Robert McClosky, even Helen and Scott Nearing. On a recent literary tour of the Bangor–Brewer area, Lou Galbath and I had to cut short part of a planned itinerary because so many of the librarians and teachers, mostly from Ohio, wanted to be sure they reached Stephen King's house to have their pictures taken before it got too dark.

Students are now enrolling at Maine because of King's influence. And in the creative writing department, where I taught for a year (1978–79), his presence is strongly felt. One of my former colleagues says, "I don't mind Stephen King, but I wished he lived in Arizona. So many students try to imitate him—and badly. They think writing like this is an *easy* way to make money."

The influence of King on the university seems natural enough. The fact is that UMaine is where Stephen King started to become STEPHEN KING. Orono is where he first began to publish his work, both in his regular columns for the *Maine Campus* and the college literary magazine, and in national magazines like *Cavalier*. Orono is where he impressed his professors as a good student and was encouraged by them in his writing. Orono is where he received an important forum and feedback for his early work. Orono is where he made lasting friendships. And Orono is where he met his wife, Tabitha Spruce ('71) from Old Town.

Of course, the era he attended the university was also an important factor in the development of Stephen King. It didn't hurt to be a writer-in-the-making on a college campus during one of the most turbulent times of the twentieth century. Steve was a student from 1966 to 1970, and while no race riots or antiwar demonstrations got wildly out of hand at Maine, there were demonstrations and protests, there was a Students for Democratic Society group on campus, and there was a three-day unofficial moratorium after the Kent State University tragedy in the spring of 1970. And Maine, like other U.S. colleges at the time, was undergoing many changes, especially in the areas of students' rights and residential life.

King's popular column "King's Garbage Truck," which appeared in the *Maine Campus* from February 20, 1969, through May 21, 1970, reflects much of what was going on at the time. While mostly he reviewed movies, TV shows, and rock music (just as he still does in his work), he did call for a gen-

---

A BLESSED EVENT

"A Blessed (?) Event Announced to the University of Maine at Orono—Name: Steve King/Date of birth into the real world: June 5, 1970/Future prospects: Hazy, although either nuclear annihilation or environmental strangulation seems to be a distinct possibility/This boy has shown evidence of some talent, although at this point, it is impossible to tell if he is just a flash in the pan or if he has real possibilities."

—King's birth announcement from "King's Garbage Truck," his college newspaper column, on the occasion of his graduation

eral student strike on April 24, 1969. And he wrote in one column about what it was like to be called dirty names and have eggs thrown at you during a relatively peaceful "End the War" protest march on campus in May 1969. He attacked such establishment organizations as the All-Maine Women, Senior Skulls, Sophomore Owls, and Eagles, calling them irrelevant and elitist. In reaction to such groups, he invented his own organization which he called the Nitty Gritty Up Tight Society for a Campus with More Cools, and he handed out "gritties" or awards to those people at Maine who, in his opinion, did cool things. His columns also attacked Pope Paul, and supported the California grape pickers' strike in October 1969. On the other hand, he wrote in support of police officers and against those at the time who called cops "pigs."

In a March 3, 1970, column, he suggests that the university would be a better place if it got rid of all required courses and abolished requirements for all branches of the school. In one of his final columns (April 1970), he writes about how he changed from being a conservative who voted for Nixon in 1968 to becoming what he termed a "scummy radical bastard." The radical image of Stephen King was featured in a photo by Frank Kadi ('69) on the cover of the January 15, 1969, *Campus*. King looked as wild as one of his evil characters, sporting long hair, a beard, a deranged look in his eyes, grinning a buck-toothed grin, and pointing a double-barreled shotgun at the reader. Underneath the picture, in "coming-of-Christ" headline print, is the exclamation: "STUDY, DAMMIT!!"

In a May 1, 1969, column, King wrote about being part of the first "special seminar" created at the university during the fall semester of 1968. This was Contemporary Poetry, taught by Burt Hatlen ('65) and Jim Bishop ('61), two of King's favorite instructors, and to whom, along with fellow English professor Edward M. "Ted" Holmes ('54G), he dedicated *The Long Walk,* one of the four novels written under King's pseudonym, Richard Bachman.

According to Hatlen, the special seminar courses were created to allow faculty and students to plan classes outside the curriculum. And students needed to apply for admission. The Contemporary Poetry seminar was limited to twelve students and involved a "very intense discussion about poetics, how you write poetry, and so on." Hatlen says that Steve "wasn't very theoretical, but on the fringes." (Tabby King, who was then a sophomore, says she'll never forgive Hatlen for not letting her in.)

As a sophomore, King had taken Hatlen for Modern American Literature, and Hatlen feels that this course had a long-term influence on King, for it's where he came into contact with Steinbeck and Faulkner (King now collects first editions of Faulkner).

Before the contemporary poetry seminar, Jim Bishop had King as a student in 1966 in freshman English and he remembers "Steve's big physical presence" and how King was "religious about writing." He also remembers that King always had a paperback in his pocket, and knew all these authors that nobody else ever heard of.

"Steve was a nice kid, a good student, but never had a lot of social confidence," Bishop says. "Even then, though, he saw himself as a famous writer and he thought he could make money at it. Steve was writing continuously, industriously, and diligently. He was amiable, resilient, and created his own world."

In his introduction to *Moth,* a student literary magazine published in 1970, Jim Bishop wrote about that extraordinary poetry seminar: "From that seminar, which supposedly terminated in January 1969, came a half dozen or so energetic and highly individual young poets who have been rapping in hallways, in coffee shops, in front of Stevens Hall, or wherever any two of them chance to meet, ever since, and that original group has grown this year to a dozen, sometimes as many as twenty, who meet every other Friday in an informal workshop to read their poetry, alternatively to read and reassemble one another, and hopefully to emerge with a better understanding of themselves, their world, and their work. This anthology brings together selected works of that amazing group and marks perhaps the climax of an extraordinary phenomenon."

Besides Stephen King, whose poems "The Dark Man," "Donovan's Brain," and "Silence" were included in *Moth,* there are Tabby Spruce with six poems; Michael Alpert ('72), a Bangor publisher, who has since collaborated with King on a fancy edition of *The Eyes of the Dragon;* three of King's best friends from college—Jim Smith ('72), Dave Lyon ('70), and Bruce Holsapple ('73)— Diane McPherson (who designed the *Moth* cover); and George MacLeod ('72), King's former roommate. The others who have work in *Moth* are Susan Lienhard ('71), Stephen Black ('70), Mike Gilleland ('72), Sherry Dresser, and Jean Stewart.

The poetry workshop met frequently at the Maine Christian Association House on College Avenue, among other places, throughout King's senior year. Jim Bishop was on leave from teaching that year and living at Pemaquid Point. But he still commuted to Orono for the meetings. Tom Bailey and Graham Adams of the English faculty presided, and it was Adams who allowed King to teach a course as a senior undergraduate. Adams served as the front person, because the university wouldn't allow a student to teach a course. But King was, in reality, the teacher, and the course, naturally enough, was called "Popular Literature in America."

King's own thoughts about the poetry workshops and creative writing courses at Maine were recorded in interviews with the University of Southern Maine's *Presumscot* in 1977, and with UM's *Ubris II* in 1984.

"I realized that what I had for those years I was involved with the writing seminar was a big blank," King told *Ubris II*. "There were about forty to fifty poems, and two of them I've still got around. So for me, there was this tremendously exciting experience and nothing came of it. It was like being on a long drunk. But, on the other hand, I wasn't typical. For a lot of people, good did come of it."

When asked if he learned the craft of writing in college courses, King replied: "No, no, but I don't think it was bad. The creative writing courses at the college level are very important, but I don't think they're necessary. It's a supportive experience. . . . The best thing about it was that the art of writing was taken seriously, and that's an awfully good thing."

In 1969–70, students from the workshop were involved with much more than poetry. George MacLeod, for instance, was one of the leaders of the student strike. Members of the group would often meet at the coffee shop which was part of the old bookstore in the Memorial Union.

Diane McPherson, who is now working on her Ph.D. at Cornell, and who was a member of both the seminar and the workshop, shared tutorial writing sessions with King under Ted Holmes. "We wrote independently but then got together once a week and it was great fun, often hilarious. I was the ideal audience for Steve's wildly inventive fantasies. My thing then was to cut all the extraneous adverbs and adjectives. Steve was pretty pop. He was writing exciting stories, but with no control."

McPherson also remembers King singing. "There was this coffeehouse on campus—The Ram's Horn—and there would be these open sings, or open hoots. People brought their instruments, and Steve would always sing country and western songs about this terrible loser who never had any luck. I remember thinking at that time that Steve was singing about a version of himself that rang true."

King is also remembered hanging out at the back booth of the Bear's Den with fellow students Jim Tierney ('69—now Maine's attorney general) and Steve Williams ('60). And he was known to frequent the old Shamrock Bar across from Pat's Pizza where he would join friends and members of the more radical campus groups for folk music and beer.

At the end of the tutorial time with Professor Holmes, Ted sent McPherson's and King's stories to his agent, and soon after, King had a story accepted by *Cavalier*. "He decided early what kind of writer he wanted to be, and he went and did it," McPherson says. "He used to say, 'I'm hoping to have my own career.' Now and then I think how funny it is that I went to college with Stephen King."

Everyone agrees that the first person to officially declare King a writer was Ted Holmes. As reported in the book *Stephen King: The Art of Darkness* by Douglas E. Winter, King, as a sophomore, showed Burt Hatlen the manuscript of a novel he had written his freshman year. Hatlen in turn handed the manuscript to Holmes, who, after reading it, said ecstatically, "I think we've got a writer."

"When Steve was a junior and senior," Holmes says, "we had a lot of conferences over his work. He was a natural storyteller, of course, and his craftsmanship was always pretty good."

One of King's stories, "Night Surf"... eventually became *The Stand*. Other stories completed at UMaine were "Here There Be Tygers," "Cain Rose Up," "The Blue Air Compressor," and "Heavy Metal."

For most of the decade of the sixties, Ted Holmes was the sole creative writing teacher at Maine. Winthrop C. Libby, then president of the university, remembers a talk he once had with Holmes about King's prospects as an important professional writer. "Ted was not especially complimentary on that point. He said, as I recall, that while Steve certainly had a knack for storytelling, he wished that Steve would write more than horror stories."

Today, Holmes says of King's career, "I'm very glad that he's so successful. I respect his craftsmanship, but I haven't read all his books."

For his part, Libby remembers King as "essentially a very gentle person who acted the part of being a very wild man." Libby said that he'd see King "hovering around in the background" of student affairs committee meetings (King was elected to the Student Senate by the largest vote ever cast up to that time). "I'd always stop and chat with him; and my wife and I went to his wedding in Old Town, which was rather strange, because the ceremony was at the Catholic church and the reception at the Methodist" (Steve was the Methodist, Tabitha the Catholic).

As a freshman, King lived at 203 Gannett Hall. But after that first year, he moved off campus. In his senior year he remembers living alone in a "scuzzy riverside cabin not far from the university."

In his junior year, King lived on North Maine Street in Orono in a house that has since burned down. One of his roommates was George MacLeod, who now operates MacLeod's Restaurant in Bucksport. There were two apartments for ten people, and MacLeod remembers King had a "whole regiment" of open beer bottles around his bed. He also remembers the future novelist's avid reading habits.

"Steve read like his life depended on it," MacLeod says. "He was writing and reading all the time. Basically he was an insecure kid who hid in books."

MacLeod remembers that a lot of energy from the poetry workshop went into politics, but he says that while King would make a lot of noise and contribute to the chaos of the times, he was not an effective leader for causes.

"He's a loose cannon as far as politics go," MacLeod says. "He was a noisy radical opposed to Vietnam, and he did lead a group of students one night to President Libby's house. He was kind of an odd person: on one hand very private and yet public in a loud way."

Some of the political gains that resulted from what MacLeod terms a coalition of splinter groups from the SDS and other activist organizations were a program for independent study, and having a pass/fail option instead of grades for students. "Steve was a figurehead for some radical efforts," claims MacLeod, "but basically he was middle-of-the-road in most areas. However, he was always there with his pitchfork and torch when you needed him."

MacLeod, who was a member of both the poetry seminar and workshop groups with King, also offered some insights into the popular novelist's personality. "Steve is uncomfortable with certain people and with large groups," he says. "He's erratic because he's nervous. He's a figurehead with feet of clay, and essentially he hasn't changed."

Emily Woodcock Templeton ('70), who audited the poetry workshop class that Steve was in, has some clear memories of the late sixties at Maine. "You felt like you were part of a school that was on the vanguard of great change, a time of building," she says. "People were working hard. Reading was something everyone was doing then. In contrast to today's atmosphere, a lot of people were at college to just read and learn. It shouldn't be forgotten that at Maine no one was looking down on the soldiers fighting in Vietnam, but we were against the war. The University of Maine was the only university in the U.S. at the time that held a blood drive for the soldiers. As for Steve King, he was one of the more committed people on campus, not a rabble-rouser, but he spoke out about what he thought."

David Bright ('70) was the editor of the *Maine Campus* when King began his "Garbage Truck" columns in 1969. He remembers King coming to him and saying he'd like to write a column. "Steve named it 'Garbage Truck' because you never know what you're going to find in a garbage truck.'"

Bright was amazed at how King would stroll in just before deadline, put the paper in the typewriter, crank out his column, and hand it to the editor. It would be "letter-perfect copy," Bright remembers, that would fit the space to the inch. "This is a guy who has at least seven stories going on in his head at the same time," Bright says.

Even after he graduated from Maine, in the summer of 1970, when there was a summer *Maine Campus* edited by Bob Haskell, King wrote a regular column for the paper. This was called "Slade," the story of a western gunfighter. This column was the seed for King's novel *The Dark Tower*.

In the Afterword to *The Dark Tower* [I], King writes about how the conception for the story began to take shape in March of 1970. "During that spring semester, a sort of hush fell over my previously busy creative life—not a writer's block, but a sense that it was time to stop goofing around with a pick and shovel and get behind the controls of one big great God almighty steamshovel, a sense that it was time to try and dig something big out of the sand, even if the effort turned out to be an abysmal failure."

This statement indicates that King developed confidence in himself and his talent at quite an early age. David Bright attributes some of that development to the University of Maine.

"The University of Maine is a good place," Bright says. "You can be just about anything you want to be here." He added that he thought the times, the atmosphere, and the type of campus that Win Libby created all contributed to the development of Stephen King.

"The university served King well," Bright wrote in an article in the *Portland Monthly,* "taking a rather shy but brilliant Maine boy and turning him into an outgoing, productive asset to the state, yet leaving intact his wit, character, and eye for observing the people around him."

Bright claims that Steve would like to provide more opportunity for other potential writers to do what he did at the university. "King sees a need for a program to help new writers develop," Bright says. "He envisions some sort of a foundation-supported artists' guild, which would help writers move their families to Maine, pay their expenses, and find an environment in which to write."

Bright agrees with King that the university could do more for young writers. "The university did for King what it's supposed to do for its citizens," he says. "But the university has got to remember that some kids aren't as motivated as Steve King was."

A few years ago, King did want to endow a creative writing chair in the English department, but there were some disagreements over how the gift was to be used and the matter fell through.

King's former teachers at Maine disagree somewhat on his stature as a writer, but all seem to think highly of him as both a student and a person.

Robert Hunting was chairman of the English department and had King as a student in an English drama course. "Steve and I are good friends but I don't really read much of him," Hunting says. "I've read a couple of his books, but I like him better as a person than a writer. He's a very successful pop cult figure, and I'm a square. I have to remind myself though that Mozart also was a pop cult figure. Some of them become classics and some are forgotten.

"Steve was in my class as a senior," Hunting continued. "I was brand new here then. He was a very good student and helped me with the class. And I read his column with interest. Actually I got to know him better when he was coming back after graduation. He was always very generous with his time. He talked to the students in many classes. Then for one year, he was my colleague."

Hunting is referring to 1978, when King taught creative writing at Maine. Ulrich Wicks, the man who hired him, remembers King as a popular and effective teacher.

"Steve was very much liked and very good with students," agrees Hunting. "He had all of these creative types. He was true and candid with them, but very kind also. I remember his saying to some very noisy young fellow that he'd have more of a chance with editors if he'd pay more attention to the nuts and bolts. He said they'd like it better if he'd spell better and if he'd write grammatical sentences. The student left happy."

Hunting says he has always been fond of Steve as a person and in later years as a public-spirited citizen. "I like the positions he takes, even if I'm not his most admiring reader. I don't think he'd mind me saying that, for I do admire him in so many ways."

One of the students Steve had in 1978 in his creative writing course was novelist Margaret Dickson, who admits she didn't even know who he was. She says he was a good teacher because he was interested in all of his students, and cared about them. "I found Steve a very generous, widely read, and interesting teacher," she says.

King helped start Dickson on her way as a novelist, as he had done with Michael Kimball and Rick Hautala.

Although Robert Hunting has not read many of King's books, other veterans of the English department do keep up with their most famous student's works.

"I enjoy reading Steve," says Ulrich Wicks, "but he's a troubled person. There's a great deal in him that needs to come out. The unevenness of his work is a reflection of Steve's many selves."

Burt Hatlen thinks King is one of the most serious writers working today. And creative writing teacher Connie Hunting brushes off the criticism that King's works are shallow. "They're always saying that Steve doesn't say anything," she says, "but *The Stand* says something."

Professor Carroll Terrell says he quit the Maine Literary Association a couple of years ago over King. "I stopped going there because they had such awful opinions of him," he says. "And these opinions were based on not having read anything of his at all."

There does seem to be a group of people who refuse to read King—probably the same folks who make a big thing out of not watching TV or not listening to popular music.

Christopher Spruce, King's brother-in-law and the former manager of King's WZON radio station in Bangor, says this argument over whether King is an artist or just a good, entertaining storyteller is never-ending. "I can tell you that people should read his work seriously, because I believe he is a serious writer. He's not just out for a fast buck—why should he be at this point? There's a deep investment in his being the best writer he can be."

Connie Hunting says that although Stephen King has great influence on current writing students, they often pick up his tricks but not his deeper philosophical stances. "A novel like *The Stand* is not just a collection of horror—it's saying something very clearly. But the students only pick up on the exaggerated style and write stuff like 'the road regurgitated in front of us.' What they get is only the glitz."

Talking about her own friendship with Stephen King, Connie Hunting says, "People have very warm feelings about Steve—it's not just that he's the world's best-selling novelist. It's because he's Steve and we know him, okay? It's not that we've got a stake in him. He's the neighborhood. He's the Maine neighborhood."

It is clear that King's four years at the University of Maine were a time of tremendous growth. No, UM didn't make Stephen King into the world's best-selling author—it didn't create that horrific and prolific imagination. But it did give him a solid foundation in literature and it did provide him with an environment where writing—most especially his own writing—was taken seriously. And more important, it gave him the freedom to explore, to be accepted for who he was, and to "act the part of a wild man," as Winthrop Libby said.

By his own account, as well as that of friends and faculty members, Stephen King left Maine with self-confidence and craftsmanship. Not a bad accomplishment for any college graduate.

3
The Long, Strange Trip of Stephen King
An Overview

1. Bestsellasaurus Rex

> I have grown into a Bestsellasaurus Rex—a big, stumbling book-beast that
> is loved when it shits money and hated when it tramples houses. . . . I started
> out as a storyteller; along the way I became an economic force.
>
> Stephen King, in "The Politics of Limited Editions"

*

There is only a handful of best-selling fiction writers who produce consistently.
Storytellers who, apparently, have endless tales to tell, and whose books are the
ones reviewed, advertised, promoted, and stacked in bookstores near the cash
register. Bookstore customers don't have to make up their minds to buy these
books; the mere presence of the book in the store is the catalyst, bringing them
in droves, with cash or plastic in hand. Grisham, Clancy, Crichton, Koontz, Rice,
and King—these novelists are storytellers who, unlike most of their contem-
poraries who labor in the fields, have struck pay dirt: They can write with the
luxury of knowing that they have clout with their publishers, the book clubs,
and the bookstores, because in the end millions of readers will eagerly to
spend, on the average, $25 for a new novel from their favorite author; and they
won't wait for the paperback.

Success affects writers in different ways. John Grisham and Dean Koontz,
like King, seem personally unaffected by the heady success that has fundamentally changed their lives. Michael Crichton, too, seems unaffected. Tom
Clancy, on the other hand, has got a reputation as an author whose vociferous
complaints about his book-to-film adaptations have caused Hollywood to
state that there's just no pleasing some people. Anne Rice, of course, ignited a
firestorm of controversy about the casting for David Geffen's *An Interview with
the Vampire,* then recanted after seeing a videotape, and took out ads in

Variety, The Advocate, and newspapers to proclaim how happy she was with the final product, her earlier protests notwithstanding.

The real peril in being a best-selling author, a "bestsellasaurus," as King so aptly put it, is that precisely because of the economic clout he wields, nobody will stand in his way. The danger here is that the books have become a product, like a car timed for release for the new season, even though sometimes there's way too much steel on the chassis.

KING IN PRINT WORLDWIDE

According to Stuart Tinker of Betts Bookstore—*the* watering hole for King fans worldwide—Stephen King is published in thirty-two languages: Bulgarian, Catalan, Chinese, Czech, Danish, Dutch, English, Finnish, French, German, Greek, Hebrew, Hungarian, Icelandic, Indonesian, Italian, Japanese, Korean, Latvian, Lithuanian, Norwegian, Polish, Portuguese, Rumanian, Russian, Serbo-Croatian, Slovak, Slovene, Spanish, Swedish, Turkish, and Ukrainian.

It can happen to anyone, but when it happens to best-selling authors, an interesting thing happens: the publisher won't be the one telling the author that the king is not wearing any clothes. Case in point: After the brilliant *Jurassic Park*—the biggest grossing movie in motion picture history, based on the imaginative scenario of a dinosaur park—Crichton followed up with what was perceived as a Japan-bashing novel, *Rising Sun,* which was followed by a politically incorrect novel about *male* sexual harassment, *Full Disclosure.*

Who's going to tell Crichton that his readers want more imaginative tales and not social polemics?

Likewise, Stephen King has, in recent years, come under considerable criticism from all corners because of his tendency to *over*write. As Harlan Ellison explained in a 1989 interview, "I can't think of any King novels, with the possible exception of maybe *It* or the two *Dark Tower* books, that could not have been told just as well as a novella. This is to me the main flaw in Stephen's work."

Think, for instance, of some of King's best work. They are—not coincidentally—novellas: "The Body," the poignant tale of the narrator, Gordy Lachance, who reminisced about his long-lost youth and the heady days of when he was a teenager, growing up in Castle Rock, Maine; "The Mist," an inventive, narrative-driven story about a strange mist that rolls across the country, bringing with it the horrors that lurked within; "Apt Pupil," the tale of the boy next door who, slowly, descended into horror when he discovered his lurid fascination with Nazi Germany and the "gooshy stuff" that happened at the death camps; "The Breathing Method," a horrific tale about a mother who gives birth under unusual circumstances; and "Rita Hayworth and Shawshank Redemption," the story of an inmate at Shawshank prison in Maine, who breaks out.

Working within the novella length, King doesn't have enough rope to hang himself, so to speak; he must tell his story in an economical manner. As story length shortens, storytelling becomes more important—you must cover the ground quickly, which King does in short stories and in novellas. But at novel length—sometimes up to 800 pages—King can become self-indulgent, and will his editor at New American Library correct him? A best-selling author either edits himself, or there is no book editing—nobody at NAL is going to tell King that a book is too long. (They did at Doubleday, when he turned in *The Stand*; grumbling, he made the cuts but didn't like it . . . and restored a good part of the lost wordage to the uncut edition published years later when he had the clout.)

In recent years, even King's die-hard fans, who buy everything, spending hundreds of dollars for signed, limited editions, have confessed that they too find King's books verbose and, of late, uneven in quality. After the embarrassingly bad *Gerald's Game*—an internal novel that starts out in bondage and unravels slowly as the protagonist drifts in and out of hallucinations—King followed up with a brilliant, minor masterpiece of regional writing, *Dolores Claiborne,* the story of a woman who, up-front, admits she had a hand in killing her husband, in a way, and tells the riveting story of her life in the Maine vernacular that King has made famous.

Insomnia, King's 1994 novel, is—depending on your viewpoint—either too wordy or a masterpiece. As a reviewer for *Publishers Weekly* put it:

> Forget the lean, mean King of *Misery, Gerald's Game,* and *Dolores Claiborne.* This is the other King—the Grand Vizier of Verbosity who gave us *It, The Tommyknockers* and *Needful Things.* There's much of everything in these 800 pages, including the worthy. . . . Then there's the slam-bang final 300 pages, in themselves a novel's worth of excitement. . . . The problem is that the finale is preceded by more than a novel's worth of casual, even tedious buildup. . . . If this novel were liposuctioned, it would rank among King's best; as is, it's another roly-poly volume from a skilled writer who presumes his readers' appetite for words is more gourmand than gourmet.

In contrast, a fellow scrivener, writing in the *Washington Post,* proclaimed it a masterpiece—ambitious, admittedly sprawling, but a major book nonetheless. A $27.95 hardback, *Insomnia* was a Book-of-the-Month main selection, published simultaneously with a Penguin HighBridge unabridged audio recording, and backed by a $1 million ad campaign. (Just to make sure everyone would sit up and pay attention, King hit the road, going on tour for the first time in years, from coast to coast, stopping in ten cities and appearing at independent bookstores, where he read from *Insomnia*, answered questions, and signed 200 copies per bookstore for resale.)

Meanwhile, Viking pushed over a million copies into stores nationwide by publication date in a lay-down that created overnight mountains of *Insomnia*, especially at the chain stores that bought them at big discounts with the intention of marking them down 25 percent.

Here's what really matters: There were 1.5 million King fans just waiting for the book to hit the stores. (For those who couldn't wait, and wanted the *true* first edition, Mark Ziesing, a small press in California, published *Insomnia* in its "gift" edition of 3,750 copies at $75 and a signed, limited edition of 1,250 copies at $175—the first time in years that King has authorized a limited edition of one of his novels.)

In the first week of October, when *Insomnia* hit the bookstores, waves of King fans rolled in, oblivious to everything else on the shelves; they wanted King, and little else.

And, with the appearance of each new King book, the crushing crowds will be back, their insatiable appetites for King only temporarily fed.

Still, you must ask yourself: Isn't King entitled to be self-indulgent occasionally? Doesn't he have the right—as one bookstore owner that deals principally in King collectibles put it—to write a bad book now and then?

Of course. Now and then ...

The important thing, really, is the body of work that is extant. Everything King has written is still in print, some books in multiple editions—take your pick. This fact alone tells you that King has staying power—which fact, born with the publication of *Carrie* in 1974, has meant his publishers can count on him to deliver the goods, with a captive audience primed to buy things King.

Those numbers also mean that, at NAL, nobody messes around with the King franchise, just as at Disney, nobody messes around with the Mouse.

Ironically, in sheer numbers, there is a new kid on the block—a friend of King's, who shares a passion for Little League baseball—whose book sales top King's. John Grisham's novel *The Chamber* went to press with 2.5 million copies. The difference: Grisham's plot-driven novels, adapted for the movies, have reached deep into the nonbook audience and pulled them into the bookstores, goosing his sales by millions of copies. King, in contrast, writes character-driven novels that tend not to lend themselves to visual adaptations, which means he doesn't draw fresh blood to his novels as Grisham can. (Besides, Grisham is also more mainstream: By *not* writing about things that go bump in the night, Grisham has widened his audience to people that are willing to give him a try, unlike some potential customers for King's novels who feel that they don't read "horror" and they aren't about to start.)

King, of course, is no more a horror writer than Harlan Ellison and Ray Bradbury are science-fiction writers. Publishing being what it is, books are sold as product by category, even though King has transcended the genre. It wasn't, after all, that horror as a genre was popular; it was *King* whose books were popular, and the horror element was just icing on the cake.

In recent years, King has come back home, so to speak, writing about private landscapes set in Maine. *Gerald's Game* is an exploration of one woman's mind, as she puzzles over her dilemma—handcuffed to a bed, wearing nothing but panties, her dead husband lunch for a stray dog that wanders in. *Dolores Claiborne,* a first-person story, unveils the heartbreaking life of Dolores, and why she wouldn't help save her miserable husband's life, even when she *could.* And *Insomnia* is an introspective piece about old people and how, to some extent, they are disenfranchised in our society for the sin of being old—who takes whatever they say *seriously?*

Where now, Stephen King?

Rose Madder, published in 1995, is the story of a battered woman on the run from her husband, a policeman, with a supernatural twist.

What territories lie beyond? Another novel, King tells us in an interview with "Larry King Live" on CNN, which aired in late August 1994. Then, he said firmly, he's going to start *Wizard and Glass,* the fourth *Dark Tower* novel, and not stop until that story is told in toto—seven books.

If King were to hang it up tomorrow, breaking the pencil and deciding never to write again, nobody would begrudge him. The novels, the short stories, and the considerable body of nonfiction (largely uncollected in book form) attest to a prodigious output from a man who, at the same time, wrote numerous screenplays and spent a good part of his time *being* a writer: giving interviews, signing books, answering fan mail, appearing on television and radio, making public service announcements, and being Bangor's main tourist attraction and philanthropist.

The growing body of work that remains is what the readers celebrate. To my mind, nothing can replace the heady rush of those early Doubleday books, in which King—like a sultan of swat—batted out *Carrie, Night Shift, 'Salem's Lot, The Shining,* and *The Stand.* After those books, he could have hit the showers, and nobody would have complained, except perhaps to speculate on what he might have written.

We know now what followed: a marvelously perceptive and anecdotal book of nonfiction, *Danse Macabre,* an overview of the horror genre; more than a handful of brilliant novellas; some excellent short novels; and—let's be honest here—some very long novels like *The Tommyknockers* that needed but did not get the necessary editorial touch.

Like any overview of any writer's work, this book celebrates King in all his gaudy glory, from the brilliant work to the less successful. What you come away with is the feeling that here's a writer who, at least, was willing to take the chances; other writers could have mined a career of self-imitative stories that would sell and resell in endless variations, since some readers prefer the same story told again and again. King, fortunately, has the good sense to trust his own instincts. At his best, he gives us new work like *Dolores Claiborne;* at his worst, he gives us big books that are far too long but that contain the heart of a good novel.

King, whom Harlan Ellison called "one of the most accomplished storytellers the twentieth century has produced," continues to produce a body of work that speaks to millions of readers. And although that day may come when the readers drop off, having discovered a new writer, or having grown tired of King's work, simply stop reading, that possibility seems remote.

Ellison said that "I think it's foolish to think that anyone can sustain forever a literary career at the level that Stephen's has been at for so remarkably long." It may be foolish, but after two decades of King in print, the literary career is stronger than ever. King's not batting a thousand, but then, he never promised that to us. All he's promised is, as he put it in *Nightmares & Dreamscapes,* the thrill of a story well told:

> But it *isn't* about the money, no matter what the glossy tabloids may say, and it's not about selling out, as the more arrogant critics really seem to believe. The fundamental things still apply as time goes by, and for me, the object hasn't changed—the job is still getting to *you,* Constant Reader. . . . It's still about making you believe what I believe, at least for a little while.

Do *you* believe?

I think so. You *want* to believe. You *want* to be taken away from the real world, if only for a few hours, because it's so depressingly real. As Shirley Jackson reminds us in the epigram to *The Haunting of Hill House,* "No live organism can continue for long to exist sanely under conditions of absolute reality; even larks and katydids are supposed, by some, to dream."

To sleep, perchance to dream . . .

Again, do *you* believe? I think so, because you *want* to believe.

Does *King* believe? You'd better believe it. As he wrote in the essay that preceded the stories in *Nightmares & Dreamscapes,* "Most of all, I *do* believe in spooks, I *do* believe in spooks, I *do* believe in spooks."

And so do you . . . and I.

And that is why we continue to read Stephen King.

John Esposito (screenwriter), Bill Dunn (coproducer), and Stephen King at a press conference for *Graveyard Shift* in Bangor.

2. The Movies

> But in the end, I think it's perhaps best for [the characters in *The Stand*]
> to belong to the reader, who will visualize them through the lens of
> imagination in a vivid and constantly changing way no camera
> can duplicate. . . . The imagination . . . moves with its own tidal flow.
>
> Stephen King, in "A Preface in Two Parts," from *The Stand* [II]

✳

The earliest adaptation, and one of the best, of a King book, *Carrie,* released as a movie in 1976, was instrumental in making King a brand-name writer, bringing him to the attention of millions of viewers that otherwise would probably not have known his name. After the movie, when they went to the bookstore to find out what was available, they would find *Carrie,* his first book, and *'Salem's Lot,* his second book, a vampire tale set in small-town Maine.

As to why King's fiction has not translated well to the screen, there are several reasons, some ironic. First, King's work is very visual, very cinematic, which makes his books an easy read; the reader can visualize the book in his mind's eye, since King's writing style is colloquial and free of ornamentation—it's as if he's *telling* you a story orally, which is why his books on tape have succeeded in a way the movies have not. Second, King wrote and directed one of his own stories, "Trucks," as *Maximum Overdrive.* The presumption was that if King did the adaptation *and* he directed it, wouldn't the King flavor be retained? In this case, no. The movie turned out to be a colossal disappointment and, for critics, a focal point for criticism about his movies. Third, King's books tend to be more about character than about plot. Reduced to a plotline, even the best King books turn to mush—*Cujo* is about a rabid dog that attacks a mother and child stranded in a Ford Pinto; *Firestarter* is about a young girl whose parents unwittingly took drugs under government supervision that, in the child, produced a pyrokinetic; *'Salem's Lot* is about a vampire that comes to small-town Maine and feeds on its unsuspecting townsfolk. . . . And, finally, the demands of the medium require that every novel, regardless of length, be boiled down to 120 minutes, or 120 pages of script, which means that a lot is jettisoned to keep the momentum going.

Given those constraints, it's a wonder that any King book survives the translation to the screen. But when one does, the results are worthy: *Carrie,* directed by Brian de Palma; *The Dead Zone,* directed by David Cronenberg; *The Shawshank Redemption,* directed by Frank Darabont; and two Rob Reiner films—*Stand by Me* and *Misery.*

The lessons learned: King's nonhorror material has adapted more easily to the big screen than the horrific material. The shorter works are more easily adapted, retaining more of the King flavor and essence of the books. And the cachet of King's name is a double-edged sword: in the book world, it brings the customers into the bookstore, but in the movie world, those new to King's work will take a pass on a new King movie, assuming it is horror. (For this reason, *The Shawshank Redemption,* one of King's best adaptations to the screen, does not herald too loudly that it was based on a King novella. If it did, some would dismiss the film out of hand.)

In contrast, King has adapted to television with more uniform results, though ironically King's participation is no guarantee that the adaptation will be successful. (Witness *The Golden Years,* an original made-for-television miniseries written by King. A standard "chase" movie, once you strip away the supernatural element and the chase, only the heart of the story remained: two old people who find their lives changed forever by a bit of bad timing.)

On the other hand, *It* was adapted as a two-part miniseries that could not have been more effective had it appeared on the screen. And *The Stand*—finally produced, not for the movies as originally planned but for a television mini-series—turned out to be a wonderful adaptation, with an all-star cast giving memorable performances. In both cases—*It* and *The Stand*—the medium, though restrictive because of the network censorship, proved to be the ideal vehicle for both books-turned-teleplays, since the stories required a length that would not have been possible to accommodate on the screen: *It* ran four hours, *The Stand* ran six.

Although it's not likely that King will see the salutary effect of movie adaptations bringing him new readers—a major component to Grisham's growing audience, as well as Tom Clancy's—there will be more of King on screen, both in the theater and on television.

In the meantime, King readers will do what they've always done: after they've popped out the videocassette of their favorite King flicks, they'll pick up the books, fall through the pages, and experience his works played out in what one critic called "skull cinema," the theater of the mind.

3. The Man

After *Carrie* was published, my wife Tabby got very exasperated with me, saying, "You've made all this money, you are a success, let's spend some of it." But I was insecure inside, for a long time, saying, "Look, I don't trust this. Nobody can do this. You can't do this twice or three times." My idea was, the success would never happen again, so I should trickle the money out. Maybe the kids would be eating Cheerios and peanut butter for dinner, but—that's okay! Let them! I'll be *writing*.

Stephen King, in an interview from *Dream Makers*

✳

Success, as any creative person will tell you, is fickle.

King grew up in rural Maine, went to college on a scholarship and a work-study program because he couldn't afford the tuition, graduated, and immediately went to work as a gas-pump attendant, a laborer in an industrial laundry, and eventually a high school English teacher earning $6,400 a year.

No wonder King was nervous when *Carrie* sold in paperback to NAL for

$400,000. He was thinking: Is this a one-shot fluke, or do I actually have the talent to write another novel that could do as well, or better?

The financial ghosts that haunted him have long since fled, but the demon that drives him to write has not, and since *Carrie,* King has become, as he put it, America's favorite bogeyman. Introducing him at a breakfast gathering at the ABA, Joyce Meskis spoke of *Carrie:*

> It was the first work of a man who in catering to a public's worst nightmares would become a publisher's dream. It was the start of a record-breaking career that would redefine a genre and would push publishing into numbers that movie producers dream about. The book was *Carrie* and the author was Stephen King.
>
> Seventeen years and a phenomenal thirty books later, Stephen King has over 150 million copies of his books sold, and [had] a record five books on the various *New York Times* bestseller lists simultaneously last winter.
>
> His catalog of novels reads like a "Who's Who" of the horror world: *It, Four Past Midnight, Misery, The Dark Half, The Stand, Needful Things.*
>
> But how has King managed to grasp the minds and raise the blood pressure of the world's readers so consistently? How is he able to make us care about killer clowns, malevolent cars, pet cemeteries and their remains? Why is he so incredibly popular? It isn't just great writing, although he is a great writer; it is perhaps we tend to think of him as ours—America's Horror Writer Laureate.
>
> Where he leads, we gleefully follow. And whatever he writes, no matter how outrageous, we believe it.

The problem with being a writer is not the writing—that's always there, the one thing that serves as a compass pointing to true north—but *being* a writer: attending bookstore signings, giving interviews, signing books by mail, answering fan mail, giving lectures to librarians and other groups, and being interviewed endlessly, answering the same questions time and again.

King has, over the years, done more than his fair share of it. Because of it, he has become recognizable in a way that many writers are not. Though King complains about his celebrity, you have to ask yourself: How much of it did he bring upon himself? As he voluntarily did these things, what does this say about his private need to be recognized on a mass scale?

You've probably seen Michael Crichton and Tom Clancy interviewed on TV enough to recognize them, but would you recognize Dean R. Koontz if you saw him on the street? Probably not, although his photo is on the jackets of all his hardback books—and he's a best-selling author.

King, for whatever reasons, enjoys the limelight but, increasingly, has seen that the downside is the loss of privacy that affects not only him but his family: his wife, Tabitha, whose books are reviewed with the inevitable mention of her husband; his daughter, Naomi, who was pestered by a neighbor about her famous father, forcing her to change residences; and his two sons who live in the shadow of their famous father.

There is now the necessity to barricade themselves behind iron gates and fences, with closed-circuit TV cameras scanning the landscape, since they've been rudely surprised more than once by out-of-town fans that were drawn to Bangor to meet the master of the macabre. King is not keen on such security.

No wonder they maintain a private residence in the lakes region of southwestern Maine, a contemporary house in Center Lovell, where the locals are understandably mum on its location, and life is as normal as it can be for a bestselling author who is a celebrity in his own right. Back in Bangor, at the office, the secretaries will open the mail, answer it, woman the phones, take care of the incoming fax messages, perhaps check the electronic mail on America OnLine, and open the packages. Long since moved out of King's personal residence, the office staff keeps normal office hours. And after his four-hour stint in front of the word processor, King puts in a half day at the office, going over the business details of being one of the most famous and celebrated writers in our time.

Despite all this, King has not become a recluse like J. D. Salinger, who adamantly refuses to be interviewed or photographed. Instead, King has become a prominent philanthropist, donating time and money to worthy charitable causes in his adopted hometown of Bangor.

In Bangor everyone knows who he is and respects his privacy. It is, perhaps, one reason why King likes Bangor so much: he is treated as one of the locals as he goes about his business; they don't bother him because they know he'd prefer to be left alone, and they respect that.

It's a comfortable fit. Bangor's far enough away so that it keeps some of the media away, big enough to have its own airport, yet small enough to have a small-town feel, although it's the third-largest city in Maine.

From a kid with an overactive imagination who grew up in rural Maine in lower-class circumstances most of his life, Stephen King became larger than the state he calls home. All over the world, millions of people read him in dozens of languages. His movies are likewise seen worldwide, scaring the bejeezus out of foreigners who enjoy a good scare, just as we do.

Approaching fifty in a few years, King, like so many of his fellow baby boomers, has settled in for the long haul. The days of sporting long hair and protesting the Vietnam War are long over; the days of meetings, business calls, and deals have replaced them, as King has become part of the literary establishment—a symbol of what other writers want to achieve: fame and fortune on their own terms.

A family man, a philanthropist, a pillar of the Bangor community, a major figure in contemporary American fiction, and a celebrity who sometimes wishes he weren't, Stephen King has never lost sight of the one thing that *really* matters—the one thing that brought him to where he is today: his ability to tell stories.

In the end, the writing is what matters. Good or bad books, it ultimately doesn't matter, because the body of work is there. And that considerable body of work says: I was here and this is what I wrote and this is what the world looked like to me, and maybe—just maybe—I'll have a writer's immortality by having my books in print . . . forever.

King's story is far from finished. Because creative people tend to live long, productive lives—fueled in part by the work that keeps them perennially young—we may expect a few more decades of stories to amaze, frighten, and delight us.

Oh, God, how the years pass! Has it *really* been two decades since *Carrie* was published? Yes, but it doesn't feel like it. Looking back, I am reminded of the impermanence of time, as King described it in "The Body." Therein the narrator reminisces about Ace Merrill, who terrorized him when they were both younger; no longer a hellraiser, Ace goes into the Mellow Tiger and sits on a barstool and drinks beers . . . and the narrator has become a famous, best-selling writer who thinks it's so funny that he can make a living playing make-believe.

Ace's dreams will never be realized, but the narrator, Gordon Lachance, has seen his come true. And although his best buddies have gone, he is still around. "My story sounds so much like a fairytale that it's fucking absurd," Lachance tells us, echoing King's life.

"The Body" ends with Lachance looking back on a long life and reminiscing:

> I looked to the left, and beyond the mill I could see the Castle River not so wide now but a little cleaner, still flowing under the bridge between Castle Rock and Harlow. The trestle upstream is gone, but the river is still around. So am I.

4
An Evening with Stephen King

*I would just say to you as students who are supposed to be learning:
as soon as that book is gone from the library, do not walk—run
to your nearest public library or bookseller and find out what your elders
don't want you to know, because that's what you need to know!*

Stephen King, on censorship, from "Virginia Beach Lecture"

*

Twice a year the Friends of the Library, a nonprofit group affiliated with the public library system in Virginia Beach, Virginia, holds an annual book sale. In support of the summer sale, which can gross up to $12,000, teenage volunteers—according to Martha J. Sims, the library director—assist the group by sorting books, making signs, unpacking books, and carrying books for customers to their cars. In return, the Friends of the Library donates half its proceeds to bring a favorite author to speak to the volunteers.

In 1985 Mary K. Chelton, then the library programming and community services director, enlisted the aid of the local school system. The school polled its students for the author whom they considered their favorite. According to Sims, "By a tremendous margin, Stephen King was designated as the first choice."

In September 1985 Chelton wrote to Stephen King in care of his publisher, New American Library. A month later King responded through his secretary, Shirley Sonderegger, saying he would appear for expenses only, and what date did she have in mind?

Chelton responded immediately, suggesting April 6–12, 1986. That date conflicted with King's schedule, since he was not only directing *Maximum Overdrive* in North Carolina but also assisting his publisher in an unprecedented publishing event—four of his novels were to be published in a fourteen-month period, later termed the "Stephen King Firestorm."

King suggested a later date, perhaps fall, and Chelton recommended September 21 or 22. King picked the latter—the 21st was his birthday.

Initial Planning

Once the date was confirmed, preparations began in earnest. A promotional poster and a handbill were designed and printed. The poster went up in area libraries and the handbills were distributed freely. Almost immediately, two concerned Virginia Beach citizens wrote a letter to the local paper, asking: "Is Stephen King the type of writer we as parents and responsible citizens want to see the library promoting?"

The citizens were clearly in the minority. By and large, everyone was anxious to hear King speak. The word began to spread, beginning with the local science fiction fan group, the Hampton Roads Science Fiction Association, which put out the word through its meetings and mailings. But the wildfire really started spreading when the official King newsletter, *Castle Rock,* published information about the event in its July issue:

> If you live near Virginia Beach, Virginia, you might want to note September 22, 1986 on your calendar. Stephen King will speak at the Virginia Beach Public Library. Check with them about tickets and time.

That did it. The phones at all the branch libraries of Virginia Beach began ringing off the hook as out-of-town King fans who subscribed to *Castle Rock* called in vain for information about the availability of tickets. Unfortunately, the announcement was premature and unintentionally misleading, since tickets wouldn't be distributed until late August. Besides, the free tickets would be distributed only locally—no tickets would be mailed to anyone for any reason.

The original plan to book the largest room at the Virginia Beach Pavilion had to be scrapped. The demand was far greater than they had imagined. Instead, the main auditorium—capable of seating several thousand—was booked, and four thousand tickets were printed up and distributed to Virginia Beach public libraries, free for the asking.

The Saturday before King's scheduled arrival, an interview with King conducted by phone by William Ruehlmann appeared in the southside newspaper, the *Virginia Pilot-Ledger Star*—the only interview King gave local media preceding the event. Predictably, that story set off another round of frantic phone calls as local King fans burned up the lines trying to get tickets, now long gone.

To ensure that these people would be able to hear King speak, albeit after the fact, plans were made to videotape King's visit, and air it on a local cable TV channel.

In the interim, the details of the trip were worked out: what King would talk about, the flight arrangements, and King's schedule.

Chelton wrote to King, suggesting he talk about "how he became a writer and where he gets all his crazy ideas," and about experiences with his readers, and about the right to read—the latter an especially appropriate subject since Banned Books Week would coincide with King's visit, and King was one of the most frequently banned authors in the country.

As for the flight arrangements, because of the problems inherent with connecting flights, delays in layovers, and the possibility of late flights, King rented a private jet for the trip, picking up most of the cost of the charter.

King flew into Norfolk International and was met early in the day by a small contingent headed by Chelton. Checking into Virginia Beach's Pavilion Towers under an assumed name—Richard Bachman?—King spent most the day signing books for resale at the Pavilion right before his lecture would start. (Estimated at nearly $50,000 worth of books retail, hardback and paperback, all copies sold out in a matter of minutes, attesting to King's popularity.)

At 6:00 P.M. King dined in the hotel with eight teenagers who assisted in the summer sale. Within three hours he would speak to the assembled crowd of several thousand fans who would soon fill the parking lot to capacity.

King Signs . . . and Signs . . . and Signs

The books to be autographed arrived in boxes, packed with Styrofoam pellets. Not knowing what to do with the pellets, King put them in a dresser drawer, leaving an apologetic note for the maid. He then signed the books for hours, until his writing hand temporarily froze. The bigger problem, however, was King's strep throat—that could make speaking for hours difficult. The remedy: pocket a couple of beers from dinner and pull them out as needed during the talk to lubricate his throat.

At 8:00 P.M. the main doors to the Pavilion were opened and a predominantly middle-class crowd streamed in, rushing to the table where a local bookseller had set up, offering signed copies of King's books. Since there was to be no separate autographing, this was the opportunity to get signed books, and the lines were understandably long as books and money changed hands.

At 9:00 P.M., flanked by two security guards, King took his seat behind the podium, as he received a standing ovation—thunderous applause.

The evening with King began as Kelly Powell, one of the library's teenage volunteers, stood at the podium and read his introduction.

Introducing Stephen King
by Kelly Powell

Our guest, Stephen King, is no stranger to most of you. He's taken all of us on some very peculiar trips to a place called Castle Rock on many occasions. It's not a place you want to visit for fun all by yourself, but somehow, you get a kick out of it when you go with him. There's probably nobody here who sees fog without thinking about being trapped in a supermarket in the mist—with Stephen King. I'll bet some of you look at your cars a little funny after riding in Christine—with Stephen King. And nobody wants to sit with Gramma—after meeting Stephen King's. And prom night is just fine without Carrie. Let Stephen King be *her* date. And just hope when you die of possibly mysterious causes, that somebody can pay for your funeral with a MasterCard like Stephen King did in *Pet Sematary*. He's not exactly unforgettable, this Stephen King.

Unfortunately, some people don't think the rest of us should read him. Stephen King's books have been banned in the following places:

- Las Vegas, Nevada (1975)—*Carrie* challenged at the Clark High School Library as "trash."

- Vergennes, Vermont (1978)—*Carrie* was placed on a special closed shelf in the high school library because it could "harm" students, especially "young girls."

- Rankin County, Mississippi (1984)—*Cujo* was challenged because it was considered "profane and sexually objectionable."

- Bradford, New York (1984)—*Cujo* was removed from the shelves of the school library "because it was a bunch of garbage."

- Campbell County, Wyoming (1984)—*Firestarter* was challenged because of its alleged "graphics description of sexual acts, vulgar language, and violence." *The Shining* was also challenged because "the story contains violence, demonic possession and ridicules the Christian religion."

- Washington County, Alabama (1984)—*Christine* was banned from all school libraries because the book contained "unacceptable language" and was considered "pornographic."

- Hayward, California (1985)—*Cujo* was rejected for purchase for school libraries because of the "rough language" and "explicit sex scenes."

- Vancouver, Washington (1986)—*The Shining* was removed from four junior high libraries because the book's "descriptive foul language" made it unsuitable for teenagers.

Stephen King gives new meaning to the old phrase: "If you're not controversial, you have nothing to offer," so it is especially appropriate that he is the Friends of the Library featured speaker for Banned Books Week, 1986. This event proclaims his right to write the books that he wants to write, and our right to read them if we choose; and, obviously, a great many of us do so choose, despite those who would like to keep us from doing so.

Ladies and gentlemen, I present the contemporary master of horror fantasy—Stephen King.

After the applause, King read from a forthcoming manuscript, Misery, *and then spoke extemporaneously and answered questions, pulling them from a box stuffed by people who had come to hear him speak.*

Banned Books and Other Concerns: The Virginia Beach Lecture
A public talk
by Stephen King

That's the most uplifting introduction I've ever had. Think of all those places I've been banned.

I've always wanted to start one of these things by coming out and saying, "Hello, I'm Johnny Cash," but I guess I can't do that now. I do have sort of a strep throat, but I brought a little vitamin B along with me to take care of the problem.

How many of you are sort of bored with Banned Books and the whole discussion on Banned Books?

Me, too. I don't go out on purpose to talk about it, and I'm not going to talk about it too long tonight.

I don't lecture because I don't really know how, and I don't make speeches because I don't know how to do that. What I do is let my jaw fall open and let it run by itself. See, I used to be a high school teacher and it's sort of like Pavlov's dogs: the bell rings and your jaw falls open. You continue to talk until another bell rings, so you guys could be here all night if somebody doesn't ring a bell.

But I wanted to tell you a couple of stories about books and the sort of situation you get into with controversial material, or material that some people consider to be controversial.

The first thing happened just after I published *'Salem's Lot,* which was well received by my relatives, but not too many other people. This was just before the movie *Carrie* came out and made me sort of a household name like Spiro Agnew. I went to a ladies' reading group in western Maine where I spoke and ran my jaw for a while and asked for questions. A lady who was about sixty-five going on eight hundred stood up and said: "Well, you know, I like that story, but I didn't like all that foul language. And I don't know any reason for anyone to tell a good story with all that foul language in it."

Photo by GB

Stephen King lecturing in Virginia Beach during Banned Books Week.

And I replied, "Well, think of it this way: Think of the way guys talk in the barbershop on Saturday morning."

She said, "Well, I've been in the barbershop on Saturday morning, and they don't talk that way."

I replied, "Madame, I am writing about the Saturday mornings you *didn't* come."

I've written a lot of stories about desperate people in desperate situations, and it gets to the point where you say to yourself: Here's a guy who's building something in his garage. He's all by himself, and he's hammering a nail into the board and hits his thumb instead, and blood squirts out. Now, does this guy say, "Oh, pickles"? Use your imagination. In other words, what I'm talking about is telling the truth. Frank Norris, who wrote *The Pit, McTeague,* and other naturalistic novels that were banned, said: "I don't fear; I don't apologize because I know in my heart that I never lied; I never truckled. *I told the truth."* And I think that the real truth of fiction is that fiction is the truth; moral fiction is the truth inside the lie. And if you lie in your fiction, you are immoral and have no business writing at all.

The other story, about banned books: A few years ago I did a film called *Creepshow.* And when the film was in postproduction, there was a controversy in the Pittsburgh school system. A kid who had been assigned to do a term paper on work picked the steelworking industry. And a book that he took out of the school library was a book called *Working* by Studs Terkel.

The way Terkel works: He sits in bars with working guys after they get off work, and his great genius is that he turns on the tape recorder and doesn't ask them any questions—he just lets them rap on about what they do. And, of course, steelworkers are the same as the guy who is missing the nail with the hammer and doesn't say "Oh, pickles." The steelworkers used a number of words that the lady would have heard on those days she wasn't in the barbershop . . . and they were all in the book.

The boy's mother saw the book, read it, and was horrified by some of the language. There were words that rhymed with *shuck* and words that rhymed with—well, never mind; you know those words. George Carlin calls them the seven words that you can't say on TV.

The boy's mother was horrified and demanded that the book be taken out of the Pittsburgh school system, and that it be banned because it would be harmful to high school kids to read those books. They might read those words and their eyes might turn to jelly and run down their faces, or possibly they might be incited to go out and rape women, children, porcupines—who knows?

Anyhow, you know how impressionable teenagers are. They can't be trusted to do anything; they are totally useless human beings who will do anything their friends tell them to do—give them Golden Books and they'll grow up to be responsible adults capable of facing the world.

It went to the school board and there was a protracted fight, after which *Working* was actually taken for a time out of the Pittsburgh school system.

The real kicker to the story was when the kid who had to do the report took the book out, there was one stamp in that book—his. The book had been in the library for three years, but nobody had taken it out. By the time the school board decided to remove it, there were sixty-three stamps in the book.

I was involved with an antiobscenity referendum in Maine. The referendum question was very simply stated: "Do you want to make it a crime to sell or vend obscene material?" This is sort of like saying, "Do you want to make it a crime to kill Santa Claus?" Well, most people said, "Of course." But when they went into the voting booths, I think that they thought a little bit different, and I'm happy to say the referendum was voted down, 70 percent to 30 percent, because they realized that *obscene* is one of those words that exists in the eye of the beholder. What's obscene—what's *not* obscene? What's bad—what's *not* bad? What's moral—what's immoral?

We live in a democracy, a place that limits free will where it's supposed to reign. Democracy is a two-edged sword, which is to say there are all sorts of rock-ribbed Republicans and conservatives who argue that you'll take the gun from their hands when you pry their cold, dead fingers from it. . . .

Okay, that's fine, and there are people who say, "You can't make me wear a motorcycle helmet when I ride because it's my God-given right to ride any way that I want, and it's not *your* business to tell me how to ride."

Man, I love that law. We have a no-helmet law in Maine, and as far as I'm concerned, it gets a lot of the dreck out of the gene pool, because these guys hit the wall and they're gone, baby. If they're not smart enough to wear a helmet, screw them: they're gone—they won't have a lot of kids and be on welfare and all this other stuff.

Okay, we understand that democracy is a two-edged sword. If you give people the right to have guns, sooner or later someone is going to get gut-holed. And we understand that if you give people the right to ride without a helmet, sooner or later somebody's brains are going to get turned into something that looks like what's in a Mixmaster. But for a lot of conservatives and fundamentalists, there is a point on the blade of democracy where that double edge becomes a single edge—and that point occurs when their own personal sensibilities are offended.

The greatest offenders are fundamentalist preachers and teachers. They are people like Jimmy Swaggart and Pat Robertson who, if they could jump into a time machine and go back to the Garden of Eden, would point up and say:

"God, you've got this tree. It's the tree of good and evil. Now, you are going to put a barbed-wire fence around it *right now!*"

Well, God didn't put any barbed-wire fence around it. Jesus said render unto Caesar those things that belong to Caesar, and render unto God those things that belong to God. And as far as I'm concerned, they can keep their noses out of what I read.

Don't tell me I can't have a gun if I'm a moral, upright citizen. Don't tell me I have to wear a mouthguard when I ride my motorcycle, which was a law that existed for a while in California. And don't tell me what goes on the shelves in my living room.

I would like to say one other thing that has to do with public school libraries. They are in a situation called *in loco parentis,* which means that they have to adhere very carefully to the idea that *they are the parent.* And if there's a consensus that decides a book should be taken out of the library, I believe they should take that book out.

I have no problem with that at all, if they take *Cujo* or *'Salem's Lot* or *The Shining* out of a public school, or if they take *Working* out of the Pittsburgh system. I would just say to you as students who are supposed to be learning, that as soon as that book is gone from the library, do not walk—*run to your nearest public library or bookseller and find out what your elders don't want you to know, because that's what you* need *to know!*

Don't let them bullshit you and don't let them guide your mind, because once it starts, it never stops. Some of our most famous leaders have been book-banners, like Hitler, Stalin, Idi Amin.

Anyway, enough about banned books.

Let me see, what questions I'm most often asked.

Where do you get your ideas? I don't really know; they come.

How does it feel to be famous? No different than anyone else, but it's a little bit strange. One of the odd things that happens is that you learn to always button your fly or to zip it because people say, "That's Stephen King and his fly's undone!"

The story about being famous is the Pittsburgh story. I don't know if you've heard this or not, but I'll give you the abbreviated version. The first book tour that I ever did was for *The Shining*, which Doubleday decided to push. I went on an author tour, which means you do everything in a city that gives you media. The last thing that I did was a banquet/dinner with Julius Feiffer, Brendan Gill, and a couple of other writers. And somebody said, "Well, let's go and get drunk after it's all over," which sounded like a very sensible idea at the time, because when you sit up on a stage, you know that you have to make a speech and two thousand people are watching you eat chicken, seeing which fork you use—it's a little bit unsettling.

So we went up to a bar that was way up on top of a mountain, which Pittsburghians call the Incline. I started to feel what is politely called Montezuma's revenge: a real sort of earthquake was going on inside me, so I excused myself and ran into the gentleman's facility, a fantastic place with gold and marble. The bathroom attendant was eight hundred years old with a bald skull and pulsing veins—you know what I'm talking about—with a towel over his arm and a couple of quarters in a dish to show you what you were supposed to do in case you were unlettered. The only thing this ornate bathroom didn't have was doors on the stalls, but I was past caring at that point. My situation had reached the redline, so I rushed in and I never felt more sorry for myself in my entire life.

I had been away from home for a week; I was homesick and I was physically sick, and I thought that things could not get any worse, until the attendant approaches me with a silver pen in his hand. "Aren't you Stephen King? My mother saw you on the 'Morning' show. She loves all your books. Could I have your autograph for her?" So there I sat with my jeans around my ankles, giving this guy my autograph. What a good time it was. . . . And *that's* what it's like to be famous.

Now, let me see . . . Let me reach into the box and see if we have any Lotto winners! [King is holding a handful of papers with questions scribbled on them.] This ought to be enough to take us through tomorrow morning.

[From the audience: "Happy birthday!"] Thank you. I turned thirty-nine yesterday. Like Jerry Lee says: thirty-nine and holding onto anything I can. Not really; I don't mind being thirty-nine. I got all this figured out: This midlife crisis business is bull. The actuarial tables say everybody croaks by seventy-two—that's the average—so I figure I passed my midlife crisis around thirty-six and didn't even notice it when it happened—it just went by. You figure the three stages of life: Being young, being middle-aged, and being old, okay? According to the actuarial tables, you are middle-aged as soon as you turn thirty-five—that's when you should have your midlife crisis. As soon as you are forty-eight, you are an old fart and you can forget it. But, okay . . .

The first question: "What do you think about God and what do you think about Pat Robertson? PS: When is PBS going to make *The Stand* into a miniseries?"[1] PBS may be the only hope, because you can't do it on a network. You can't have the end of the world brought to you by Charmin Toilet Tissue—they just aren't into it. As to what I think about God: He's out there. A more important question is what God thinks of *me*. As far as what I think about Pat Robertson running for president: Baby, you don't want to know. That's like asking me what

---

1. This lecture was given in 1986. In 1994, *The Stand* aired as a TV miniseries on ABC-TV, which drew its highest ratings for a miniseries in almost two decades.

I think about if Christ had run for the emperor of Rome. I don't think the place for a preacher is in politics, and I don't think the place for a politician is in preaching. I think that one person who proved that admirably was Jimmy Carter, who at least understood the difference between Caesar and God, and God and Caesar. Maybe he wasn't such a great president, but he was okay.

Here's a question that says, "What do you think of Virginia Beach?" Well, I saw a hotel and a hall. The outside of this place [the Virginia Beach Pavilion] has got an interesting construction. It looks sort of like something Trashcan Man might burn up—all these round things all stuck together. But I think Virginia Beach is great because they asked me to come here. Actually, you are very sweet to have me; you've all sat there while I've run my chops.

This question says, "Who is my favorite comic book character?" Batman, without a doubt; Spiderman is in second place, but what I'm sort of into is G.I. Joe.

I have a word processor which I only use for rewrites. The brain is called a CPU, which is a great big box that just sits there—it's a little bit intimidating, so I cover the top with G.I. Joes fighting each other. Sometimes, when I'm road-blocked, I push them together and people come in that you don't know and you get a little embarrassed and say, "I'm just trying to figure out something the kids can do when they get home from school."

For my birthday yesterday, Owen, my youngest son, who is nine, knows the truth. He gave me a Doctor Mindbender—he's so cool . . .

"Do you scare yourself sometimes?" The answer is: Yes. I've scared myself three times. A lot of times it feels like you've got a bulldozer inside your head and you know that you are going to scare people, but it doesn't feel bad. My idea about what a really good book is, is when the writer—whether he's alive or dead—suddenly reaches out of the page and grabs you by the throat and says: *You're mine, baby! You belong to me! Try to get away! You want to cook some dinner for your husband? Too bad! You want to go to bed? Tough shit! You're mine! You belong to me.*

That's my idea of what it's supposed to be about. You're supposed to go out there and get them. You are not supposed to mess around and be delicate— *you're supposed to run them down.*

I have scared myself on three occasions—one of them is in the book I just read to you, where something extremely nasty happens later . . . and I just passed that point in the rewrite and realized to myself that I'd been dragging my feet, because I knew when I got to the axe and the blowtorch, things were going to be nasty, and I didn't want to write that.

And there's one in *The Shining,* where this kid goes into this room and there's a dead lady in the bathtub. He keeps telling himself those things aren't there, but he turns around and, man, *she's still there.* I got so freaked, I couldn't believe it.

It usually comes up on you the worst in the rewrite when you realize that you've got to face that whole nightmare again.

The third time would have been toward the end of *Christine,* when I began to see how badly everything would turn out. I really didn't like it very much, because the whole book started out to be sort of a joke: "Happy Days" gone mad: Boy gets car, boy loses car, boy finds car.

I thought it was hilarious, until the kid started to run people down. Sometimes stories get out of control and they are like the car itself—they start to run by themselves and don't always turn out the way you think they are going to turn out.

I'll answer a couple more of these, and then I'll ask for a couple more from the audience. [Pulling questions from a box] is like no interaction whatsoever—I can't stand that. There's got to be some feedback, I think.

"What's the average and the longest hours a day you might spend writing?" I think the longest I ever spent in front of the typewriter was when I was working on *The Talisman.* I was writing about the Sunlight Gardner home and realized that seven hours had gone by, and that my kidneys hurt like hell, but I could barely get out of the chair. That was a weird experience, but that was with the word processor, which I've since given up.

Have you ever seen that James Bond movie [*Thunderball*] where he gets hooked into the exercise machine and the thing starts exercising him to death? That's what a word processor is like—it's insanity. I've given it up. I used to write six pages and I was out, but a word processor just keeps scrolling up and up—there's no end.

"Some of your readers can find a moral story in many of your stories. Do you intend this and, if so, do you intend your stories to be the next set of Mother Goose stories for the coming generations?" The answer is I try to be as moral as I can, because you walk a fine line in this field. There's too much exploitation. There's too much slasher stuff—too much like the later *Friday the 13th* movies.

My criterion here is that you don't come to see people get away—you come to see people *die.* And, to me, at that point you've crossed the line into immoral territory. I have always wanted my characters to be alive, and I've always wanted my readers to like the characters and to find them good and hopeful, and I want them to live.

I got a lot of letters about *Cujo* when the little boy, Tad Trenton, died. Well, I didn't think he was going to die. I didn't mean for him to die—I thought he was going to live. So I get letters saying: "Oh, you son of a bitch . . . the kid died. How could you *do* that?" I would write back: "I don't know—he died. I was working away and I thought she was going to get him back to life, but the kid just croaked. I couldn't help it." The fact is, that's a moral ending because kids don't always live—sometimes they die. That's the truth: sometimes they die, and sometimes they can be saved.

Well, I thought, then let him live in the movie, because I think we would have been lynched from pillars outside every movie theater in America. Also, I was curious to see what would happen if the kid *did* live, because that's what I had intended all along. But, unfortunately, after the movie ends, I think in the context of the movie, the kid dies an even nastier death because after the dog has been bitten by the rabid bat and licks the kid's face, I'm sure he ended up with rabies, and he died an even worse death. But that's after the end.

Do you have any other questions?

[A question is asked about *The Stand* being made into a movie.] I hope *The Stand* will come out as a movie. We've been talking about it. There has been a script for a long time. I think it would make a wonderful movie. To me, it doesn't look that terrible or expensive to do.

Luckily, *Stand by Me* has been made based on "The Body," which has been a success. Maybe that will make a difference and unlock some of the funds— I don't know. The real problem isn't money, it's time. The movie would probably run two and a quarter hours, and they don't like movies that run longer than two hours because it makes it tough to run three shows a night.

Pet Sematary as a movie? I don't know. It was scheduled and unscheduled and rescheduled. Hollywood people are crazy; they're not like us.[2]

[A question about a restored version of *The Stand*.] He asked me about *The Stand* and whether or not it was true that it was going to be reissued, and that pages were cut from it.

The truth was that *The Stand* was four hundred pages longer than it was when it finally appeared. The reason those pages were cut was that this was my last book with Doubleday, and they wanted to publish it at $12.95. I was called into a meeting and told, "This book is four hundred pages too long. Do you want to cut it—or shall we?"

So I said, "Well, maybe I better do it," because I didn't know what they would cut. I made the best cuts I could, but there was a lot of good stuff in those pages, so we're going to republish it and reinstate the stuff that's gone. It's real nice stuff—a lot of it is real cool, complete with pictures by Berni Wrightson. It's going to be a nice book.[3]

[A question from the audience about how much of Bill Denbrough of *It* came from Stephen King.] It was to an extent, but when writers write about themselves, they always lie. . . . So you change things around a bit.

The actual physical character of Bill Denbrough is based on Peter Straub. The Bill Denbrough character is bald—and while I've started to show a little snow on top of the mountain, I don't seem to be losing too much of my hair.

---

2. The movie was eventually released in April 1989.

3. The uncut edition was published by Doubleday in 1990.

Photo courtesy of the *Bangor Daily News*

King in tuxedo makes Bob Haskell "eat crow."

Some of my marbles, I think, but not too much of my hair. . . . And when Peter was three years old, like the character in *It*, he and his seven-year-old brother had been allowed to go down to the market to get ice cream cones. On their way back, a car, driven by a drunk driver, struck Peter and drove him into the wall. His older brother picked up his ice cream cone, walked back to the house, and said, "Peter's dead. He was a good brother." But Peter wasn't dead. . . . I showed Peter the manuscript and asked if I could use it.

It's funny, for instance, but in "The Body," which turned into the movie *Stand by Me*, almost every incident in that book actually happened, but I twisted everything around. I have leech scars in several places on my body, some of which could not be shown without really getting Pat Robertson mad. (If you see the movie, you'll know what I'm talking about.) You twist things around to fit the story—that's all.

[From the audience: "*The Talisman* is good. Do you plan on collaborating again?"] Not in the near future. Collaborating was tough, but it was fun, too. It was a good story.

Fanny fatigue seems to be settling in with some people, so I'll tell you what: I'll take two more questions.

And I do want to say that, generally, I don't have any problem with autographing, but [autographing here] would be like having a wine-and-cheese party for the entire Democratic party. And once you start, you can't stop, because you can do about forty people, and the first forty are insane collectors who have books in wrappers that they don't even want you to touch without gloves on. And what you end up with is three hundred autographs and a hand that looks like one of Jerry's kids—and everyone else is sort of left out and they're not happy about it.

[In response to a question from the audience:] Am I a big Boston Red Sox fan? Do ursine mammals excrete in high foliage inside the woods? I'm such a big Boston Red Sox fan that I can't wait for the Red Sox–Houston World Series. And if they play those wimps the Mets, it'll be over in four games, because the Mets are so soft and Houston is a scrappy little team.

I made a bet with a Bangor sportswriter who foolishly declared that Boston would be out by Flag Day. He ate some chicken in his skivvies—I ate mine in my tuxedo. That was one of the best days—as the guys say in the song—of my life.

＊

After ninety minutes, when it was obvious that questions would pepper King all night, Mary Chelton—concerned about King's aggravating strep throat—cut off the questions and closed the evening's activities by presenting King with a Friends of the Library T-shirt, which he gratefully accepted.

Then, just as he had arrived, King left, escorted by two security guards.

The Aftermath

The following day, a local radio show took questions from its listeners about King's visit to Virginia Beach. Not surprisingly, some listeners were concerned about the "negative" image King has presented by drinking beer in front of an impressionable young crowd and also using mature language during the talk itself, but they were clearly in the minority.

The mayor's office received one complaint about King's "public drinking and advocacy of sex and drugs," and the library had received one complaint about the beer King consumed. (Ironically, King's talk—presented as part of a Banned Books Week event—was banned from local cable television.)

Afterward, King sent Mary Chelton a thank-you note and enclosed a personal check, refunding the amount of royalties he would receive on the books sold before the lecture.

5

You Know They've Got a Helluva Band
The Rock Bottom Remainders

This band plays music as well as Metallica writes novels.

Dave Barry, on the Rock Bottom Remainders

✳

One of the nicest things about being a famous writer—or semifamous, or a best-selling writer—is that you can indulge your fantasies, even if they're as far-fetched as being in a rock and roll band with an audience that really doesn't care what you play: just play it REAL LOUD! as Robin Williams in the role of a disk jockey in Vietnam reminded us.

For a handful of writers, including Stephen King, the dream came true when Kathi Kamen Goldmark, a book publicist from San Francisco, decided to form the first rock and roll band of best-selling authors. (The ones that couldn't play the guitar or sing were members of the Critics Chorus or Remainderettes, depending on whether or not you looked good in a black sequined skirt that rode pretty high up your hips.)

In her liner notes to "The Rock Bottom Remainders" video—ironically out of print because the publishers who own "Teen Angel" objected to King's improvisation to its lyrics—Goldmark picked up on a general comment that she heard a number of authors voice: "Writing is okay, but I was in a band in college and it was the most fun I ever had."

Writing, you see, is *work*. It's what you do to make a living, and although it's fun, it's, well, okay . . . but nothing like being on stage in front of a thousand screaming fans who really don't care how well you play; they just want to boogie to the music!

On May 25, 1992, at the Cowboy Boogie in Anaheim, California, the Rock Bottom Remainders gave their first "plugged" public performance—earlier in the evening, they sang in unison "unplugged" at an anticensorship benefit. Playing to a capacity crowd of booksellers—tickets were not available to the general public—the band took to the stage and soon had the audience screaming . . . for more!

How good were they? On the BMG video, "The Rock Bottom Remainders," Dave Barry, a competent guitar player but weak on vocals, perhaps spoke for all the members of the band in saying, "I don't think we're really bad—I think we're medium garage-band level."

King, as you'd expect, was a big draw. In fact, standing in line outside the Cowboy Boogie, a number of fans showed up simply because of King. (That BMG headlined his name first on the cover of its video of the first performance underscores the brand-name appeal of King, even as a part-time rock band member. To underscore the point: In Joel Selvin's piece in *Mid-Life Confidential,* he wrote: "All along the way, our fellow members of the press evidenced zero interest in the Critics Chorus. Dave Barry, yes. Amy Tan, maybe. But as long as Steve King was available, everybody was happy. 'Stephen King, Others Killed in Crash' went the joke on board the tour bus.")

Humorously introduced by Roy Blount Jr. each member had a part to play:

- **Dave** (His Mind May Be Full of Boogers and Dog Poop, But His Heart Is Full of Love) **Barry** . . . guitar and vocals.
- **Tad** (Just a Tad Toooo Bad) **Bartimus** . . . Remainderette vocals
- **Michael** (Whoever Heard of a Man Named) **Dorris** . . . percussion
- **Robert** (But Then I Forgot It All in Grade School) **Fulghum** . . . mandocello, guitar, and vocals
- **Kathi** (the Queen of the Book Tour) **Goldmark** . . . Band Mother and Remainderette vocals
- **Matt** (Happy Families Are All Alike) **Groening** . . . Critics Chorus
- **Stephen** (and Still the) **King** . . . guitar and vocals
- **Barbara** (She May Be the Answer to Stephen) **Kingsolver** . . . keyboard and vocals
- **Al** (He May Be a Mother-You-Know-What, But We All Call Him Dad) **Kooper** . . . keyboard and guitar
- **Greil** (Elvis is Dead in My Book) **Marcus** . . . Critics Chorus
- **Dave** (I'll Say 'Fuck the Police' If I Want to) **Marsh** . . . Critics Chorus
- **Ridley** (He Do Know Diddly) **Pearson** . . . bass and vocals
- **Joel** (If You Rearrange His Name It Spells Nelvis) **Selvin** . . . Critics Chorus
- **Amy** (If You Can't Stand the Heat, Get Out of My Kitchen) **Tan** . . . Remainderette vocals

Logo design by Gretchen Schields

King, who plays the guitar better than he can sing, took center stage to croon "Sea of Love," which, in my recollection, sounded much better than it did on the poorly recorded BMG video from that same night. (Was I, like the others, caught up in the moment or did BMG just give us a muddy recording? A little of both, I think.) Enveloped in a sea of blue lights and rising mist—appropriate touches—King obviously had a lot of fun on stage with this song.

At the end of the concert, King closed with one of his favorites, "Teen Angel."

Though this was planned as a one-shot event, the Remainders were never remaindered. Instead, they played in Miami in 1993 and in Los Angeles at

1994. They even toured professionally in May 1993, playing in Boston; Providence, Rhode Island; Northampton and Cambridge, Massachusetts; Washington, D.C.; Philadelphia; Atlanta; Nashville; and ending up at Miami, where they made their second ABA performance—a whirlwind tour aptly chronicled in *Mid-Life Confidential: The Rock Bottom Remainders Tour America with Three Chords and an Attitude,* with contributions from each member and illustrated with one hundred photos by Tabitha King.

For my money, though, neither the book nor the video could capture the spirit of camaraderie and plain fun that marked their debut appearance, as they belted out "Money," "Nadine," "Sea of Love," "Louie Louie," "Bye, Bye Love," "Gloria," "Good Rockin' Tonight," "Double Shot of Love," "Take Out Some Insurance," "Ripple," and "Teen Angel." No rap, no heavy metal, no grunge; just some classics that middle-aged Americans grew up on when they were teenagers, when rock and roll burst onto the scene in the fifties and defined a generation that adopted it like a rebel flag.

Those were the days, my friend, and I thought they'd never end . . . but they did, and a lot of the writers in the group grew up and never played in the rock bands beyond high school (like King) and college (like Dave Barry). Instead, they pounded the typewriter or computer keyboards instead of the piano keyboards, and gave us words instead of music, and then they grew up and became famous, best-selling authors, and things came full circle.

For King the circle, finally, had been completed. Previous to his appearance in Remainders, he took the stage with John Cafferty and the Beaver Brown Band (see the back cover photo on the hardback edition of *It*), but that was just an interim, spur-of-the-moment thing. It really began back in Durham, Maine, when he and childhood friend Chris Chesley discovered the wonders of the guitar together, when all they had was a friendship, a shared belief in writing, a love for the fantastic, and a love for rock and roll.

How good, in King's estimation, was that first performance? In "The Neighborhood of the Beast" (read his piece to understand the allusion), King wrote: "We weren't very good that night at Cowboy Boogie—I have hidden my copy of the videotape of the show and refuse to tell anyone where it is—but we were loud, and the audience was enthusiastic."

In the end, that was enough, and that was all that mattered.

King front and center at Cowboy Boogie (Anaheim, California).

Photo by GB

6
Stephen King's Field of Dreams
The Shawn Trevor Mansfield Complex
by Daniel Golden

Stephen King told an interviewer in the late eighties, "There is a baseball book in me. I didn't mention it because that's the one that's closest to happening." King never wrote that novel—or if he did, it went into his trunk of unpublished books—but he did write a lengthy nonfiction piece, "Head Down," which recounts the tribulations of the Bangor West All-Star team, for which his youngest son, Owen, played.

King, who coached Little League baseball during his college days, felt compelled to record their story, taking a month out of his life to help coach the team and, with his novelist's eye, observe and write about what is surely every young boy's dream: to play on a winning all-star team.

Originally published in the New Yorker, *King's piece was reprinted in an anthology of the best sportswriting for that year. It's a pity that he doesn't write more nonfiction, especially pieces about baseball, where his personal interest and professional skill can combine to give us a memorable piece that anyone can enjoy. As for the piece itself, King admits that it was "the best nonfiction writing of my life . . ." and cites Chip McGrath, the editor of the* New Yorker, *for his part in encouraging and helping King—the role of a good editor.*

A steadfast Boston Red Sox fan, King lamented that there was no appropriate Little League field in Bangor and decided to make a dream come true for Little Leaguers. He donated the money to build a field in the park behind his house, which is informally known as the Field of Screams (a play on Kinsella's baseball novel, Field of Dreams) *and is formally known as the Shawn Trevor Mansfield Complex, named after the son of Dave Mansfield (the coach who led the Senior Little League All-Stars to victory), who died at age fourteen.*

In the piece that follows, originally titled "Field of Screams," Daniel Golden, a staff writer for the Boston Globe *magazine (August 1992), tells the story of the $1 million-plus ballpark that King built.*

✳

"Who wants it more?" A hulking, awkward man in the standard Penobscot County coaching attire of jeans, baseball cap, and scruffy Converse All-Stars leans on the top step of the first-base dugout, barking encouragement to his team of nervous teenagers. The right-field scoreboard, raised only a few hours ago, isn't working yet, but the manager's voice—oddly urgent, strangely obsessive—conveys that the game, if not the fate of the world, hangs in the balance.

Whatever demons possess him aren't shared by the hundred or so fans scattered in the 1,500-seat grandstand above the dugout. On this sunny July afternoon in Bangor, Maine, they're cheering for schoolmates or children to get a hit, munching hot dogs or home-baked brownies on sale for a quarter from the concession stand, and occasionally visiting the portable toilets erected in the parking lot until the stadium restrooms are ready.

They've also come out of curiosity about the ballpark, an unexpected gift wrapped in a palette of baseball colors: orange clay infield, Kentucky bluegrass outfield, pink warning track made of stone dust from Mount Desert Island. Beyond the outfield fence stand clumps of forest and three-deckers and a flag-topped water tower marking the highest point in Bangor. In foul territory, toddlers clamber over a fanciful playground that resembles a medieval city.

The manager is too busy to enjoy the view. He records every pitch on his scorecard. He signals to the third-base coach, rubbing his chest and scratching his neck as if suffering from poison ivy. And he exhorts his West Bangor Senior Little League all-stars to dig down deep against Brewer.

"Who wants it more?"

The voice belongs to Stephen King, and, to answer his question, nobody wants this victory more than America's self-described "literary bogeyman" himself. Right now, King, whose thirty horror books and half-dozen Hollywood screenplays have made him one of the world's wealthiest authors, is as possessed as any of the ghosts, vampires, or telekinetic girls that haunt his fiction.

That's not surprising, because this tableau, this hard-fought contest between West Bangor and its archrival across the Penobscot River, is as much King's creation as are his novels. Two years ago he helped revive Senior Little League in Bangor so that boys aged thirteen to fifteen could play organized baseball.

King became coach of the WZON team, named after the Bangor rock station he used to own. And when he discovered that his team had to play on a field that he describes as a "sad, neglected, overgrown, frost-heaved, guilty afterthought," he spent $1.2 million to build a proper ballpark for Bangor.

"These kids have been cheered all their lives," says the forty-four-year-old King. "When Little League ends, the cheering stops and the crowds are gone. They have to play under field conditions that are not only poor but dangerous. At age thirteen, they find out what it is to be a washed-out rock star."

Photo courtesy of the *Bangor Daily News*

Stephen King at a local Little League baseball game in Maine (1990).

By joining what his wife, Tabitha, calls the "surrogate dads' community among amateur coaches," King could experience the father-son bonding he had missed as a child. Abandoned by his father before he was old enough to play catch or swing a bat, King was eager to share the joys of baseball with his younger son, Owen, a slugging first baseman, and Owen's friends. The novelist ran errands for Owen's Little League team, then moved up to Senior Little League with his son. Since *Field of Dreams* is a popular movie about a farmer who builds a ballpark to make peace with his father's memory, it's small wonder that some Bangor residents joke about King's "Field of Screams."

The park's official name alludes to another father-son story. Dave Mansfield is a Little League coach who led West Bangor to the Maine championship in 1989. He also coaches third base for King's Senior Little League all-stars. At King's suggestion, the park will be named after Mansfield's son, who died of cerebral palsy in 1980 at the age of fourteen. A plaque near the entrance will be dedicated to "Shawn Trevor Mansfield and all the other boys who never got to play baseball."

Mansfield, whose sun-toughened face and salt-and-pepper beard give him the look of a retired sea captain, was moved by King's gesture. "Steve's a good friend," he says.

Shawn Trevor Mansfield Complex, aka the Field of Screams, is as idyllic as Ray Kinsella's Iowa cornfield. It is intended, King says, to re-create the atmosphere of town baseball early in this century, when barnstorming semi-pros would challenge the local nine before a shirt-sleeved crowd.

The field has no dome, no artificial turf, no television cameras. A press box was canceled because it cost too much; reporters peek at the game from a ground-level stadium window. When Coca-Cola and Pepsi offered to pay for the $20,000 scoreboard if it would display their logos, King vetoed the deal and picked up the tab. The concessionaires are volunteers, mostly Little Leaguers and their parents.

Aside from an ornate clock with Roman numerals, the House That *Carrie* Built is also bereft of horror clichés. King's faithful would search in vain for gnarled oaks, creaking iron hinges, or cobwebbed dugouts. No cemetery lies under the field, just a mile of drainage pipe and a computer-driven sprinkler system. Tabitha King had hoped to drape vines on the chain-link outfield fence, which might have been a tad creepy, but the fence couldn't take the weight.

Although King is a rabid Red Sox fan, his field is not Fenway Park North. No Green Monster lurks here. Designed to meet college standards, in case King's alma mater, the University of Maine, in nearby Orono, should need to use the park, its dimensions are symmetrical: 330 feet down the lines, 375 to the gaps, 400 to the straightaway center.

The city of Bangor owns and operates the ballpark, but King keeps an eye on it from his nearby twenty-three-room Victorian mansion—and from the dugout. His players praise its smooth surface and true hops. "It's so different from our other field," says pitcher Mike Pelkey. "That was like sliding on cement. Every time someone slid, they were cut open."

Yet playing on an adult-sized diamond means a major-league adjustment for teenagers accustomed to the miniature confines of Little League. Some Senior Little Leaguers thrive in a world of ninety-foot base paths. Others discover their inadequacy and begin to consider alternative careers.

"The kid who had a rocket arm in Little League finds he can't throw from third to first," King says. "The kid who used to hit homers when the fence was 200 feet now finds they're just pop flies."

Through seven games of the five-team district tournament inaugurating the ballpark, nobody has hit a home run yet. Like the field itself, the style of play is a throwback to the deadball era, before the Bambino revolutionized the sport.

Rather than swing for distant fences, West Bangor has adopted Mansfield's system, which King calls "Davyball." It requires a lot of bunts, steals, and hit-and-runs—and signals between King in the dugout and Mansfield in the third-base coach's box. "The two of them are signaling back and forth all day," says Gary Crowell, whose firm constructed the park for King. "They have more fun than the kids."

Most of West Bangor's players, including Owen King, were on the 1989 Little League team that parlayed Davyball into a state title—a season recounted in an article for the *New Yorker*. Now they're fifteen years old, gearing up for one last drive at a Senior Little League championship, under King's guidance. "He's fun to play for," says second baseman Travis Demmons. "He hardly ever yells at you."

West Bangor defeated Millinocket in its first game in the double-elimination tournament. Before it meets favored Brewer, King is so preoccupied with vital strategy, such as picking his pitcher, that he declines to be interviewed until the game is over. He finally decides to start right-hander Pelkey, proud possessor of a seventy-five–m.p.h. fastball.

Shortly before game time, the team runs through a quick practice at a junior high school field. The field, where Senior Little League games were sometimes held before the new ballpark opened, is scruffy, weedy, and prone to bad hops.

Hiding his own butterflies, King clowns around to relax his players. He pitches batting practice wearing a catcher's mitt. When Pelkey laces a drive to left field, King kiddingly brushes his back with the next pitch.

Several players worry that the Brewer pitcher might hit them in the ribs with his sidearm curve. "Coach King," one asks, "if I get hit, can I be the first one to charge the mound?"

King leers. "Nobody's charging anyone," he says. "We're going to be perfect young gentlemen."

Soon it's time for the perfect young gentlemen to ride to the ballpark. Left fielder Nick Trzaskos brings the team's good-luck charm, a child's sandal that he found in the outfield during the 1989 season and named Mo.

Inconsistent over the last two years, Mo is potent today. As Mansfield shouts at the West Bangor hitters to choke up on the bat, they eke out one run in the third inning and three more in the fourth. And while the Brewer pitcher does not hit anyone, the Brewer batters stand in against Pelkey with less zeal after he plunks two of them with sidearm hummers.

Trailing 4–3, Brewer has its final at-bats in the top of the seventh inning. With one out, there is a single; then a double to right center. The hit seems certain to tie the score, but a quick relay erases the runner at the plate.

As his players rejoice, King yells hoarsely from the dugout, "Hey, we're not done. We're not done. No celebrating."

There's still one out to go. Or, since King's best-sellers usually italicize moments of suspense, try it this way: *One out to go.*

The ballpark is not King's only gift to young people. He has donated $750,000 for a pediatrics unit at Eastern Maine Medical Center in Bangor, and $30,000 for the varsity swimming and diving program at the University of Maine. He also donated the profits from his *Dark Tower* trilogy—an amount in the "low millions," according to one insider—to build an Elizabethan theater at Milton Academy in Massachusetts, a prep school from which his two older children graduated.

The theater is named after King's mother, Ruth. Speaking at its dedication last year, King recalled that his mother, a concert-trained pianist who worked as a laundress to support her two sons, used to relax by playing "boogie" music. "Although I'm not much of a musician, I've been playing boogie on a typewriter ever since," King said.

King's mother taught him to enjoy another pastime: baseball. Her black co-workers at a Stratford, Connecticut, laundry rooted for the Brooklyn Dodgers, the first integrated team in the major-league baseball. One day, she joined the other employees for an outing to see Jackie Robinson's Dodgers play at their home ballpark, Ebbets Field. She was entranced.

Her son became a Dodgers fan, too. "A latchkey kid before anyone knew what a latchkey kid was," he watched their games alone at home after school while his mother earned their keep. "Baseball has saved my life," King told an interviewer last year. "Every time I needed a lifeline, baseball was it."

The Dodgers abandoned Brooklyn in 1958, before King could attend a game at Ebbets Field. But he would later memorialize the park, which was leveled for an apartment complex, in a poem, "Brooklyn August," and a 1991 novel. In *Needful Things,* the devil tempts an eleven-year-old boy to play pranks on neighbors by selling him a rare 1956 baseball card of Dodger pitcher Sandy Koufax.

The card transports the boy in a reverie to Ebbets Field, where he imagines Koufax giving him the same kind of advice ("Practice your fundamentals") that King now dispenses to his Senior Little League charges. According to Pamela Dorman, King's editor at Viking, the publicity-shy Koufax was irked by the use of his name—even though the baseball card turns out to be a hoax, relieving the Hall of Fame left-hander of any association with Lucifer.

As in *Needful Things,* King often mentions ballplayers or games in his books. But he has never written a baseball novel. (His wife, Tabitha, is the author of *One on One,* a novel about high school basketball.) "It's daunting," King says. "There are so many great baseball novels, like *The Natural* and *Bang the Drum Slowly.* But it will happen sooner or later."

Then, again, no fiction could be more frightful than the Red Sox. They became King's favorite club after the Dodgers moved to Los Angeles and he moved to Maine. It was the perfect marriage: a horror novelist and a haunted team.

King was teaching at the University of Maine in 1978 when the Sox blew the pennant to the Yankees on Bucky Dent's pop-fly homer. He promptly canceled classes for the rest of the week.

In 1986, King won a bet with *Bangor Daily News* sportswriter Bob Haskell that the Sox would still be in the pennant race on July 1. Haskell paid up, by eating a chicken dinner on the lawn of the newspaper office in his underwear. That same year, King bought four Red Sox season tickets, which he still owns.

He usually attends a dozen games a year, occasionally with luminaries such as actor Tom Selleck and author Robert Parker, more often with his son Owen, a baseball-trivia maven. They fly from Bangor in a private plane and take a limousine to Fenway. Once the game starts, King concentrates ferociously, charting every pitch and brushing off celebrity hounds with a polite, "Nice to see you, but I don't give autographs at the ballpark."

King himself has been known to ask for autographs on his occasional visits to the Red Sox clubhouse. One of his favorite players was now-retired relief pitcher Bob (Steamer) Stanley, whom King mentioned in the novel *Cujo.* "Everybody would be booing him and we'd be yelling, 'Go, Steamer!'" says Daniel Casey, King's former limo driver and frequent Fenway companion.

In 1989, King rewarded the Little League state champions from West Bangor by renting a bus and taking them on a vacation that included visits to the baseball and basketball halls of fame. The tour culminated at Yankee Stadium, where the Red Sox were playing the Yankees. Stanley, whose wife, Joan, is a horror buff, traded autographs with King.

Team management has not always reciprocated King's loyalty. Although King has written that his box seats are "as close to the first base bag as the security forces allow," they are actually way down the right-field line. King made the best of his bad seats, becoming friends with the grounds crew, who camp out in a nearby runway. Intermediaries have beseeched the Red Sox to upgrade his seats, to no avail.

King yearns to throw out the first ball at a home opener or a postseason game. According to his friends, the team has raised his hopes several times, only to bump him for a war hero, a retiring athletic director, or the oldest living Red Sox widow. Perhaps team officials scouted the 1989 Maine Little League tournament, where King threw out the first pitch—halfway up the backstop. "He had too much mustard on it," Mansfield says, "and it just took off."

But these personal rebuffs alienated King less than last year's firing of manager Joe Morgan, whose hunches—some of them more bizarre than the novelist's plots—had succeeded often enough to earn the sobriquet "Morgan magic." Butch Hobson, Morgan's successor, "looks like he should be the second lead on the soap opera: *The Line Drives of Our Lives,*" King has said. "He has the Vegas hairdo and the gold chain and everything."

Disgusted by the team's poor start, King has boycotted Fenway this year. The novelist, who plays rhythm guitar in a band of writers and critics, may be induced to return by reports that the public-address system now plays rock music between innings.

There's one easy way that King could improve his seats, throw out the first ball, and reinstate Morgan. He could buy the team. The post-Yankee Red Sox are expected to be sold in the next few years, and King could afford the anticipated $150 million price tag. King has 150 million books in print worldwide. *Gerald's Game,* his latest novel, is expected to sell five million copies in the United States alone.

King has been churning out horror novels for two decades now. Is he ready for a new challenge? Could he be the ghost-buster to exorcise the fabled curse of the Bambino?

"It's a very interesting idea," says Harvard paleontologist Stephen J. Gould, who has seats near King's. "I'm very worried about the future of Fenway. If Steve did own the Red Sox, it would save Fenway."

But King demurs. Citing the example of humorist Mark Twain, who went belly-up following poor business investments, King says that he has to be careful financially. Besides, he doesn't want the publicity. "I've got enough problems," he says.

No matter how famous Stephen King was, Dave Mansfield wanted to treat him the same way he would any other player's parent. So, in the spring of 1989, Mansfield called to introduce himself and ask the writer to rake a Little League field.

King agreed. Soon he was sanding muddy infields, driving players to road games, hauling aluminum bats, and behaving as if charting pitches for Little League games was more important than inking a contract for a Hollywood screenplay.

The truth is that King needed Bangor baseball as much as it needed him. "There was a time before baseball when I was kind of an isolated guy," he says. "I was in the community, but I didn't belong to the community."

Now, he belongs. "I paid my dues," King says. "I'm in without buying my way in. This field is my way of saying, 'The trial marriage is over. I'm here, and I'm staying.'"

So is his team. The last Brewer hitter flies out, leaving West Bangor undefeated in the tournament. King jogs, whooping, onto the field, shaking hands with everyone in sight.

"Stick around," King shouts. "We play for the championship Saturday."

Stick around.

Photo courtesy of the *Bangor Daily News*

The ballfield under construction.

WZON—the AM radio station that King used to own and that played rock and roll— is back from the dead, reported King's hometown newspaper, the Bangor Daily News, *August 7–8, 1993. And the new owner is a previous owner: Stephen King.*

Broadcasting on the AM band at 620 on the dial, the all-sports station is helmed by Dale Duff, a veteran TV sports broadcaster, who does double duty as WZON's programming manager and sports director.

*

New York Yankees games on the air in Red Sox country? That is just one of the many programming chances in the works for a local radio station.

WZON (620 AM), a Bangor radio station also known as Talk Radio, will begin shifting to more sports-oriented programming on Monday with the debut of former WLBZ-TV sportscaster Dale Duff's live talk show.

Bangor authors Stephen and Tabitha King, Duff, and other new members of the WZON staff held a press conference at King's Bangor office Friday to announce the new changes in the station's format and personnel.

"I've been a sports mom for several years now, and I've noticed that there were many moments when radio could have had a real function," said Tabitha King.

"I'm thinking of all the times I went to Bangor–Old Town basketball games where the auditoriums were full and there were people who couldn't get in. That certainly encouraged me that this was one serious format consideration."

Duff is the new programming manager and sports director. He joins new station manager Brent Slowikowski and sales director Linda Cummings.

Slowikowski was formerly known as Brent Stevens at Brewer country western station WQCB, where he was promotions and operations director. Cummings was vice president of sales at WWMJ and WDEA in Ellsworth.

Can sports radio work in a limited market such as Greater Bangor? Duff and Slowikowski think so.

Photo by GB

The original sign outside of WZON in Bangor.

"Sports radio has shown some strength across the country," Slowikowski said. "A lot of the seventy or so stations with sports programming aren't in major markets with pro teams. They focus a lot on local and college."

"With me, it's a gut feeling that the area needs more local sports coverage, and that's why I joined the team," said Duff.

Duff added that the chance to have more of a say in what gets covered and how also motivated his decision to leave WLBZ.

"It was a tough decision. I loved TV," he said. "But this was a unique opportunity to have more of a say and have more freedom."

Stephen King is certain that sports radio can work in this area.

"I left our summer place early to make the [Little League] playoff game in Belfast [between Bangor and Waldo County] and got started a little late and was thinking how great it would be if I could catch that inning or two that I was gonna miss on the radio," said King.

"There's really no reason why that shouldn't happen."

The station is still officially owned by NEB Communications Inc.—owned by Nancy E. Boyd of Falmouth, Mass.—but a bankruptcy court judge approved the sale of the station to King's The Zone Corporation in March.

The sale will not be completed, however, until the Federal Communications Commission approves the transfer of the station's broadcasting license to King's company.

"The ownership is essentially the same as it was when the station went into Chapter 11 bankruptcy proceedings in December," said Gary Growe, the bankruptcy trustee for WZON appointed by the U.S. Trustee's office.

"We expect that [the license transfer] ultimately will be approved sometime in the next thirty to ninety days."

Meanwhile, Duff will get things rolling with the introduction of a daily talk show from 6 to 10 A.M., broadcasts of New York Yankee games beginning on Tuesday, and sports updates every half hour.

Duff also plans to broadcast at least seventy-five high school games through the next year including baseball, soccer, football, softball, hockey, and basketball.

"That doesn't include the tournament and the playoffs," said Duff.

"And we're not doing just Bangor or Brewer, but what we think are the most important games of the week . . . as well as reporters at other games," Duff said.

Brewer Junior High Principal Rich Kimball, a veteran TV and radio announcer, and former Old Town football coach Jim Walsh will be the primary high school announcing team.

Duff will also do high school games in addition to University of Maine football and basketball games.

WZON will start the third year of a three-year contract to broadcast UMaine football and basketball games this fall and may add other colleges in the mix as well.

"We'll be talking with Husson, Maine Maritime, and others," Duff said. "We can do most anything in terms of being able to go where the big game is."

The daily programming schedule is still in limbo. Duff said that he has talked to representatives of various sports radio services such as ESPN Radio, and Slowikowski held out the possibility of broadcasting twenty-four hours.

"We haven't committed to a twenty-four-hour format, but we're licensed to . . . so it's a possibility," Slowikowski said, adding that the station programming with be mostly sports, but not entirely.

Slowikowsi said the station's popular Rush Limbaugh and Larry King syndicated talk shows are being evaluated and will continue to run through their current contracts.

The "Leo in the Morning" show has been replaced by Duff's "Sports Zone," but V. Paul Reynolds will continue to do news updates.

"What community sports-oriented radio is supposed to be up to is mirroring the community itself," King said. "We want to be a community radio station, not just a satellite downlink for syndicated, talking, guns-for-hire."

8
Stephen King Trivia

First published story: "I Was a Teenage Graverobber," published in a fanzine, *Comics Review.*

First fiction sale: A short story to *Startling Mystery Stories,* for which he received $35.

First book advance: $2,500 for *Carrie.*

Most expensive collectible as published: A limited edition of *My Pretty Pony,* published at $2,200, with a built-in, functional digital clock on the cover.

Most unusually bound book: The asbestos-bound *Firestarter,* published by Phantasia Press.

Highest price for a King letter: $440 for a letter to Forrest Ackerman, offering a story for *Famous Monsters of Filmland* (the offer was rejected).

Most expensive holographic manuscript: $6,600 for a school notebook containing work in progress and private notes.

Jobs held before becoming a full-time writer: "Janitor, bagger, dyer and sewer in a mill, a baseball coach, library shelver and stacker, industrial washroom worker, and for a while in a laundromat"—all termed "shitwork" by King. His first professional job was as a teacher at Hampden Academy.

Most controversial book: *The Dark Tower I: The Gunslinger,* which was originally published by Donald M. Grant, Publisher. The book was controversial because it was included in a list of King's published books in *Pet Sematary,* which created a firestorm of inquiries from fans who never knew it had been published. (King for years refused to allow it to be published in a trade edition, but finally relented. Now NAL reprints each new *Dark Tower* novel after its original appearance in hardback by Donald M. Grant, Publisher.)

Longest book: *The Stand:* 1,153 pages.

Most revised book: The original version of *The Stand.*

Worst film adaptation: A tie—*Children of the Corn* and *The Lawnmower Man.*

Best film adaptations: *Carrie, Stand by Me* ("The Body" from *Different Seasons*), *The Dead Zone, The Shawshank Redemption,* and *Dolores Claiborne.*

Only movie King directed: *Maximum Overdrive.*

Most prolific King critic: Dr. Michael R. Collings.

Most frequent occupations of King characters: Teachers and writers.

9

King of Horror
by Bill Goldstein

We have had exorcism, ESP, ghosts, UFOs and doppelgängers.
Now we have telekinesis—the apparent ability to produce motion in objects
simply by control of the mind, without any physical contact. And a fine,
eerie, haunting tale this results in. Carrie is 16, lonely, the butt of all
her Maine classmates' tricks and jokes, an object of scorn even to her own
mother. . . . Carrie begins to put into effect her awesome telekinetic
powers, powers with which she has only toyed before. The result is sheer
horror for all concerned. Not the least of Mr. King's talents lies in
his making Carrie always more pitiable than evil.

from *Publishers Weekly* review of *Carrie*

Bill Goldstein, then a staffer at Publishers Weekly, *wrote this overview piece on King's career for its January 21, 1991, issue.*

✳

On February 25, 1974, *Publishers Weekly* published the first review of Stephen King's debut novel, *Carrie*, which Doubleday would release on April 8, 1974. No one could foresee the history-making career that would follow upon the publication of this slim book, which was listed eighth in importance on Doubleday's spring 1974 list. King is so popular now that his career seems to be simply one of numbers: there are more than eighty-nine million copies of his twenty-seven books in print in mass market paperback alone; he had a record five books simultaneously on the various *New York Times* best-seller lists last winter; he routinely makes millions of dollars per title; he is the best-selling author in Germany and Sweden. It is almost as if King is most notable for *his* telekinetic powers, an ability to move books without any physical contact. But in reality, Stephen King's intoxicating power is his ability to tell stories. "If the stuff you're writing is not for yourself," King says, "it won't work. I feel a

King holding a macabre memento.

certain pressure about my writing, and I have an idea of who reads my books; I am concerned with my readership. But it's kind of a combination love letter/poison-pen relationship, a sweet-and-sour thing." Readers write King and tell him they want to read more, and he wants to provide more: "I feel I ought to write something because people want to read something. But I think, 'Don't give them what they want—give them what you want.'"

Stephen King acknowledges that long before he became the successful writer he'd hoped to become, "I wanted people to leave jobs, to ride past their stop on a bus or train, to burn dinner—because of my books. I wanted to make them prisoner." Without false modesty, he says, "What is true is that I'm living this truly fulfilled life. God made me the kind of person who wanted to write stories, and God made me the kind of person who likes to make people happy. There's really a simple and egotistical idea at the bottom of it all, one that has sustained creative artists since time immemorial. It's that feeling, when you're really into it, that 'I'm great, they're going to love this, they're going to love me, I'll be rich and famous and never suffer—and never be constipated again.' But that's only partly true. It's just life. Nothing really changes. I'll still be told by my wife, 'Steve, we need a loaf of bread,' and so I'll go out shopping. And if I forget, and come back instead with an idea that I tell her will make us $2 million, she'll still say, 'Steve, I'm delighted, but we still need a loaf of bread.'"

The Storyteller's Dilemma

You're not likely to find a writer as serenely down-to-earth as Stephen King. Or a writer as productive who maintains as high a standard throughout his work. Or a writer who conveys so articulately the dilemma faced by a storyteller who sells books in an American society obsessed not only by the "dark-half" of life *he* writes about, but also by a definition of "literature" that historically has excluded writers like himself. Stephen King is a writer who is read, and his fame is everywhere but in the proverbial academy.

"I'd like to win the National Book Award, the Pulitzer Prize, the Nobel Prize; I'd like to have someone write a *New York Times Book Review* piece that says, 'Hey, wait a minute, guys, we made a mistake—this guy is one of the great writers of the twentieth century.' But it's not going to happen, for two reasons. One is I'm not the greatest writer of the twentieth century, and the other is that once you sell a certain number of books, the people who think about 'literature' stop thinking about you and assume that any writer who is popular across a wide spectrum has nothing to say. The unspoken postulate is that intelligence is rare. It's clear in the critical stance; I hear it in the voices of people from the literary journals where somebody will start by saying, 'I don't read Stephen King,' and they are really saying, 'I don't lower myself.' But the fact is that intelligence is fairly common. What's rare is education—or it used to be."

Disdain for writers like himself, King feels, "is the hangover from the late-nineteenth, early-twentieth century when the people who were reading were reading penny dreadfuls, or Horatio Alger kind of stuff. Many readers then were not educated; much popular writing was bad. But education is no longer rare, and there *is* popular literature that has much to say. You can't explain the popularity of fine books like *The World According to Garp* [by John Irving] or *Tender* [by Mark Childress] any other way."

King says he has always wanted to "build a bridge between wide popularity and a critical acceptance. But my taste is too low, there is a broad streak of the *vulgate,* not the 'vulgar,' in my stuff. But that is the limitation of my background, and one of my limitations as a writer. I've got a lot of great things out of a small amount of talent."

"I'm Not That Hard to Please."

Looking back on his books wouldn't seem to be something King would have the time to do with all the time he spends writing or reading ("I'm not that hard to please," King says. "I'm the quintessential audience and I've blurbed a lot of books because I *like* a lot of books.") But "a retrospective by way of Ouija board" brings surprises, which is probably just what one should have expected from King.

Carrie probably lies lowest in King's estimation of his works. "I remember once years ago seeing the author of *The Third World War* on a television chat show in England. And when the interviewer asked John Hackett about his book, the first thing he said was, 'Oh, yes, it's just some old trash I put together.' I do think of *Carrie* that way." (Maryann Palumbo, vice president of marketing at NAL, King's publisher, said, "I'm glad we thought otherwise," when she heard of King's self-criticism.)

Still, for NAL, as for King himself, *Carrie* was a landmark book. NAL paid $400,000 for paperback rights to *Carrie*, which it released in 1975. But the book had not been as big a success in hardcover as NAL had hoped. Sure of the book's potency but concerned about its own huge investment (NAL paid $500,000 for *'Salem's Lot* before *Carrie* came out in paperback), NAL issued *Carrie* without a title or author's name on the cover. Instead, the first printing of 700,000 copies had on the cover only: "A novel of a girl possessed of a terrifying power," and a double-image picture of a young girl. The break with tradition continued with *'Salem's Lot,* King's second novel, which NAL published in paperback in August 1976. This time, there wasn't any copy on the cover—only a three-dimensional embossed image. *Carrie* had 1.33 million

A KING'S RANSOM

Carrie — 30,000 first printing
'Salem's Lot — 20,000 first printing
The Stand [I] — 70,000 first printing
The Dead Zone — 80,000 first printing
Firestarter — 100,000 first printing
Christine — 250,000 first printing
Pet Sematary — 335,000 first printing
It — 1 million first printing
Misery — 900,000 first printing
The Tommyknockers — 1.2 million first printing
The Dark Half — 1.2 million first printing
Four Past Midnight — 1.2 million first printing
The Stand (uncut edition) — 400,000 first printing

—from a sidebar to Goldstein's article on King in *PW*

copies in print by the end of its first nine months of paperback life (now there are nearly four million copies in print); *'Salem's Lot* did even better—2.25 million copies in print after six months (now there are about five million copies in print). King says, "What the book did do was give me a little running room to write a better book, which was *'Salem's Lot*. No one was more surprised than I was about *Carrie*." Palumbo remembers King once told her, "I have a cold spot in my heart for *'Salem's Lot*."

When asked which of his books a newcomer might best start off with, King hesitates to be specific (although, clearly, *Carrie* is out of the running). "If I were Agatha Christie, who wrote something like one hundred little books, I'd say the first one to read would be the first good one. A lot of Christie's books weren't very good, but interspersed among them are true classics that redefine the mystery genre. I'm not like her—I've written twenty-five fairly long books— but I have redefined the genre of horror-writing in this country. I'm not trying to say they're great books, but for better or worse I have changed the genre." Of course, the word "genre" doesn't define King's writings, in any case.

"You're Living His Books"

Ralph Vincinanza, the literary agent who sells foreign rights to King's work, says, "It's not just that Stephen writes good books and frightens us to death." He offers the best explanation of how King has redefined his genre: Vincinanza believes that King is a phenomenon because, "You're not just reading his books—you're living them. It's a good writer who can make you feel he's sharing his experiences with you, but it's a genius who can make you feel that you are sharing your life with him. Reading *It,* I remember thinking, 'Yes, Stephen is drawing on his background here. But there was a shift, and I actually began to think that this novel was about me. You feel so comfortable in Steve's world that you feel as if the author has become the person who is listening. Somewhere along the line, you begin to feel you're telling the tale."

In Vincinanza's view, there are three stages to King's career so far. First, the 1970s—from *Carrie* through the first version of *The Stand,* published in 1978—when King was extraordinarily popular in paperback but only mildly successful in hardcover. For example, *The Shining* was a best-seller briefly: it sold under 50,000 copies in hardcover in its first year; in paperback the same book had nearly 2.3 million copies in print after only a few months. Sales of *The Stand* reached the same level as *The Shining* in hardcover and paperback. Second, the early eighties, when King began to be published by Viking, under an unusual arrangement: NAL bought world rights to King's books and then sold hardcover rights to Viking, which was not yet its sister company. During that phase, his books began to sell several hundred thousand copies in hardcover—sales went from 175,000 for *The Dead Zone* in 1979, to 285,000 for *Firestarter* in 1980, to 350,000 for *Cujo* in 1981. In 1983, 657,000 copies of *Pet Sematary* were sold by Doubleday and 303,000 copies of *Christine* were sold by Viking, making 1983 the first year King had two books among the year's top ten fiction sellers.

King's third stage—1983 to the present, according to Vincinanza—has made publishing history. *Pet Sematary* was followed by *The Talisman,* written with Peter Straub, which had a first printing of 600,000 copies—a record number at that time, which several of King's later novels would surpass. The first printing of both *It* (1986) and *The Tommyknockers* (1987) was one million. The first printing of *Four Past Midnight* was 1.2 million copies, and 1.7 copies of it were in print four months after publication. King now sells as many copies in hardcover as his early books sold in paperback. (An odd record of sorts is the thickness of *The Stand:* the spine of each copy measures 1⅞"—probably the widest paperback ever. First printing of the book is 2.5 million copies.)

King is "something akin to the Beatles," says Vincinanza of the author's worldwide appeal. "The Beatles were very British, but everyone in every mar-

THE KINGS OF THE BEST-SELLER LISTS

"Surviving Success: Bestselling Authors Tell (Almost) All," a videocassette recording, VHS format, 60 minutes; 1994. $20. John Grisham and Stephen King, moderated by Barry Hannah.

At a conference to celebrate books, John Grisham and Stephen King sat on a panel moderated by Barry Hannah, who remarked that this was the only time he could ever think of that these two giants of the best-seller lists had ever shared the same forum—and he is right. Of the two, King comes off much better than Grisham; and, of the two, King is the more experienced at such public gatherings. For this reason, this videotape highlights King's observations on the trials and tribulations of being a best-selling author, though Grisham does manage to squeeze in a few comments.

ket around the world felt them as their own. We think of him as an archetypal American, but Stephen addresses problems that are intimate to everyone everywhere in the world. 'He's American, but he's our American,' is how foreign publishers seem to take him, and I think foreign readers, too." Historically in Europe, as in America, hardcover publishing "catered to the intelligentsia," Vincinanza says, "but Stephen changed all that. Here and abroad."

Good-bye to Castle Rock

Another thing King will change is the landscape of the Maine world in which many of his greatest novels have been set. Castle Rock, Maine, will not survive catastrophe in *Needful Things*. "I'll never leave Maine behind," King says, "but Castle Rock became more and more real to me. It got to the point where I could draw maps of the place. On the one hand, it was a welcoming place to write about. But there is a downside to that. You become complacent; you begin to accept boundaries; the familiarity of the place discourages risks. So I am burning my bridges and destroying the town. It's all gone—kaput. It's sad but it had to be done." According to King, "Everybody who's ever been in Castle Rock comes into the book to take a kind of curtain call." King himself probably will not be taking curtain calls for quite a while yet. Maybe not in Castle Rock, but everywhere in the real world. Of course, Castle Rock was in the real world for everyone who's ever read and loved a Stephen King novel.

10
The House That Horror Built

The most famous residents of Bangor, Maine, live in a twenty-three-room Italianate villa originally built in 1854 for $6,000—land and house. Girdled by a wrought-iron fence, the stately manse looks normal from a distance, but when you get up close, you see that *this* house is different from the others on the street: the main gate, with its spider and cobweb design, is flanked by a pair of bats that perch on high; on the right corner of the fence, a three-headed creature perches, looking in three different directions. More recent additions include a keypad entry device for the gate that bars the driveway, and—strategically positioned—closed-circuit TV cameras that keep an eye out for errant passersby.

A drawing card year-round, the house becomes a holy mecca on Halloween, as befitting its owner: the master of the macabre, the bogeyman of Bangor, America's horror writer laureate—Stephen King.

King could have set his castle anywhere in the world—even in Transylvania, in the Carpathian mountains, where Dracula commanded the night—but he preferred, in the end, to stay close to home, to his roots.

But why Bangor? Why not Portland? Or why not a small town where the tourists couldn't find him, and the out-of-town wackos wouldn't bother to come looking?

As Bob Haskell, a columnist for the *Bangor Daily News,* wrote:

Bangor has always seemed an ideal place for Steve King and his family to live. . . . I have told a few people who think I know Steve a lot better than I really do, "Now, look, he was born in Maine. He lives ten minutes from an airport that can get him anywhere in the world. And he doesn't get hassled like he would if he lived in Boston or New York. Everybody takes him for granted around here. So why should he want to live anywhere else?"

When the Kings bought, and later renovated extensively, the William Arnold house in 1980, King told the hometown newspaper, "We're going to make Bangor our winter home for good." And they did.

*

A Girl's Dream Comes True in Mansion Fit for Kings
by Joan H. Smith

In the early years, the Kings' home served double duty as a private residence and an office from which King handled his business affairs. Originally, managing the King empire became a family affair—sister-in-law Stephanie Leonard worked as his secretary, and later published the informal, official King newsletter, Castle Rock; she was joined by her brother, Chris Spruce, who made the newsletter look more professional, and who became its second publisher. Meanwhile, Chris would go on to manage WZON, King's radio station in Bangor, a hard-rocking station that changed hands several times, only to wind up eventually in King's hands.

At some point, it became obvious that managing King's business affairs required more room, at which point office space was rented in Bangor, now occupied by Shirley Sonderegger—King's major-domo who was hired during the time Stephanie Leonard worked out of the house—and other secretaries.

Because of security concerns, both the office and the home were wired for closed-circuit TV, after an obsessed man intruded in King's life, raising concerns about the personal safety of his office staff and family.

Photo courtesy of the *Bangor Daily News*

A side view of the King residence—the house that horror built.

King, who works out of his house, writes four hours a day, every day. From his office window on the second floor, he can look out over the front lawn and see the tourists that line up in front of his famous front gate, cameras clicking. (His wife, Tabitha, writes her novels downstairs, in a room that, like Stephen's, looks out across the front lawn.)

After lunch King drives over to the office, where he takes care of business. There's always mail to read, books to sign, phone calls to return, and matters to discuss with his staff.

Because the home is now private, open only to family and close friends, this rare glimpse circa 1984 by a Bangor Daily News staffer of the King residence is a behind-the-scenes tour of what by necessity became the most private residence in Bangor. The days when anyone could walk up to the front door, ring the doorbell, and ask for autographs or bring books for signing, are long gone. Today, of course, the Kings' castle is off limits to the public except for occasional Halloween events. In lieu of the traditional moat with drawbridge, the wrought-iron fence, five feet tall with barbed points, keeps most of the onlookers out. But just in case someone takes a notion to jump over the fence, the video cameras that never blink will see you.

The old days of open house are gone. Those were the days, my friend, we thought would never end . . . until the high price of fame made entry impossible for all but family and friends.

✳

As a girl she strolled down West Broadway with a friend and dreamed of living in one of the mansions. She leaned toward the red one with the towers. She certainly never thought she'd live there one day.

But the wide-eyed girl grew up to be author Tabitha King and married the man who became the most famous horror author of our time, Stephen King. He decided the barn-red Victorian mansion at West Broadway replete with towers, secret passages, and unbeknown to them at the time of purchase, a ghost, was his kind of place.

"I thought it was destiny," said Tabitha.

The oldest house on the street, built in 1854 for $6,000 by a man who couldn't afford it, had to go through a transition before it fit the needs of three children, two writers, and their entourage.

It took a crew of craftsmen from Center Lovell, where the Kings have a summer home, four years to modernize the mansion on the inside, yet maintain period architectural integrity on the outside.

"The historical commission is quite pleased with it," she said.

The house proper remained unchanged except for the kitchen and the addition of some closet space and a laundry. The major overhaul took place in the barn, which had been used to store relatives' old couches, but which is now the most-used living space in their home.

She feels they aren't quite done yet; he's had enough of the constant construction. If the movie version of Stephen's book *Pet Sematary* is filmed in Bangor this summer—and she believes it will be—Tabitha will be spending the summer in Bangor and will have time to plan period gardens of peonies and roses to surround the house.

Through the decades, the 126-year-old house has had many changes, such as the addition of the front porch and the carriage port. Yet, most is original, including the bright golden oak entry, considered a utility wood at the time, but probably the best the builder could afford.

The rooms are decorated mostly in cool pastels of green or blue, which contrast with the warm oak and mahogany woodwork.

The living room is large and beautifully decorated in period furniture. Over a baby grand piano is a photograph of their summer home, which is featured in Tabitha's book *The Caretakers*.

"It was a cold room and for some time after we moved in no one—the kids, the animals—wanted to go in it. I added a rug and re-wallpapered, but the vibes were bad. We knew it must be the room with the ghost."

"Bruce [their seal point Siamese cat] likes to sleep on the couch in here; it's his couch," she said.

In the square tower, to the right, is a collection of light oak period furniture, one of Tabitha's many "nests," which are in nooks throughout the mansion.

In this nest she wraps packages and organizes clothes. Parked next to her oak desk is a large orange telescope, which her husband, an amateur astronomer, moves out onto the front lawn on clear nights. This quantum leap in time is a hint of what is to come toward the back of the house.

The Kings combined six small rooms to create a labyrinth of a kitchen. Seated at a lunch bar is a man sipping coffee and chatting with the housekeeper. Tabitha introduces him as the man who maintains their Wang word-processing equipment. Today is a social call. Behind him is another of Tabitha's nests. She calls this one her "concierge nest," where she plans menus and pays bills. A bulletin board plastered with slips of paper and a fast-food restaurant menu is above a small counter covered with books and paper.

On a bar in what was once the butler's pantry is a caged albino guinea pig named Butler. Around the corner is a higher-than-average counter custom-made for six-foot-three Stephen to knead his bread. Around another corner is the brick warming oven, where he sets his bread to rise.

The indoor swimming pool at the King residence.

"They're Royal River bricks, where Steve grew up," Tabitha said.

The kitchen is a modern room with a brilliant red sink, butcherblock countertops, and sleek off-white cabinets trimmed in oak. A red electric dumb-waiter is used to transport linens to the laundry on the second floor.

"I can show you mistakes all over this kitchen, but the pool is perfect," said Tabitha, who led the way through a long corridor, down a step, which follows the lay of the land, past a number of tiled dressing rooms, which were once box stalls in the pool room, a swimming shrine.

Beyond the forty-seven-foot length of the pool is a window designed by the architectural firm I. M. Pei, which also did the Portland Museum of Art. The mosque-like shapes of the window and pool repeat a motif found in the shape of the front porch floor, a medallion adorning the outside of the house, and a handsome wrought-iron fence added by the Kings.

The small, square windows that once admitted light into the horse stalls remain along the south side of the pool room. From the outside, it appears to be a well-maintained nineteenth-century barn. Inside is Tabitha King's fantasy—a plaster pool twelve feet at its deepest, which she swims in every day.

"For Steve, it's now and then, but the kids and I swim every day and my father, who has a heart condition, uses it, too," said Tabitha, who did not learn to swim until she was thirty, but said she then fell in love with it.

She said she "fell insanely in love" with the creations of Barbara Lambert of Orono, whose stuffed cloth sculptures hang from the rafters around the pool. Lambert's fantastical sea creatures are "evolution gone mad," according to Tabitha, who said she reads a lot of biology and believes there is very little in fantasy that does not actually exist.

The sculptures are vividly colored in many shades of blue and green, accenting the pool's color, which change with the quality of the day and season's light.

Above the pool's dressing rooms is an office with a stained-glass window depicting a bat in flight. A secret entrance to the office is up a narrow low-ceiling staircase, through a foot-thick door that closes and disappears as part of a bookcase. Skylights, hanging lights, white walls and white plush carpeting brightly light the writing digs of Stephen King.

He said he wanted a bright office because he doesn't "see all that well." It took two of the largest desks the Kings could find to hold his Wang word-processing and printout equipment. Beside the printout machine is a neat stack of paper titled *It* by Stephen King, his latest work. Beside that is a chrome drive-in movie speaker presented to him as King of the Drive-in Horror Movie. The room is rimmed with bookcases. One section has a copy of each of his books, including those in foreign languages.

Half of King's books have been best-sellers, and eight were made into movies, with three more in the works.

The seating area beyond the office was once a hayloft where the groom slept. Secret passages through the eaves led to the maid's quarters in the attic over the house.

"There was some concern, I was told, of the grooms' getting to the maids . . . ," said Tabitha.

A New Hampshire license plate with the word "Cujo" is on one wall. A jig-saw puzzle of Marilyn Monroe and another of Humphrey Bogart hang on the wall above a loose-pillow charcoal gray couch. A plastic model of Frankenstein's monster graces the coffee table.

THE WILLIAM ARNOLD HOUSE

Only one stylist Italianate villa was built in Bangor. The William Arnold House . . . dates from 1854 to 1856. It was the first house built on West Broadway on the former Davenport lands, between Hammond and Union Streets.

William Arnold (1806–75) was a prosperous livery stable owner who lived on Union and Ohio Streets before building this house. Arnold's tax lists show that the lot was valued at $1,700 before the house was built; upon its completion in 1856, it was valued at $6,000. Arnold sold the house to William H. Smith of Old Town for $6,148.93 in July 1857.

Though he sold the house for one reason or another, William Arnold continued to prosper. He was later the president of the Penobscot Mutual Fire Insurance Company, and was prominent in the Unitarian and musical circles. When he died, his estate amounted to $19,000; this was a comfortable estate but not the fortune of a rich man, which supports the idea that the West Broadway house represented too large an investment for a man of his fortune.

from *Bangor, Maine, 1769–1914, An Architectural History*

"The only time I realize it's a barn is in the summer, when I roast in the loft," said Stephen.

Beyond the sitting room is his bath with black Jacuzzi tub and black pedestal sink. His secretary's office is in the hayloft, too. Tabitha shares the secretary along with the printout machine, to which the word processor in her office in the other end of the house is connected.

Tabitha's office on the first floor of the cylindrical tower was Stephen's when they moved in four years ago. Although she had insulated interior wooden shutters installed in the massive windows, he found the street sounds too distracting. She enjoys watching the color changes in the original spiderweb stained-glass windows as the sun floods through them.

"Steve wrote three books here. He never had an office that was really his and he felt he earned it," said Tabitha. "He finally has his own place."

Photo by GB

The William Arnold House, now known as the King residence.

She soon encountered the "King's Garbage Truck" column in the school
newspaper: "I remember reading it and getting furious," she says,
"thinking *Who's this joker who just moved in?*"

Douglas E. Winter, *Stephen King: The Art of Darkness*

✻

*Ever heard of a fictional place called Nodd's Ridge, Maine? No? Next question: Ever
heard of a fictional place called Castle Rock, Maine? Okay, you can all put your hands
down.*

Nodd's Ridge is Tabitha King country.

*A poet, novelist, and photographer, Tabitha King goes to great lengths to avoid a
linkage to her famous husband in the bios of her books; she wants to be considered
on her own terms, and not just as the spouse of Maine's most famous citizen.*

*According to Stuart Tinker, Tabitha King's work is taken seriously, and a grow-
ing number of readers are discovering her. (The Special Collections at UMO, which
has considerable Stephen King holdings, had asked Tabitha King for her papers, too,
some years ago.)*

*Beyond Maine's borders, those in the know—notably Harlan Ellison—praise her
work for "a quality of kindness that is missing from Stephen's work. Tabby's stuff is
quite different from Stephen's, and in some ways is far more mature."*

This piece appeared in the Bangor Daily News, *March 1993.*

Early one morning nearly ten years ago, Tabitha King was driving along the road
that hugs Pennesseewassee Lake in Norway, Maine. From her car window, she
saw a huge ice sculpture proudly displayed on the frozen water.

It would be improper to describe the [phallic] shape in a family newspaper, but King describes it with great delight and detail in the opening chapter
of her new novel, *One on One*. The image, she says, made a big impression on
her, but not for the reasons you might think.

Photo courtesy of the *Bangor Daily News*

Tabitha King

"There it was in the middle of the lake—the work of someone's heart," she says. "They really put enormous effort into the thing. Not only was the image incredibly startling to encounter that early in the morning—and unexpectedly—but the evidence of the energy was very pleasing to me. I just thought: You know, there were some kids who had a hell of a good time and who are, at this moment, reveling in it."

King brings up a laugh that has been waiting to come out as she related her story. She appreciates a good teen-instigated prank, and a quirky brand of satisfaction pours from her eyes as she talks about the one in her novel. (She does, in the book's preface, thank the unknown artists for their inspiration to her.)

As writers will, King has altered and embellished the scene for her work. (A group of mischievous high school boys mount the eight-foot statue above the main entrance to their school.) Just because something is funny in real life, she instructs, doesn't mean it will translate well to fiction, and the writer's job is to give it a little boost.

"There are always sources for fiction, but the fact is, you make it all up," says King.

Backlit by the snowy sky behind the glass of the sunroom in her home, King is sipping peppermint tea and sitting on a wicker chair. She has just returned from a book signing at the Bangor Mall, and, to honor the basketball players in her book, she wears a tie painted with a player making a jump shot. She bought the tie earlier that week while in Utah with her husband, Stephen King. In the next room, there is the hum of televised sports, and, further away, the Kings' corgi barks at the doorbell.

One on One, an opposites-attract love story about two pithy star players at a high school in a fictitious mill town in Maine, obviously finds much of its source in the personal experience of this writer, who is also a mother of three children, a native of Old Town, and a community-minded citizen.

As with the parents in her book, King has spent a lot of time on the sidelines of high school basketball games. She has guided her own children from puberty into young adulthood. And even though she declares that the characters in her book are like no kids she knows in real life, she has spent ample time observing her children's peers, who often hang out at the King mansion.

"I like kids," she says, and her faces take on a teen animation. "I love their energy and their grossness and their excitement about being alive. As a mom, I'm a relatively invisible person around teenagers."

In particular, King adds, she loves the music of young people. Although son Owen, the only offspring still living at home, likes rap—the backbeat of which can be heard and felt from an upstairs room—King is partial to thrash metal.

Photo courtesy of the *Bangor Daily News*

Stephen and Tabitha King are presented a plaque from the Greater Bangor Chamber of Commerce in recognition of their civic contributions to the community.

Her real preference, however, is fusion, and the lyrics cited in her book also show a devotion to the music of the 1960s, during which she was a student at John Bapst Memorial High School in Bangor.

King, forty-four, has tapped into those distant days, too, in crafting this novel, which took her two years to write. Elsewhere, she has written that her teen years were difficult because she wasn't popular with the main crowd. If that was the case in high school, the opposite problem has been true in her adult life, which has been marked by an unrelenting public exposure due to a fame that is not her own.

"I'm sort of invisible to many people, and there's been a cost to Steve's fame for the whole family in terms of privacy and identity," she says.

Yet, with five novels published, another in manuscript form, and others floating about in her mind, King is a successful writer in her own right. She is dedicated, working most mornings in her office, which is at the opposite end of the house from her husband's (they often act as first reader for each other's work), and she is driven to voice the dreams of her culture.

With its soap-operaish sequences and hip teenspeak, *One on One* is sure to bring King more recognition than the previous books did. And the life-is-a-lot-like-basketball theme is even likely to catch a young-adult audience.

King expects *One on One* will incite some anger among parents, who are likely to be shocked at the language, sex, and drug abuse in the novel. But, offers King, too many parents are in denial about those realities in American high schools, and she hopes her book will get parents and children talking, particularly about sexual abuse issues, such as statutory rape.

"We need to be frank," she defends, "because we're living in a scary, scary world. I think I'm going to continue to write with some explicitness, and that's probably going to upset people. If the explicit sexuality gets in the way of some parents, I'm sorry about that."

During the next month, King will also be doing national book signings, an aspect of publishing she dislikes because, up until her recent appearance on "Good Morning, America," she has not had the face recognition of her husband. *One on One* is also under consideration for movie rights.

And then, too, King has been publishing for more than ten years, and her increased confidence and skill are apparent on each page.

"I don't think I'm a particularly gifted writer," she says. "I don't have the sort of wild inventiveness that Steve has . . . and I don't have the enormous energy that has allowed him to produce thirty-six novels. I guess maybe I have a feeling for character. If I can make people get interested in someone else's life, that's great, because that's what I want to do."

King suspects that she will write a sequel to *One on One*, but she is currently gathering information and inspiration for another book about college sports. In that one, she says, she will not paint quite as favorable a picture of the sports culture. Similarly, if there is a sequel to *One on One*, it won't be as happily-ever-after as its predecessor. Real life is never so comfortably wrapped up, says King, even in fiction.

Paul Bunyan surveys Main Street in Bangor from a statuesque perspective.

12
King's Main(e) Haunts
by David Lowell

Sometimes bad things happen to good people.

Take David Lowell, for instance. Now here's a good ol' Maine boy, a writer who puts black and white the old-fashioned way, with a typewriter, not a computer. (Personally, I think Dave would find a computer much easier, but he sticks to what works for him and doesn't listen to what this gentleman from Virginia tells him.)

So, naturally, when it was time to publish a small-press book for fun—there's very little money in it when you're printing only 300 copies—I asked Dave to contribute a piece about Maine haunts, and he did.

His manuscript was impeccably typed. When I asked him how he managed to do that, he said that when he discovered an error, he retyped the whole page. It drives him crazy to see a typographical error.

Unlike the other contributors to the aforementioned book, all of whom submitted their stuff on computer diskette, Dave assumed typewritten copy would be retyped in error-free fashion, just as he had submitted it.

As I said, sometimes bad things happen to good people, and in this case, when it rained . . . it poured.

In the introduction to Dave's piece, I gave his address—with the wrong zip code. Then, in the worst possible places, I inserted typos in the final text that made Dave's piece a challenge to read. (In one instance, I retyped ". . . Main Street, where people shot . . ." instead of "shop," which was unintentionally funny, but Dave wasn't laughing.)

I promised Dave that I'd set things right and publish the piece just as he had written it—without my bloopers inserted. So here it is, finally, the way we both intended for it to appear in print. (By the way, in the piece, there's a reference to a drink called Moxie. Unless you live in New England, you've probably never heard of it, much less tasted it. Depending on your taste, it's either ambrosia— or bitter medicine.)

✳

Beyond New Hampshire's border lies the land of Stephen King. A fictional world where vampires roam, rabid dogs run amuck, and innocent children disappear on full moon nights or attain some mystical powers.

It's the site of rural towns filled with rat-infested mills, spooky Victorian homes that hide cold, dark secrets, and strange people who speak with accents (Oh Ayuh!) as thick as a Moxie float. But in all truth, much of what King incorporates into his fiction *can* be found—at least as far as actual buildings and locations are concerned.

Take, for instance, the setting of his novella "The Body," where a group of juveniles set out in search of a missing boy. The tale is deeply autobiographical: King has cleverly drawn from his hometown of Durham and nearby Lisbon Falls to create his now-famous Castle Rock.

During the quest, the boys travel a stretch of railroad tracks which leads to the Royal River. The Shiloh Church, Route 136, Hillcrest Chicken Farm, and WLAM, a Lewiston/Auburn radio station, are mentioned.

In fact, the Shiloh Church, which sits high atop a hillside off a wooded road in Durham, is probably the inspiration for the Marsten House in *'Salem's Lot*.

King's brother Dave disagrees, claiming that the building was inspired by an old North Berwick house Stephen lived near in 1973 before moving to Colorado. That house was a spooky Victorian with a turret and a widow's walk, and sat on a hillside, overlooking the town like a haunted mansion.

King's boyhood friend Chris Chesley feels that the inspiration for the Marsten House came from an old, deserted barn he and King played in as adolescents.

It's possible that all three of these actual Maine sites were incorporated into the Marsten House mystique, but of course only King himself knows for sure.

But there is little discrepancy insofar as other King haunts are concerned.

Harmony Grove Cemetery is just up the road from King's boyhood home in Durham. In *'Salem's Lot,* it appeared as Harmony Hill Cemetery.

In *The Dead Zone,* Runaround Pond was where six-year-old Johnny Smith, who fell during skating, was knocked unconscious. Runaround Pond, incidentally, is also the name of the Durham road where King grew up. The road has a deep country setting, and on it is the Methodist church and the one-room schoolhouse King attended as a boy.

Lisbon Falls is just over the bridge from Durham. Old, decrepit mills, the setting for *Graveyard Shift,* line its riverbanks; and Main Street, where people shop, hasn't really changed in over thirty years. On the corner sits a general store, where Moxie is the specialty. Down the road is a barbershop, a stationery store, and a pool hall where a visiting King fan would expect to see Ace Merrill ("The Body") come walking out with greased-back hair and a Winston pok-

Photo by GB

The Shiloh Church in Durham, Maine, considered to be one of the inspirations for the Marsten House in *'Salem's Lot.*

ing out from the corner of his mouth. Lisbon Falls is truly Castle Rock, one hundred percent!

Traveling Lisbon Street to Lewiston, where King went to high school, more sites from "The Body" can be found. Along a steel-gray river, railroad tracks stretch on for several miles, surrounded by a tranquil pine tree forest.

In Lewiston more textile mills can be seen, as well as the Ritz theater—no longer in business—where King viewed his first horror movies.

Kennedy Park is just a few blocks away, where a bandstand gazebo has stood for over a century. The gazebo is not only stylish and historic, but greatly resembles the one King describes in *The Dead Zone*.

Other Lewiston landmarks include Bates College (mentioned in *Four Past Midnight*) and Lewiston High School (in *Carrie*); Central Maine General Hospital appears in "Gramma" where Buddy Bruckner was taken when he broke his leg while playing baseball, and in "The Woman in the Room," where John and Kevin's terminally ill mother underwent a cortotomy.

In nearby Auburn, off Route 136, one can easily locate the Rollerdome (*Rage*), where Ted Jones took Sandy Cross skating. And the Auburn Novelty Shop ("The Mist"), still standing near city hall, is where Billy Drayton bought a set of wind-up chattery teeth.

But the easiest sites to locate are in King's home base of Bangor.

Not only can his West Broadway home be found, complete with bat-winged fence, but much of the surrounding community appeared in *It,* including the Stand Pipe, a water tower, and a statue of Paul Bunyan off Main Street.

Bangor has also been the backdrop for *Creepshow 2, Pet Sematary, Graveyard Shift,* and *The Langoliers.* A drive down Main Street should look quite recognizable to many visiting fans, particularly the church steeple in the city square.

En route north to Orono is the Mount Hope Cemetery, where King did a cameo of a preacher in *Pet Sematary.*

And, of course, no visit would be complete without a stop at King's alma mater, the University of Maine, an important site that he has mentioned in several of his novels and short stories.

All in all, there are many King haunts to be explored while visiting the great state of Maine. All one has to do is simply find them and, of course, *hope to get out alive!*

Part 2
The Unreal World of Stephen King

The real world is where Stephen King—family man, philanthropist, pillar of the Bangor community—physically resides. But because King writes fiction, he spends most of his time in his imaginary worlds where anything can, and does, happen.

King's job, as he sees it, is to "report on what he sees" when he looks out from his unique perspective, as he explained in "A Note on 'Secret Window, Secret Garden'": "Sitting down at the typewriter or picking up a pencil is a physical act; the spiritual analogue is looking out of an almost forgotten window, a window which offers a common view from an entirely different angle . . . an angle which renders the common extraordinary."

The unreal world of King is the world of his celebrity, of which he has a unique view. At the eye of the storm, he sees the fans that encircle him, the book publishing that defines him, the interviewers that seek to understand him, the critics that dissect him, and the writing that consumes him. Demon-driven, King moves effortlessly from the real world to the unreal, from the mundane day-to-day world to the twilight zone of a writer's world, which at times probably seems the most sane, especially when compared to the craziness that defines celebrity and the fans that deify him.

13
Your Number-One Fan

umber whunnn
yerrrnnn umber whunnn
fayunnn
These sounds: even in the haze.

from *Misery* by Stephen King

✳

Misery, King's 1987 novel, is oddly described by his publisher on the flap copy: "He owes his fans a love letter. *Misery* is it."

Misery is the story of Paul Sheldon, who is held captive by a crazed ex-nurse, Annie Wilkes, and forced to write *Misery's Return,* bringing Wilkes's favorite character, Misery Chastain, back from the dead. In the process, Sheldon gets amputated, blow-torched; Wilkes get barbecued; and a sheriff gets shot-gunned to death.

How, I ask, is *this* novel a love letter from King to his fans?

It isn't.

It is, perhaps, King's way of saying that he's tired of celebrity and very tired of being the focal point for millions of fans worldwide who, on average, write him nearly five hundred letters a week—according to Stephanie Leonard—and, among other things, ask for donations to charity auctions, send books for autographs, ask for autographed pictures, ask about when the next *Dark Tower* novel will be out, ask questions for school papers, and complain about faults in his novels. As Stephanie Leonard explained to Stephen Spignesi in an interview for *The Shape Under the Sheet:* "We've been party to his life for a long time and we've seen the fan mail and the people who hang around in front of his house snapping pictures, and the way the fame and money has affected his life. Basically, we know all the little things that inspired *Misery.*"

Since the beginning of his career, King has had to deal with his burgeoning

Stephen and Tabitha King sign books at a Bangor bookstore.

Photo by Scott Haskell, courtesy of the *Bangor Daily News*

fame and popularity, which meant getting an unlisted telephone no matter where he lived, checking into hotels under an assumed name; flying on private jets instead of on commercial airlines on occasion, refusing to attend book signings for fear of turning away, and thus angering, more readers than he could possibly accommodate; receiving hundreds of letters per week from readers worldwide (the majority requiring an answer, and many not accompanied by a self-addressed, stamped envelope); receiving books in the mail for signing, with a note asking would he please sign them and send them back in a hurry. . . . And, finally, not being unable to venture beyond Bangor without getting mobbed.

Like other famous writers, King has discovered that it's impossible to deal with the mountain of correspondence generated by readers, many of whom are hopeful that he'll reply in some fashion, even if it's just a note on a postcard.

Why, they ask themselves, can't he write back if I take the time to write him? On occasion, King does. Several of my readers have written to tell me that they've got postcards from King—brief notes answering specific questions—but, for most, there is no reply.

It's understandable. If King were to answer all his mail and sign all the books people want him to sign, he'd have no time left for writing, which is the reason his readers have written to him in the first place.

In "Letters from Hell," a limited-edition, signed broadside from Lord John Press, King talks about the fan mail he receives. King says that readers expect two things from authors: writing books and, more important, "The primary function of writers, it seems, is to answer readers' questions."

Not content merely to read a book, readers feel compelled to write letters, to ask questions, to reach out and touch the writer that touched them with his words and stories. It is, perhaps, the most telling sign that a writer's work has meaning. It touches the readers so that they want to reciprocate in the only way they can—writing letters, even if it's a one-way communiqué.

In an August 1994 interview on CNN's "Larry King Live," Stephen King, in answer to a frequently asked question, said that once he gets his next novel out of the way, he'll write the remaining four *Dark Tower* novels to close out that series permanently. Writer's inspiration? To some extent . . . but the real impetus was probably the pressure from his fans who have written him—I'd guess—tens of thousands of letters asking when the next one is coming out, and the next one after that, and—you get the idea.

STEPHEN KING ON FAN MAIL

I'll tell you the truth: A lot of it I don't read because it's repetitive and a little bit scary. If you think too much about writing . . . it's like being an actor on the stage: It's all right to know the audience is there; it's all right to sense them as a bulk presence, but never look for faces. They're out there and that's enough. I can't look them in the eye, one by one.

I love the people who read my stuff, and I don't just love them because they support me. I love them because they listen.

There are people who write who believe that the act of putting it down on paper is enough, but I've never felt that was the end of it. I've always felt that to make it complete, it had to go out to some other person. What we're talking about is communication.

Donald M. Grant, Publisher, Inc., which publishes the true first editions of each new *Dark Tower* novel in illustrated hardbacks, gets more mail and phone calls about the *Dark Tower* novels than anything else it has ever published. Grant will look forward to the day that the books are finished, published, shipped, and the company can get back to publishing other fine works of fantasy by lesser-known authors who don't have a legion of fans that bombard them with letters, postcards, and phone calls.

King, being who he is, gets more than his fair share of weird mail. From a box of correspondence deposited at the Special Collections Department at the University of Maine at Orono, here's a sampling of what fans wrote him in the late seventies regarding *The Shining:*

The typical letter: "You are only the second author I have ever written to. I wanted to write because I enjoyed *The Shining* so much and haven't thought about much else since I put it down."

The puzzled thank-you: "How very odd to be writing to thank you for what was really a most unpleasant experience, reading *The Shining.*"

The junior league literary criticism: "I've always felt that the author of fearful tales is the most talented because he has to be able to take hold of the reader's emotions, and hold them throughout the story."

The reader who wisely knows his limitations: From a man who had misgivings after reading *The Shining,* wondering whether or not to read *Carrie* and *'Salem's Lot*—"Though I consider myself a strong person, I must think of my own mental health."

On King's cinematic writing style: "While reading, it is almost as if I'm right there when everything is going on."

A novice writer's plea: "All I want is for that someone to tell me that I'm a lousy writer who should stop wasting his time or that I have some potential and should keep trying. PS: If there is nothing you can do, send money."

The term-paper blues: "Due to the fact that I live in a small town, I have been unable to find enough articles and reviews of *The Shining.* Therefore, I would appreciate it greatly if you would send me your personal analysis and any other articles and reviews you may have."

Reaching into the nonbook audience: "My husband, who very rarely reads a book, could not put *The Shining* down."

On motivations for writing: "Do you write just as a money-making job, for literary value, or in hopes it will be sold for a TV show or movie someday?"

The frequently asked:

- "Why did you choose to be a writer?"
- "Why do you write horror novels?"
- "Where do you get your ideas?"

The affirmation: "I've gotten so that all it takes is the *name* Stephen King on a book, and I know it will be good."

The plain truth from a female fan: "Pardon the phrase, but you scared the shit out of this twenty-year-old."

From a novice writer, age sixteen: "I've been working (and I really mean *working*) on a novel for close to a year, and it is a lot tougher than I thought writing one would be. It's a pretty good little book, but there are many *problems!!* I really need help! Sometimes I can be writing a very gory blood-and-guts scene that should make a person want to throw up, but when I take the scene from my mind and try to put it down on paper, it just doesn't seem scary."

The question from the twilight zone: "How come all your books are about something that is possessed? Do you have any suggestions to a sprouting writer?"

The naked truth: "Really, Steve, *The Shining* is a masterpiece, considering the fact that it was written by an American hack, and I congratulate you."

14
The News from . . . Castle Rock?

In January 1985 *Castle Rock* published its first issue. For four years Stephen King fans looked forward to receiving their monthly issue of *Castle Rock,* the official King newsletter. To the subscribers' dismay, Chris Spruce (publisher and editor) shut down publication permanently with its December 1989 issue.

King fans were suddenly stranded without any reliable source of information; and although there were attempts by fans to publish King newsletters, none had staying power, and none had the voice of authority like *Castle Rock.*

As Tabitha King explained to an interviewer in 1986, King was more or less committed to "institutionalize his relationship with his fans," and *Castle Rock* was that institution.

Part of the appeal of *Castle Rock* was that it was published in Bangor, King's permanent residence. Also appealing was the fact that you knew the information was accurate, because the publisher/editor could pick up the phone and ask King himself what the "skinny" was on a piece of news reported elsewhere. But, most of all, the publication became *the* place for King fans to congregate, submitting letters, contributing pieces, sending clippings, sharing news, and placing classified ads for King collectibles.

In its heyday, when New American Library was running ads for the newsletter in the mass market paperback editions, the subscription base skyrocketed to a high of 5,500, but toward the end, it became obvious that the steam had run out of the engine: Chris Spruce—working full-time as the station manager for King's radio station, WZON, and working part-time as the editor/publisher of *Castle Rock*—decided to put both jobs behind him permanently and get his master's degree at the University of Maine at Orono.

One reason, Chris said, was that King had become less involved with *Castle Rock*—though, admittedly, he never promised to be an active participant— and it was, in those days, harder to get newsworthy pieces by and about King because he had deliberately slowed his production, letting the creative well refill.

That well, apparently, is now full. Since the demise of *Castle Rock*, King has been active on several fronts: more fiction—mostly novels—and more (and better) film adaptations, as well as more public appearances as an author as well as a member of the Rock Bottom Remainders.

A NEW STEPHEN KING NEWSLETTER

Phantasmagoria (letter-size; approximately twenty to forty pages; three issues a year, $10 in the U.S., GB Publishing/Ink, P.O. Box 3602, Williamsburg, Virginia 23187). Intended for die-hard King readers. *Phantasmagoria* is my answer to all the readers who write in to ask: "Where can I get *reliable* news about Stephen King?"

Supplementing the newsletter: "postcard alerts" are sent out by first-class mail to provide early notification of time-sensitive King projects, especially signed, limited editions, which typically sell out prior to publication.

The newsletter covers King news, forthcoming book projects announced by his mainstream and specialty publishers, film and television adaptations, audiotape and videotape recordings, and other projects. The newsletter features interviews with professionals in the King community; articles and reviews from its contributing editors (Dr. Michael R. Collings, Stephen J. Spignesi, Gary Wood, and Barry R. Levin); price guide updates from booksellers; and articles reprinted from King's hometown newspaper, the *Bangor Daily News*.

Photo by GB

Headstones at a Bangor cemetery.

Publishing

15

Plume's "Stephen King Collectors Editions"

Stephen King is the world's best-selling novelist and
undisputed master of modern horror.

from Plume book catalog

✳

It's the stuff of nightmares, but for many authors, this nightmare is a reality: Their books are out of print, unavailable in any edition—unless you are a best-selling author, in which case all of your books are available in a variety of formats, stocked from coast to coast, with prices to match.

In Stephen King's case, the problem of collecting a uniform edition of his books may in time be remedied with the ongoing program Plume—the trade paperback imprint of NAL—began in October 1991, when the first three "Collectors Edition" books were published.

Although I'd prefer a uniform set of hardback books, the trade paperbacks are an inexpensive tradeoff, appealing to people who want an attractive set of King books at an affordable price. Unlike the limited editions of King's books published by small presses—ranging in price from $38 to $75 for their "trade" editions—the Plume "Collectors Edition" books are kept in print, and are more affordable. (My preference, from a collector's point of view, is for the "trade" editions from the small presses, though.)

While these Plume books—as Betts Bookstore owner Stuart Tinker points out—are not true collectibles, they are to my mind worthwhile additions to your King collection for one reason: the introductions prefacing each book were commissioned especially for this series.

The other virtues of this series—the reset type, the layout, the bold covers, the color frontispiece reprinting the original hardback dust jacket—are what you would expect. But who would have expected to see, for instance, Tabitha King writing an introduction to *Carrie*? Or Ken Follett writing an introduction to *The Shining*?

My favorite introduction, though, is Clive Barker's piece prefacing *'Salem's Lot*. Not only is *'Salem's Lot* my favorite King book, but the choice of Barker was inspired. (After reading Barker's first collection, *Books of Blood,* King observed, "I have seen the future of horror . . . and it is Clive Barker.)

After the publication of the first three books, it wasn't until 1994 that the next three were published: *Cujo, Firestarter,* and *The Dead Zone*. All novels, these three retained the same look and feel inside the covers, but were in stark contrast to the black and gray covers on the first three books in the series; the second set—and, presumably, the books to come—sports striking full-color covers. Against a black background, the titles pop out (white against the black), King's name pops out (in three-inch letters), and full-color artwork (symbolic, not representational) suggests the interiors.

As with the first three books in the series, the second trio features newly commissioned introductions, hand-picked by (presumably) King: Dan Simmons for *Cujo,* John Grisham for *Firestarter,* and Anne Rivers Siddons for *The Dead Zone*.

Though all the Doubleday books are now available in new editions—with gorgeous, photographic art for the dust jackets and, it appears, sturdy bindings—they merely reprint the text. They contain no new material: no introductions, no afterwords, and no critical analyses putting the book in context with King's other works.

Plume's "Collectors Editions" have been sporadic offerings, but they remain, if the series is brought to its logical conclusion, the only uniform set of King books available in any edition, affordably priced, each with an introduction that properly sets the stage for the fright show that follows.

In other words, make room on your King bookcase for these editions, because they are a visual and textual delight.

16
Collecting King

An Overview of King's Book Publishers

Unlike some authors whose books are published by numerous houses, King has kept things relatively simple for the reader.

First, all of King's books are in print. If you want reading copies, mass market paperbacks are available from NAL of every major book, with the exception of King's nonfiction study, *Danse Macabre*.

Doubleday finally got the hint and reissued its titles in handsome editions, with matching dust jackets and reset type. A far cry from the usual, cheesy production values that have marred their original editions, the current editions are fitting showcases for King's macabre fiction. (The dust jackets are imaginatively designed, using photography and art to achieve the proper effect.)

Viking is King's hardback publisher—now a sister company of NAL—and, like clockwork, issues its new King book annually, usually in October, timed for Christmas release.

NAL is King's main publisher, issuing him in mass market paperback, but also issuing a very handsome set of trade paperbacks, which sport full-color reproductions of the original hardback dust jacket illustrations, and newly commissioned introductions by major writers.

In the small presses, Donald M. Grant, Publisher, is the source for the true first editions of the *Dark Tower* novels. (NAL reprints the Grant editions in trade paperback, but the edition of choice is Grant's.)

Commonly Asked Questions About Collecting King Books

Since its original publication in 1989, *The Stephen King Companion* has generated a sizable amount of mail, all duly forwarded from the publisher to me. Often the same questions arise, typically from my younger readers new to King who seek direct answers to puzzling problems, things the more seasoned collector takes for granted.

The questions, and answers, that follow address some of these problems.

Is it expensive to collect King books?

It *can* be, depending on how elaborate a collection you wish to assemble. For most King fans, the priority is in collecting recently published first editions from King's trade publishers, which is fairly easy and affordable. The important thing to remember is that condition is important. So before you leave the bookstore, *inspect your copy carefully:* take the dust wrapper off and make sure the store hasn't put one of its own stickers on; inspect the wrapper for cuts, tears, or scuffing; look at the book itself, to ensure that the corners are not dented in; and leaf through the book to ascertain that you don't have a misprinted copy with pages missing.

Also, be sure to check the "legal" page (the page that the copyright notice is on), to ensure that it is a first edition. For a Viking book, a first edition is not noted as such. Instead, you must look at the row of numbers and make certain that the number "1" is on the far left side; if it is, you have a first edition; if it isn't, you have a subsequent printing. Thus, look for the following to ensure the book is a first edition: 1 3 5 7 9 10 8 6 4 2.

Books in bookstores tend to get manhandled, so don't buy the top copy of any stack. Go down a few books, and check that copy carefully.

Alternatively, you can order from a specialty dealer that will ensure a mint copy is sent to you, properly packed to survive shipment by UPS.

If you must buy from a bookstore, strike up a friendship with a clerk, who can lay one or two copies aside for you, avoiding the price-stickering that many bookstores employ. (One of the local bookstores uses a special sticker that is impossible to remove without damaging the book. The chain bookstores, like Waldenbooks, generally do not sticker books, but independent bookstores do.)

What should I collect?

It really depends on your budget. Certainly you should collect the first editions of each trade book, which (these days) will cost under $30 each. Viking releases on the average one King book a year, in the fall to take advantage of Christmas sales. Thus, a King book scheduled for October release is generally shipped in late September.

If you have more disposable income, consider buying trade editions of King's books when available in small-press editions. *Insomnia*, for instance, was published by Mark V. Ziesing Books in a "gift" edition of 3,250 copies, a far cry from the 1.5 million copies that Viking printed. Likewise, the "trade" edition of Grant's *Dark Tower III: The Wastelands* was published in a print run of forty thousand copies—and, in this case, it is a hardcover, whereas NAL published a trade paperback reprint.

If you want to think about investments, consider buying signed, limited editions. But these are expensive—the average price today is $175 because, typically, King limits them to 1,250 copies. Because the demand for these few copies outstrips supply, you must order immediately upon hearing the publisher is taking orders. Usually, these are issued by small presses in the horror, fantasy, and science-fiction fields. Collector's note: Because these are sold out before publication, copies sell for twice retail once the book is officially published—thus, *Insomnia* (1,250 copies, $175) will cost $350, or more, because that's what it will command on the secondary book market.

Beyond the limited editions, you're getting into rare stuff: uncorrected proofs ($175 and up), advance reading copies, presentation copies (given by the publisher or author to close friends), and lettered states of limited-edition books. These are, frankly, collectibles of the first order and priced accordingly.

My recommendation: There's so much King material out there that the beginning collector should proceed cautiously, building up his collection slowly, adding a new book when the budget permits. (Even if you were to try and collect one copy of each signed, limited edition, it would cost thousands of dollars. But because these are always available from secondary sources, when you have the money you can always add them to your collection in the future.)

What kind of books should I avoid?

Don't buy ex-libris books (discarded from the library), because they are generally marred by glued-in pockets, stamps ("Property of Castle Rock Library"), protective covers, and the like. Don't buy book club editions, which are usually cheap reprints or—if Book-of-the-Month Club—overruns bearing the club's indicia on the legal page: "Book-of-the-Month Records® offers a wide range of opera, classical and jazz recordings. For information and catalog write to BOMR, Dept. 901, Camp Hill, PA 17012." (You can also tell a BOMC/BOMR edition by the dust jacket: sometimes it reads "book club edition" where the price usually is, or the ISBN and retail price are simply omitted. *The legitimate trade editions always have an ISBN number and a retail price on the dust jacket inside flap.*)

Beware of book club editions jacketed with legitimate dust jackets. You *must* check the legal page to ascertain that it is, indeed, a first trade edition and not a book club edition.

What's a first edition?

Generally speaking, a first edition refers to the "first edition, first printing" of a book. In the King world, however, the confusion results when a small press issues its own edition—with the same text—prior to the release of the trade edition. The key factor is the book's distribution date.

For instance, Mark V. Ziesing has published two states of *Insomnia,* in a limited edition and a "gift" edition. These would properly be termed the "true first edition," to make a distinction between his and Viking's edition.

Viking, of course, went to press and labeled its copies first editions, too, which leads to confusion. It is, indeed, a first edition, but can best be termed "first *trade* edition," which is why some small presses note that theirs are the "first *limited* edition" instead.

The matter is further complicated by the fact that when King's British publisher jumps the gun and publishes its edition *before* the U.S. edition, it is, technically, the first *world* edition, which means that of all the published copies of the book, the British edition came out first. (For example, *Rose Madder* had an official publication date of August 1995 in the U.K. However, as early as April, copies of the first printing were sold in bookstores, which made it the true world first edition, beating out the U.S. edition.)

Generally, when a small press publishes a King book, it does so *before* the corresponding trade edition, but not always. *Skeleton Crew,* published by Scream Press, appeared *after* the trade edition, which did not make it the true first edition.

The important thing to remember is that when examining trade editions from Viking, look at the row of numbers to ensure that "1" is in the row, on the far left; if it's missing, then you've got a first edition in a subsequent printing. For instance, if "4" is the lowest number, then you've got a first edition, fourth printing. Which means you don't have as collectible a book because it is not the first edition, *first* printing.

How can I identify a book as a first edition?

Unfortunately, this is an area that should be standardized within the book publishing community but is not, which fact can lead to a lot of confusion.

Again, insofar as King's books are concerned, Viking does not indicate "first edition" on its books. Instead, it uses a row of numbers to indicate the printing of the book. If you see a "1" on the left, it's a first edition, first printing.

New American Library specifically states that a book is first edition, first printing. In *Pearl,* the legal page notes: "First Printing, November, 1988 / 1 2 3 4 5 6 7 8 9," which translates to: first edition, first printing. (If the number "1" is missing, it is a *subsequent* printing, and thus worth less as a collectible.)

It is critical that you understand how to identify a first edition, because inept book dealers in the mainstream can unknowingly sell you a subsequent printing of the book and tell you it's a first edition, when in fact it's not. My recommendation is to buy from a legitimate book dealer who knows what he's selling—the specialty dealers I've listed in this book are all knowledgeable about the different editions, states, and points of King books, which have become increasingly difficult to track.)

What makes a book valuable?

Many things. Generally, with King, demand far exceeds supply, so the prices will escalate rapidly, especially when a King book goes out of print, at which point it usually doubles in value.

First, condition. A book in fine condition (or mint, as some dealers term it) looks "as new"; it is a fresh, clean copy without any defects whatever. Even a minor cut or bumped corner can greatly diminish the value.

Unfortunately, some of King's books haven't been constructed well—notably, the early Doubleday editions, and books like *Skeleton Crew* that, although hardbound, have insufficient bindings. Thus, they fall apart easily under several readings, creating a scarcity based on book condition alone.

Second, print run. As King's career grew, the first printings grew too. The Doubleday books when originally issued not only had modest print runs, but many went to libraries that, eventually, put their copies out of circulation. Thus, the potential number of copies in fine condition has been reduced, escalating the prices of the books, even though they are trade editions.

Third, scarcity. The fewer the copies, the more rare and costly the book. In the case of lettered copies, there are usually twenty-six, and not all of these may have been offered for sale. (The asbestos-bound *Firestarter* from Phantasia Press is scarce—even if you have the money and want to buy a copy, you may not be able to locate one; and when one does surface, the price keeps going up. For instance, when John McLaughlin of the Book Sail put his collection up for sale at the Pacific Book Auction Galleries, the estimate for *Firestarter* was in the $6,000 to $9,000 range; the book went for $6,000+, according to Michael J. Autrey, who catalogued the book.)

Fourth, desirability. Because *Carrie* was King's first published book, it will always be a cornerstone of any major King collection. Of course, signed or inscribed copies are even more desirable—if the signature is authentic—and the very few bound galleys of *Carrie* that were distributed are also highly collectible.

When *The Dark Tower* was listed in the front of Doubleday's *Pet Sematary*, King fans deluged his publishers with requests for information on how they could get the book—an edition of only ten thousand copies plus five hundred signed copies. (Later, King authorized a second printing of ten thousand copies, which was far from adequate to meet the demand; finally, King relented and allowed NAL to publish trade paperback reprints, presumably because he wanted to keep the cost down. The fans, however, wanted a hardback edition, and thus drove the price up of the Grant editions, now among the most costly King collectibles.)

Similarly, after ABC-TV aired *The Stand* on television in 1994, the demand for the signed, limited edition of Doubleday's *The Stand* [II] spiked upward. People wanted *that* edition, and no other.

What is the importance of the dust jacket?

All of King's trade books, and many of the limited editions from small presses, come with dust jackets, or dust wrappers, as they are sometimes called. They are an integral part of the book from a collector's point of view. A book in fine condition without a dust jacket is worth substantially less.

Dust jackets are very fragile, so make sure that you protect it with a cover, and make sure the price has not been clipped off, which happens when bookstores want to add their own prices to their stock, or when someone buys it as a gift but doesn't want the recipient to know what the book cost. (In the case of a King book, it cost the recipient the collectibility of the book!) Also, make sure the dust jacket doesn't bear the words "book club," which means you've been burned badly.

How can I tell what my book is worth?

Your specific copy may vary depending on condition, but generally you will know what it's worth by checking listings of comparable copies in book catalogs. If you want more exact information, consult with a specialty dealer to see what his current appraisal is. (I wouldn't expect a dealer to do this for free, though; his time and knowledge are worth money, like those of any other professional.)

Keep in mind that prices can fluctuate sharply, based on demand for the book, as well as on recent discoveries regarding various points or states of it.

Caution: Do not assume that because a book dealer deals in collectibles he's charging the going rate—he may be charging more. Although this generally is not a problem in the fantasy and science-fiction/horror field, there have been dealers that have engaged in price-gouging, preying on the ignorance of buyers who have more money than sense. (I will *not* tell you who they are; you'll know them when you run into them, because they'll charge you substantially more than their counterparts. Obviously, shop around.)

If King signs a book, how does it increase its value?

Presuming the book is in good condition, and presuming it's a hardback instead of a cheap mass market paperback, and presuming the signature is authentic, a King signature does indeed increase its value.

King, from all accounts, typically dates his signature thus: month/day/year. For example: "11/2/88," which means November 2, 1988.

Ideally, you'd want the book to be signed as close to the publication date as possible—a book signed years later just doesn't have the same cachet.

Also, unless King has signed the book to a notable person in the field, an inscribed copy is generally worth *less* than an autographed and dated copy, on the assumption that if the person is a stranger—like a customer at a bookstore signing—there's no personal connection. In cases where there is an obvious connection—like the inscribed copy of *The Plant—Part One* and *The Plant—Part Two* to one of his publishers, which appeared as auction items from the Book Sail collection—the inscribed copies are worth more.

I checked with an autograph dealer who dealt exclusively with rare signatures—including people like Napoleon!—and asked if he had anything signed by King. He did—a half-dozen portrait shots provided by movie studios of King on location. The average price for an eight-by-ten-inch glossy was $75.

A King signature is not rare, unlike J.D. Salinger's, a recluse who refuses to sign copies of his books, which make his very valuable indeed. Still, King does not attend conventions anymore, nor does he attend bookstore signings, as a general rule, but he does sign books at the office, presumably copies dropped off by locals. (By the way, I do *not* recommend that you send him books unsolicited; the word I have is that he will send them back, unsigned, if you have enclosed postage, or will donate them to the local library, or may even throw them away. You are well advised to write to him first and ask permission, and limit your request to one book, and he *might* accommodate you. In any event, you're on your own here. I'd think long and hard before sending a first edition of, say, *The Stand* [I] with the hope of getting your book signed, and wondering years later why you never got it back.)

Why are King's limited editions so valuable?

For these reasons: scarcity, demand, and desirability. In most cases, these limiteds are the true first editions—the trade edition inevitably follows. Also, in most cases, these are the only editions to be substantially illustrated, a concession that the publisher can make, knowing that the edition will sell out.

Unlike some authors, King does limit the number of books he signs for a given limited edition. He appears to have set the limit at 1,250 copies; more than that, according to his essay in "The Politics of Limiteds," he doesn't consider limited.

Even more limited: the lettered states of the signed, limited editions, which are generally not advertised and often sell out immediately upon word of their availability, since the savvy collector knows this is the most desirable state.

If King signs a limited edition that isn't one of his own novels, how collectible will that book be?

In numerous instances, King has signed limited editions to which he has contributed a story, like *Prime Evil,* edited by Douglas E. Winter, published by Donald M. Grant, Publisher; the special Stephen King issue of *Gauntlet,* published by Borderlands Press; and his own Philtrum Press edition of Don Robertson's *The Ideal, Genuine Man,* to which he contributed an original introduction.

Because it is a limited edition and because King has signed it, the book is obviously collectible. But it falls into the category of being a secondary signed collectible, as I term it: valuable, but not as valuable, or as desirable, as a limited edition of a book King has written, like a novel or a short-story collection.

Unlike one by King, a book with a King short story or introduction will generally sell out, but it may take much longer—months, in some cases. (At this writing, the signed copies of *The House Next Door* by Anne Rivers Siddons, published by a specialty press in Georgia, is still available; King contributed a very brief, one-page introduction and signed the book.)

Because King is very selective in the projects he endorses, all signed King books have traditionally proven to be prudent investments.

How important are low numbers on limitation pages?

Some collectors seem adamant in asking for a low number, as if it means the book is more valuable. It isn't, unless there has been an unusual situation, like King's signing copies of *Firestarter* (Phantasia Press) on three separate days, *and putting the date under each signature,* which is why the earlier the day, the more valuable the copy.

Also, the first copy is generally more valuable, since it presumably is kept by the publisher for his own files.

There is, in the King market, a distinction that must be made: in cases where a set of books exists, like the *Dark Tower* novels, which are offered to original subscribers first and then made generally available, it is desirable to have matching numbers because that's how the sets were issued.

According to Grant, there are only a few hundred complete sets of *Dark Tower* available, which means that they are worth more than a comparable set with different numbers. Grant's policy is to offer the limited, signed edition to the current owner on record, requiring a photocopy of the limitation page as proof of purchase, so to speak. In the case that a subscriber of record has bought all three *Dark Tower* books, and continues to buy each new limited, he will eventually own a complete set of the projected seven books in the series with matching numbers—a valuable set of books indeed, since there will likely be only two hundred to three hundred at most in existence.

In the case of *The Plant,* numbered sets are difficult to come by because the recipients did not get matching numbers of the three published installments.

If low numbers are important to you, or you are trying to collect a certain number for all your collectibles, get your order in early and specify what number you wish. Some publishers may accommodate you. It's worth a try, at any rate.

Why is an advance copy so valuable?

First, let's explain what an advance copy is. It is generally a bound set of pages from unproofed and uncorrected type printed in trade paperback format for advance review purposes.

For instance, Viking typically prints for sales purposes advance copies— galleys—for the chain bookstores, as well as review sources like *Publishers Weekly* and *Library Journal,* which require advance notification months in advance.

Companies like Crane print galleys specifically for the book trade. The cover is usually plain and states, "This is an uncorrected proof. It should not be quoted without comparison with the finished book." On the cover, typically, publication information is provided: the publication date, the price, any pertinent information (whether it has been bought by a major book club), and the first printing—information designed to position the book as a "hot" title.

These being trade paperbacks with perfect binding, they are fragile and their spines can crack easily if you open one too quickly. For this reason, they are treated very gingerly. (The publisher, of course, is not concerned with whether or not it survives a first reading; it's intended as a throwaway.)

In the case of King, galleys are always made of each new book, but they are difficult to obtain because the print runs are low and, technically, they are supposed to be controlled items. (In practice, copies of *Insomnia* were available from a rare-book dealer in New York City almost immediately upon publication.)

The going price of an advance, uncorrected proof of a King book is $150 to $200, depending on condition and the source. (Reviewers, knowing that these are valuable, resell their copies to rare-book dealers—one benefit of book reviewing, I guess.)

If Viking puts these items under more strict inventory control—under lock and key—it may be more difficult to obtain these from any source.

How valuable are King manuscripts?

Very valuable, and for a good reason: Very few have come onto the market. Mostly they are auction items for charity purposes that have been sold and resold. On occasion, King has given them as gifts, too.

In the Book Sail auction, lot number 28 consisted of three hand-written pages from *The Napkins,* later titled *The Eyes of the Dragon.* A gift from King to publisher Stuart David Schiff of Whispers Press, the pages were appraised at $1,500 to $2,000.

At the same auction, lot number 57 consisted of eleven hand-written pages torn out of a loose-leaf notebook; the pages belonged to "The Raft," which was written by King while on location in Philadelphia for the filming of *Creepshow.* The pages were appraised at $4,000 to $6,000.

It is not likely that we will see a sudden flood of King manuscripts on the market. He either has donated the material to UMO's Special Collections or is keeping them for himself.

I bought a King novel as a remainder. Is it worth anything?

It depends. A remaindered book means the publisher has decided that he's sold all the copies he can through normal channels. He has therefore discounted it heavily, and it will be sold at chain stores on their remainder tables and at re-mainder bookstores.

Usually, a remaindered book will be marked in some fashion, so that the book won't be sent back for credit from a bookseller. Viking, for example, puts its mark on the edges of the pages, where it is sometimes impossible to remove, even when using bleach. Also, remainder books, usually overstocked items, have been returned from booksellers, and thus may show a bit of wear and tear.

Chances are, the remaindered book is not a first edition. In most cases, the book will be a subsequent printing. That means the publisher, in the end, over-printed the book—an easy enough thing to do, since books are fully return-able and bookstores will overorder what they perceive as "hot" books because they know they can return unsold books for credit.

Are book prices negotiable?

Herb Cohen, a professional negotiator, wrote in *You Can Negotiate Anything* that everything is negotiable. Much depends on how badly the dealer wants to make the sale, how badly you want the book, how the dealer has sized up the situation, and how you've sized it up. In other words, if you think the price is too high, make a counteroffer. At the worst, the offer will be declined.

To be honest, though, most of the book dealers I've dealt with have arrived at prices that they deem fair market value, and they aren't inclined to dicker on prices. Still, you can always give it a try.

I notice that some King books, really rare items, go up for auction. Should I bid?

It depends on whether or not you really want that book. Because of the nature of the beast, auction items tend to be collectibles, since people aren't going to bid for run-of-the-mill material that is readily obtainable elsewhere. When a major King collection goes up for auction, it is usually broken into lots, and you can bid in person or by mail.

In any event, write and get the catalog describing each lot, and outlining the bidding procedures. Most auction houses have procedures they follow to the letter. You must follow them too.

Keep in mind that the people who are bidding probably know what the auction items are worth and may be willing to pay top dollar, especially if bidding fever erupts. In any event, it's not likely that you will walk away with a bona fide bargain.

I'm thinking of putting personalized bookplates on my King books. What do you think?

Not a good idea. If you are a private collector—as opposed to being Stephen King, or someone associated with him—your bookplate will *devalue* the book's worth.

Are King books good investments?

Generally, yes. Over the years King books have risen, not fallen, in value. And the more scarce material has skyrocketed in value, depending on the item.

King is one of the few authors who have both a mass audience and a fan audience, which means that he's extremely collectible. And because there are so many King readers, the demand for King collectibles will always outstrip supply.

King's first book, *Carrie,* was published in 1974, over two decades ago. As an author, King has demonstrated staying power, with print runs averaging 1.5 million copies in hardback. Since *Carrie,* his books have gone up in value, some dramatically. And collectors who have turned their collections into cash have found that there are specialty dealers who will make offers on single titles as well as on collections. (Keep in mind that when a dealer buys your book, he will pay you less than market value, because that's what he's going to sell it at.

Depending on the dealer, you may get 50 to 75 percent of fair market value. The dealer has to make a profit, or he has no incentive to be involved in the transaction.)

In some cases, specialty dealers will take the books on a consignment basis—you get paid when the books sell. This arrangement keeps him from tying up funds on a speculative basis, which is a consideration, especially if the market is temporarily glutted with a King product.

Are paperbacks collectible?

Generally, no. However, in the case of the Richard Bachman novels—originally published in mass market paperback, in fairly small runs, and published under Bachman's, not King's, name—the books have sold for $100 to $125 each.

As King's novels go to press with three million copies in mass market paperback, the law of supply and demand swings into action, and the net result is that these editions are good for reading purposes only. (In other words, if you're thinking of collectibles, think hardback.)

I notice that specialty dealers are offering other King items for sale. Are these collectible?

It depends on the item, its condition, its demand, and its relative scarcity.

Just because it has King's name on it does not mean it is a valuable collectible. In a case of what I consider to be blind optimism, Viking published *Nightmares in the Sky*, a coffee-table book of photographs, with an introduction by King. According to David Streitfeld, the initial sales were lower than expected, and he predicted a good part of the print run would be remaindered. He was right. Within months after publication, the book was remaindered, available for under $10, a big discount from the originally published price, $24.95. What Viking never took into consideration is that the primary market for King material is new, novel-length fiction. Everything else, especially nonfiction, is of secondary interest.

In cases where the item has special significance, like "The Raft," which was published as a separate pamphlet, the item is indeed collectible—hard enough to find under any circumstances.

I'm really confused about points, states, and other fine points of bibliographic distinction. Can you recommend a book that will explain these things in plain English?

Yes. Get John Carter's *ABC for Book Collectors* (fifth edition, revised), in hardback, published by Alfred A. Knopf, at $18.95. Witty, wise, and authoritative,

STORING BOOKS

Books may look sturdy, but like anything else, they can be damaged easily if not preserved.

Here are some ways to keep your books in "as new" condition:

- Store them upright. They should be snug, but not jammed together. (Obviously, do not stack them like cards.)

- Keep them in an air-conditioned room at approximately 50 percent humidity and a temperature range of 60 to 70 degrees. (Heat and moisture are the two big enemies of book preservation.) Putting books in the attic, where they are subject to the extremes of heat and cold—depending on the season—can do much damage over time.

- Do not expose books to direct sunlight. Over time, the sun's rays can "bleach" a book of its color, especially dust jackets.

- Protect dust jackets by encasing them with Gaylord wrappers (used by libraries to protect dust jackets).

- Handle books carefully. Do *not* pull books out by the headband.

- With slipcased books, let the gravity pull the book out—*don't* pull them out manually.

- With especially rare books, you may want to store them archivally, in special wrappers or boxes that are used by libraries for the rare books in their collection. This is a good, long-term way of preserving the books if your intent is to resell them at some future date. (Plastic bags are not necessarily a good substitute. Plastic "breathes" and, unless it is Mylar®D, you will have a long-term storage problem.)

Bill Cole Enterprises, Inc., points out that for years comic book collectors have stored their valuables in polyethylene and polypropylene bags, which are "coated with chemicals and contain additives that migrate into paper and cause premature aging. Even the manufacturers of polypropylene warn that only uncoated and untreated Mylar®D is suitable for archival protection. This exceptionally strong transparent film will resist moisture, pollutants, oils, and acids."

Similarly, archival boxes are the preferred method of long-term storage, preferably a genuine, acid-free box with an 8.0 to 8.5 pH with a 3# calcium carbonate buffer throughout. (Write to me and I'll send information on where to order these specialty items.)

the book is a real education for any bibliophile. (Besides, how can you resist a book penned by an author who shares the same name as the protagonist in Edgar Rice Burroughs's Mars books?)

In the last edition of this book, you published a price guide, written in cooperation with Barry R. Levin. Why isn't it in this edition?

For these reasons:

1. This book was turned over to the publisher in early November 1994. By the time it appears in October 1995, the price guide will already be out of date, yet people would be using it as a reference for pricing books for resale, for assessing values for insurance purposes, etc.

2. Barry R. Levin has, since 1988, discovered many new points and states that are not in the original price guide. To ensure 100 percent accuracy, it is necessary to take the time and catalog everything properly, which would make it impossible to have a manuscript to the publisher in time for a fall 1995 release date.

3. The ideal format for a price guide would incorporate photographs (the more, the better), a detailed price list (preferably updated), and background information on each book or collectible that gives the story behind the item itself, as Sheldon Jaffery had done in *The Arkham House Companion.*

After discussions with Levin and other booksellers, as well as private collectors who have expressed a desire to assist in a new price guide, I've decided it's best to publish this information on an ongoing basis. Again, rather than print it in book form, which will go out of date quickly, I've elected to publish the price guide in my King newsletter, *Phantasmagoria.*

What are my chances of getting signed, not inscribed, copies of each new King novel?

Not very good. On a tour to promote *Insomnia,* King signed thousands of copies and, predictably, those same copies surfaced immediately on the collector's market at inflated prices—a clear case of profiteering. As a result, King, according to my sources, has become disenchanted with "flat" signing (autographing books without personal inscriptions) and in the future will likely limit signings to inscriptions, which adversely affect the collectibility of the book, unless it's an associational copy.

17
Kingly Collectibles
Limited Editions

He could see tiny dents in the surface—they had been made by the
point of the pen Sandy Koufax had used to sign his name ... Sandy Koufax
had held this card in his hand and had imposed his mark upon it,
the mark of his living hand and magic name.

from *Needful Things*

＊

Within the fan community that collects King, the big news in 1994 was not that
King was going on tour—who, after all, might live close enough to the ten cities
he would visit to be able to stop by?—but that King's big fall novel, *Insomnia,*
would be rolling off the assembly line at the King Works.

As Viking geared up its presses to run 1.5 million copies in hardback of an
eight-hundred-page novel at $27.50—or $79.95 if you wanted King's reading
on unabridged audiotapes, nearly thirty hours' worth on twenty-four cas-
settes—the real excitement was a 1,250-copy edition at $175.00 that was pub-
lished by a small fantasy press in southern California, which was selected by
King to publish a signed, limited edition of his latest novel. (There is also what
the publisher terms a "gift" edition, which is $75.00, limited to 3,750 copies,
but not signed or numbered.)

King, who had not had a signed, limited edition of any of his novels since
the 1991 edition of *The Wastelands,* signed 1,250 copies of *Insomnia,* which
meant that, upon publication, the book would go out of print and command
an out-of-print price of twice the cover price: $350. (Even before the book was
out, one dealer who had recieved a small allotment offered his copies at $450,
knowing that there would be fans who would pay it, rather than go without
or risk paying more later.)

Among King fans, the most collectible books are the signed, limited editions,
which have usually been published from the small presses in the fantasy,

Stephen King and Kenny Ray Linkous hold up artwork for *The Eyes of the Dragon.*

science-fiction, and horror community. (The notable exceptions were Double-day, which published a sumptuous edition of *The Stand [II]*, and the Whitney Museum, which published a $2,200 edition of a King short story.) The names of the publishers who have issued signed, King limiteds include the most celebrated houses in the field, including Donald M. Grant, Publisher, who issues the *Dark Tower* novels, and published *Christine* and *The Talisman;* Mysterious Press, which published *Cujo;* Land of Enchantment, which published *Cycle of the Werewolf,* with illustrations by Berni Wrightson; Everest House, which published *Danse Macabre;* Lord John Press, which published *Dolan's Cadillac* and a broadside, "Letters from Hell"; Phantasia Press, which published *Firestarter;* Scream Press, which published *Skeleton Crew;* and, most recently, Mark V. Ziesing, which published *Insomnia.*

Even King has been involved, self-publishing with his Philtrum Press: three installments of *The Plant* (a work-in-progress published as pamphlets, given out as Christmas greetings); *The Eyes of the Dragon,* a sumptuous hard-back with delightful illustrations by Kenny Ray Linkous; and *The Ideal, Genuine Man* by Don Robertson, who heavily influenced his writing style.

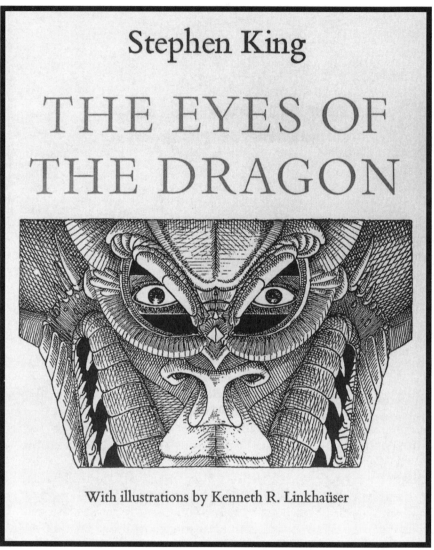

Title page to *The Eyes of the Dragon.*

That King has signed tens of thousands of copies of his trade books, which are staples in rare-book catalogs, doesn't explain the appeal of the limited-edition books, which are now averaging $175 for each new book. Even investment potential doesn't suffice as an explanation, since King's fans who buy these books hoard them like Smaug, from *The Hobbit,* sitting on his piles of gold treasure. The real reason, I think, is more basic: the limited-edition book—despite its high price—is typically a work of art in itself, with imaginative design, typesetting, and artwork that give the story an added dimension a trade edition cannot.

These days, companies like QVC hawk "limited editions" that, to be honest, are limited only to what they think they can sell. The chances that a signed photo of a television celebrity will be worth more than what the mark—ah, customer—paid are not likely. There is no value added, and simply saying that it's a limited edition, when there are five thousand of them floating around, doesn't make it rare or valuable. What make it rare and valuable are its perceived intrinsic worth and its limited number.

In his long essay "The Politics of Limiteds," King says he doesn't consider a trade book—no matter how beautifully bound, printed, and illustrated—to be a limited edition, because the text is the same and what you're really buying is an autograph.

In King's mind—at least back in the mid-eighties when the piece was published—a true limited edition exists in no other form, which means uniqueness is the issue. He considered true limiteds to be his own Philtrum Press edition of *The Eyes of the Dragon,* and his *Dark Tower* novels that Grant had issued. In both instances, the books in question were, at that time, not available in any trade editions.

The Eyes of the Dragon was available only by lottery, one to a customer. It was published in two main states—250 copies numbered in red ink were given as Christmas gifts; one thousand copies numbered in black ink were sold for $120 through a lottery. An exquisite book, *The Eyes of the Dragon* was designed by Michael Alpert, illustrated by Kenneth Linkhaüser (the pen name of Kenny Ray Linkous), and printed by one of the finest printers in New England, the Stinehour Press. Oversize, printed on napkinlike paper stock (an allusion to a pivotal scene in the book itself, as well as the original title, *The Napkins*), and exquisitely encased in a slipcase, the book was advertised in three science-fiction and fantasy magazines, which meant that most of King's readers never knew the book had been published.

Working closely with King, Alpert worked out the basic design for the book itself: "We decided that the finished book would be quite large in format, printed from metal type on fine acid-free paper, illustrated with black-and-white line drawings, bound attractively in a sturdy binding, and housed in a matching protective slipcase. This was the general basis from which I began to work on the details of my design."

The result, to which anyone who owns a copy can attest: a book which was a perfect marriage of text and art, form following function. Alpert, who considers reading to be a private experience, likened the book's presentation to a private theater in which the design itself invites the reader to read on, ensuring that "nothing interferes with a reader's immersion into the text."

Even if the book had not been an associational item from King's own small press, it would still be regarded as a major King collectible because it is the true first edition of the book. Indeed, it is the only edition, for the text itself was changed in the trade edition that followed. Thus it is, truly, a limited edition. Of the edition proper, only 1,250 copies were printed, plus a small handful of other states.

Obviously, King could, if he wished, sign several thousand copies of a new novel, and all would sell out. King, however, is an exception, perhaps *the* exception. His audience is sufficiently large, and his fan following so loyal, that without exception, every signed, limited edition of a King novel—as well as any limited-edition book that sports his signature because of the inclusion of a short story of his—*has sold out,* usually before publication.

For a small press, the advantage is obvious. There is no need to sell the book; simply announce the book and, for months prior, fans will frantically phone in, send checks by FedEx overnight, and besiege the publisher with requests for ordering information.

King could self-publish his books through Philtrum Press. But he chooses to spread the wealth around to small presses in the field that can use the infusion of cash a King project brings. That says much about King's character, and his desire is to give back to the community that he cut his teeth on when he was younger. (In fact, King was a frequent attendee at conventions, until his fame made it impossible to attend without being mobbed.)

Typically, when a small press issues a limited-edition book, it will only print, in some cases, as few as a thousand copies, which may take years to sell out. But when it's a Stephen King novel, you can count on a sell-out of the limited edition. Or, put another way, in a field where there are no guarantees, *publishing a signed, King limited-edition book is a guaranteed sell-out.* Even your banker would smile broadly when he looks at the numbers: 1,250 copies, with an average price of $175—that's one hell of a shot in the arm for any small press.

The word within the small-press publishing community is that King does want to spread the wealth around, so there is no one publisher that benefits from the King phenomenon excessively. (There are exceptions to the rule: Donald M. Grant, Publisher, has published limited editions of *Christine, The Talisman,* and

MARK V. ZIESING BOOKS
INSOMNIA

The most recent limited edition—*Insomnia,* published by Mark V. Ziesing Books—is a textbook example of how imagination and love and a lot of attention can produce an objet d'art. The signed, limited edition is handsomely protected by a custom slipcase that uses a three-piece design, allowing it to wrap around the entire book—the book and slipcase are matching burgundy red. The dust jacket, in full color, is by Phil Hale. The endpaper art, again in full color, is by Hale. The limitation sheet, printed on heavy, speckled art stock, uses raised ink (similar to that used to print business cards). The text has been reset, printed in two colors (black ink for the basic text, and a powder-blue ink for the running heads); and throughout, Hale's illustrations lend the appropriate, macabre touch. Finally, to ensure that you don't lose your place in this 591-page book, a silk ribbon is sewn in. As with all previously published limited editions signed by King, this one sold out immediately.

Recognizing that the demand for the limited would far outstrip the supply, Ziesing wisely printed a "gift" edition, which is essentially the same book, sans the limitation sheet, the burgundy boards, and the wraparound slipcase. A good buy at $75, the gift edition is bound in blue boards with matching slipcase, stamped with silver lettering.

A handsome book in its own right, an example of small-press publishing at its best, Ziesing's *Insomnia* is an attractive addition to any King collection.

all the *Dark Tower* novels.) Also, according to the publishers of these limited-edition books, King is concerned that the edition be limited to 1,250 copies, a figure consistent with his own limitation on the run of *The Eyes of the Dragon,* and the figure he mentioned in his essay, "The Politics of Limiteds."

In publishing a King limited, everybody wins: King gets a beautiful edition of his book, the publisher gets a financial shot in the arm that is not possible with any other author, King's die-hard fans get a collectible and an investment, and rare-book dealers who buy and resell these collectibles make a profit too. (You could argue that the people who don't benefit are those that were unable to buy them because they didn't know of the availability—a valid point, which is why King reissued a second printing of *The Dark Tower I: The Gun-slinger,* after vowing that there would be no further editions.)

Today, all of King's major books are available in affordable trade editions, in hardback and paperback, and that is as it should be. There are many King readers who wouldn't think of paying $175 for a signed, limited edition. They just want to read the story, and don't care if it is printed on cheap pulp paper with a cheap glue binding sufficient to hold it together for one reading—in other words, a mass market paperback edition. That is as cheap a book as can be printed, one step up from the pulps of the thirties and forties, so called because of the pulp paper they were printed on, with staples to hold the pages together. (In time, as oxidation sets in, the pulps and the paperbacks will literally crumble to dust—a far cry from, say, *The Eyes of the Dragon,* published by Philtrum Press, which will last hundreds of years if stored properly; a family treasure that can be handed down to the next generation of readers that will increasingly view printed books as artifacts and perhaps even antiques, as we move into an electronic age of CD-ROM books and books on diskette.)

Beyond the investment potential and the book as collectible, the signed limited edition offers something that, insofar as King fans are concerned, has become an increasingly scarce commodity: King's signature.

King has said his autograph is commonplace, but the fact remains that only a tiny fraction of the estimated 150 million copies of his books in print could possibly be signed, which is why all books signed by King have gone up in value.

There is a practical limit to what King can, and will, sign. And, from all accounts, that limit has been reached and he's restricting the number of books he's signing for any given fan. (He could, if he did nothing else, sign books for the rest of his life, twenty-four hours a day, seven days a week, and still not meet the demand for autographed books.)

It's understandable why people want signed books. Beyond the obvious and crass—the increased worth of the book as a collectible—a signature from the author means that, for a brief moment in time, he signed *this* copy and it establishes a link, however tenuous, between the writer and the reader. Even a trade hardback bearing a signature can make the book special: it is no longer just one of 1.5 million copies printed, but one of perhaps a few thousand that the author has signed.

To me, there are several reasons why signed, King limiteds have such special appeal: at a time when the phrase "limited edition" has become so generic as to lose its meaning, like the word "sale," a King limited edition is truly limited, usually to 1,250 copies or less; at a time when books are being manufactured by the cheapest printing and binding methods, guaranteeing that even a $27.50 hardback will crack in two under repeated readings, a "trade" edition of

3,750 copies, like Ziesing's *Insomnia,* seems like an absolute bargain at $75, with its two-color printing, oversized pages, full-color art, smythe-sewn binding, and protective slipcase; and at a time when best-selling authors distance themselves from the readers, whether by choice or inclination, a signed limited solidifies the link between writer and reader in a way an unsigned book cannot.

In other words, the limited edition is, in some ways, an anachronism. It recalls a time when book publishing was less an entertainment industry than a profession for gentlemen, who loved books, loved stories, and knew how to publish sumptuously illustrated books, with readable typefaces and wide margins, that were bound for the ages and could be handed down from generation to generation.

I own only one signed King book, an inscribed copy of *The Dark Tower II: The Drawing of the Three.* For it, I thank Chris Spruce, who took it to King, who signed it in 1988. Someday, I hope one of my nephews or nieces will discover King, just as I did, and look over the trade editions and see this Grant edition, and open it up and see the generic inscription ("best wishes"), and perhaps gasp in astonishment. And then that book will be passed to the next generation, and the story will continue to be told . . . and retold, which is the magic of good fiction, enhanced by the signature of the author who, briefly, uncapped a pen, scribbled his name in the book, and made that copy something special indeed.

Kenny Linkous, artist for the Philtrum Press edition of *The Eyes of the Dragon.*

18
Specialty Publishers

I never knew that people cared enough to do them right. I love books—I love the way they're crafted; I love the way the pages turn; I love it when there's good paper stock in it, and if the publisher does something interesting, intriguing or imaginative. I think the imagination and the love and care someone puts into making the book are just as important as the care that goes into writing the book.

Howard Wornom, writer and collector

✳

If you depend on your local bookstore for copies of books for your collection, you will not likely see any of the gorgeous, limited-edition books published by the small presses in the horror, fantasy, and science-fiction field. Normally one-person operations, the small presses pick and choose what they publish with great care, giving each book the time and attention the book deserves.

Why, you ask, would a best-selling author go to a small press when there's not much money in it for him? The reason is simple: best-selling authors know that their trade publishers are interested in shipping book as product, manufactured as cheaply as possible, with no illustrations, and with standard paper and binding. Often, for marketing considerations, prose can be cut or dramatically altered, which can change the substance of the story.

Because small presses are typically part-time ventures, keep the following in mind when dealing with any small press:

1. Get on their mailing lists. Most small presses do not advertise extensively, nor do they get distribution in trade bookstores, because of the heavy discounts required. Instead, most rely on mailings to customers on their lists to generate interest and orders.

In the case of King limiteds, this is an important consideration because rumors run rampant when a new limited is announced; the only source of reliable information is the publisher himself, who, be assured, will take orders as soon as the details of publication are firmed up with the author.

2. Get on the mailing lists of new-book dealers. There are a handful of excellent book dealers that stock in-depth books published by small presses. (Because signed King limiteds are typically published in runs of 1,250 copies or less, and because the publisher wants to reserve the right to sell most of the copies himself, the book dealers are getting smaller allotments and reserve them for their steady customers, not the first-time customer who only wants to order a copy of a signed limited.)

3. Order early. When a King limited is announced, the feeding frenzy begins: the publisher is deluged with phone calls, letters, faxes, and overnight letters requesting ordering information. Subscribing up to six months in advance, the customers are positively frantic, concerned that they're going to miss out and have to pay out-of-print prices on the secondary market.

When you hear of a new King limited being published, write immediately to the publisher and enclose a self-addressed, stamped envelope and request ordering information.

4. Be patient. With the notable exception of one small press that, I'm thankful, has apparently gone out of business, the small presses in the field are reputable, honest, and take care to answer mail inquiries and phone calls.

Because the phone is always intrusive, it's best to write when inquiring about an order. Chances are that if a book isn't published when announced, it's still in the works. And if you are curious about your order, write and ask, and enclose a stamped postcard or an SASE (self-addressed, stamped envelope).

5. Specify a UPS shipping address if possible. The most reliable method of shipment is UPS. The post office is generally reliable for first-class mail, but I've had two limited-edition books severely damaged in shipping, despite excellent packing, because they could not survive the transit.

UPS requires a street address, so make sure that when you order, you specify UPS shipment (even if it costs extra), and give your full street address. (And type your address too; penmanship has become a lost art, and trying to decipher scribbles on an envelope simply delays your order.)

6. Inspect your book on delivery. Small presses can't inspect every copy they ship, since some books come from the printer individually shrink-wrapped. Make sure you open up the book, take off the dust jacket, look at the cover and the endpapers, and go through the pages. Printers do make mistakes, but the time for you to find out your copy is defective is when you get it, not when you're trying to resell it and the buyer complains that there's a big ink smudge on page 200.

7. Be nice. I know of no case in which a publisher has deliberately defrauded its customers—that would be enough to make you scream and press for redress. As for the publishers I've listed below, I know them personally and can vouch for them. They will answer your mail, and they will keep track of your order and ship as soon as the book is published. (One example: A week before my company received its shipment of *Insomnia* from Ziesing, a customer who had heard that other dealers already had the book in stock called me and asked, "Did Ziesing's printing press blow up?" I told him no, and asked him why he'd ask such a question. He replied that he hadn't received his book yet, so there must have been some sort of problem. Well, delays in the small-press field are commonplace; and although the books do run late, most publishers send postcards to inform you of the delay—they aren't, believe me, running off to Aruba with your cash, flanked by a pair of blonde bimbos, intent on spending your hard-earned money. After I explained to the customer that I was expecting my shipment any day, he calmed down and apologized for his abruptness. While I understand his concern, please understand that the small-press community is a small one, and most of us are one-person operations, trying to make a living and publish books on the side.)

8. Buy King, but buy other writers too. It distresses me when the publishers tell me that King fans buy nothing but King. Frankly, there are some terrific writers out there *not* named Stephen King.

Not every small press will be fortunate enough to be able to publish a King limited, but all of them care enough to publish lesser-known writers and artists whose work deserves publication in these handsome editions that aren't available from any other source.

Support the small presses by ordering something from their lists, since your continued support is what keeps them alive.

9. Ask for a catalog. Most publishers issue a general catalog or an updated list of books recently published, as well as backlist titles. Be sure to enclose an SASE, since small presses don't have big budgets for answering mail.

The following publishers are worth your support:

Borderlands Press (Thomas Monteleone, P.O. Box 146, Brooklandville, Md. 21022. 1-800-528-3310). The publisher of Harlan Ellison, Tom—an excellent writer in his own right—also publishes several other titles of interest to any fan.

CD Publications (P.O. Box 18433, Baltimore, Md. 21237). The book-publishing arm of *Cemetery Dance,* this small press has published anthologies like

Thrillers (original fiction) and *The Definitive Best of the Horror Show,* as well as books by Ed Gorman and Joe R. Lansdale. Editor/publisher Richard T. Chizmar knows how to pick 'em. In addition, he publishes a magazine that is easily the best in the field. Subscribe. His books are worth your attention too.

Charles F. Miller, Publisher (708 Westover Drive, Lancaster, Penn. 17601). Formerly half of Underwood-Miller, "Chuck" Miller is a veteran with eighteen years of experience and one of the leading small-press publishers in the field.

Best known in King circles for books about King—two books of interviews, and several books of criticism—Miller has an extensive list of art books and anthologies of interest to any horror fan.

Donald M. Grant, Publisher, Inc. (P.O. Box 187, Hampton Falls, N.H. 03884). Inspired by the late August Derleth's Arkham House, Donald M. Grant's small press was established in 1945. A first-class operation, Grant typically solicits advance orders *once a book has gone to press.* Grant does not, as a rule, take subscriptions to titles months in advance.

The long-awaited fourth *Dark Tower* novel is tentatively scheduled for publication in 1997 by Donald M. Grant, Publisher, Inc. At a public lecture on September 15, 1995, in Bangor, Maine, King said that he has not yet begun writing it but will do so in the winter. According to King, the matter of its book publication is *the* question his readers pose to his secretaries at the office. (Like everyone else, I am hopeful that King will sit down and finish the projected seven book series before moving on to other writing projects.)

Grant issues an annual catalog, which is updated with special announcements on interim titles.

Grant's most recent King book, still in print, is the "trade" edition of *The Dark Tower III: The Wastelands* ($38), issued in a print run of thirty thousand copies. Sumptuous, profusely illustrated with black-and-white decorations and full-color, double-, and single-page illustrations by Ned Dameron, this book is printed on a heavy cream-colored stock, with colored endpapers, sturdily bound with smythe-sewn binding, and a protective dust wrapper.

If you have any interest in fantasy, science fiction, horror, and the art of the fantastic, you must get on Grant's mailing list, because he's the premier publisher in the field, the standard by which all the others are measured.

GB Publishing (POB 3602, Williamsburg, Va. 23187). My small press has issued editions of my King books, as well as small-press books like *Demon-Driven: Stephen King and the Art of Writing* for the hard-core King fans on my mailing list. In addition, I publish an unofficial King newsletter ($10 for a one-year subscription: three issues).

Lord John Press (19073 Los Alimos Street, Northridge, Calif. 91326). Founded in 1977, Lord John Press publishes exquisite, jewel-like editions that, frankly, are works of art.

Wanting to publish a King book, publisher Herb Yellin contacted King, who suggested *Dolan's Cadillac,* which was originally serialized in *Castle Rock.* Yellin agreed and subsequently published two signed editions: one thousand copies at $100, and one hundred copies of a deluxe edition at $250. (Both editions are long out of print.)

Yellin also published what has to be a unique item in the King field: a broadside—a color poster—titled "Letters from Hell," which was originally published in the *New York Times* in 1987 as "Ever Et Raw Meat?" Printed in three colors (black, red, and purple) with hand-set type on a letter press, this twenty-by-twenty-five-inch print is limited to only five hundred copies, signed by King.

Still available at this late date, "Letters from Hell" is $125 plus $10 for priority-mail shipping via U.S. mail. (The print is mailed flat, and sufficiently packaged to survive even the post office.)

"Letters from Hell" is the only signed broadside by King and thus a unique collectible. And it looks splendid when framed.

Mark V. Ziesing Books (P.O. Box 76, Shingletown, Calif. 96088). The publisher of the limited edition of *Insomnia* (1,250 copies, $175, out of print) as well as its trade edition (3,250 copies, $75), Ziesing's list of authors makes any collector's mouth water. Recent titles include *Mefisto in Onyx* by Harlan Ellison (with jacket art and an introduction by Frank Miller), *Book of the Dead* (an anthology with the first appearance of a King short story), and books by hot new authors Lucius Shephard, Joe R. Lansdale, David J. Schow, and others.

In addition to publishing books, Ziesing carries books by other publishers. A catalog is $2. (The Ziesing catalog of its own titles is available for free.)

Underwood Books (P.O. Box 1607, Grass Valley, Calif. 95945). The other half of Underwood–Miller, Tim Underwood is one of the most savvy book publishers I've ever met. With distribution to the book trade through Publishers Group West, Underwood Books is the exception to the rule: its titles can be found in chain stores as well as independent bookstores.

Titles of interest to King fans include *A Look Back,* an oversize art book collecting the work of *the* macabre artist of our time, Bernie Wrightson, who has collaborated with King on *Cycle of the Werewolf, Creepshow,* and *The Stand* [II]; *Rein of Fear: Fiction and Film of Stephen King*; and the fabulous *Shadows in Eden* by Clive Barker, of whom King said: "I have seen the future of horror and it is Clive Barker."

19
Specialty Dealers

Collectors in the fantasy, science-fiction, and horror field do have the equivalent of one-stop book shopping—the specialty dealers that carry not only new titles but out-of-print titles as well.

All the dealers listed issue catalogs and will search for out-of-print books for you. (Of course, it pays to shop around; even King's books can vary substantially in price, since a dealer may have overstock on some items and want to move the inventory. Keep in mind, though, that you aren't likely to get a bargain—a mint condition of a prized King book for pocket change; these guys know what books are worth, and charge accordingly.)

Here are some general tips when dealing with mail-order bookstores:

1. Get on their mailing lists. Most of them issue regular catalogs, since the books they offer will not be found in trade bookstores. Most are mail-order, not storefront retail, operations and prefer to handle inquiries by mail. Once on the list, of course, patronize the bookstore. Postage and printing catalogs add up, and they can't afford to keep you on the mailing lists for months if you don't send in at least one order a year.

2. Send checks. Don't send cash. (In some cases, they accept credit cards, by mail, or over the phone. The details will be found in their catalogs.)

3. Provide a street address. Most will ship any way you prefer, with the appropriate surcharge for shipping. My recommendation is to request shipment by UPS, which is much more reliable than the post office.

4. Let them know your specific wants. These dealers are used to handling a lot of inventory and, if they don't have what you want in stock, they can generally locate almost any book, so long as you don't need it immediately.

5. Patronize the dealer on a regular basis. In talking with several of these dealers who sell to King fans, they often complain that the only time King fans order is when a new King book is coming out. As these dealers carry out-of-print books by King, as well as a wide selection of books by other authors, you

139

are well advised to broaden your reading horizons and sample something else—a new Clive Barker book, a Joe R. Lansdale, et al. King's good reading, but what does King himself read? Clive Barker, Peter Straub, David Morrell, and all the other authors in the field.

Barry R. Levin Science Fiction and Fantasy Literature (Barry R. Levin, 720 Santa Monica Boulevard, Los Angeles, Calif. 90401. 310-458-6111). Established in 1973, Barry R. Levin offers the *crème de la crème*—the rarest states. For most King fans, a signed, limited edition will be sufficient, but Levin's customers want more—the lettered state (sometimes not offered for sale), the proof state (rarely offered for sale), and the like.

For instance, when a King limited is published, a limitation notice indicates that there were a specified number of signed copies, and perhaps lettered copies. However, there will inevitably be other copies on hand, marked by the publisher as "presentation copy," or "publisher's copy," or "artist's edition." These are generally not offered for sale, and usually aren't cataloged.

Such rarities are Levin's bread and butter: the unusual, the strange, the bizarre, the eminently collectible. (For instance, let's postulate that a proof of *Carrie,* sent to King himself, surfaces on the collector's market. Levin is the dealer who will offer it, with provenance.)

Barry R. Levin is the source for the one-of-a-kind item that nobody else is likely to have. (Ask him, if you dare, about the unusual copies of Poppy Z. Brite's book that he sold. Go ahead, I *double*-dare you.)

Betts Bookstore (Stuart Tinker, 26 Main Street, Bangor, Me. 04401. 207-947-7052). I've always thought that a bookstore in Bangor should be—insofar as King books are concerned—King Book Central, but for years nobody came forth. Then, lo! the clouds parted and light beamed down, illuminating the hallowed ground at 26 Main Street in the downtown area.

King fans who have made the trip to this unholy mecca have not been disappointed. Just as you enter the bookstore, you know you've traveled into a time warp where all the needful things can be found: signed, limited editions; original art by King illustrator Kenny Ray Linkous; rare collectibles like a bound set of the *Maine Campus* newspaper with King's college column, "The Garbage Truck," and other goodies.

A friend of King's, Stuart has been able to offer special promotions like autographed copies of *Insomnia,* and news straight from the source, which is why you must get on his mailing list (tell him Leland Gaunt sent you).

Bud Plant, Inc. (P.O. Box 1689, Grass Valley, Calif. 95945). A mail-order dealer whose catalog offers a wealth of science fiction, fantasy, and mostly comic book material, Plant's love of limited-edition books, artwork, and collectibles makes his catalogs a smorgasbord of bibliographic delights. If ever there existed a Cave of Wonder for collectors, his warehouse would be it: books, art prints, magazines, sculpture, comics, calendars, trading cards—you name it, Bud's got it.

The Coven (Larry Coven, 2036 N. Beachwood Drive, Apt. #15, Los Angeles, Calif. 90068). Larry specializes in limited editions and carries not only U.S. but U.K. editions as well. Larry is very knowledgeable and can hunt down specific books you need, especially out of print fantasy and horror.

Jim Orbaugh, Bookseller (1500 Shadowridge Drive, #125, Vista, Calif. 92083. 619-598-2734). Jim specializes in horror and weird fantasy, mostly first editions, and many signed. King, Koontz, McCammon, Barker, Garton, Lansdale—these authors plus many more are Jim's stock in trade. (Send $1 for a three-issue subscription.)

John W. Knott Jr., Bookseller (8453 Early Bud Way, Laurel, Md. 20723. 301-317-8427). A specialist in first-edition science fiction, fantasy, and horror, John can find virtually anything you want. He publishes a catalog on a regular basis and, like others, will hunt down the rare book you want.

L. W. Curry (Elizabethtown, N.Y. 12932). A dealer in out-of-print SF (not "sci-fi"), horror and fantasy material, Curry is an expert in the field. His catalogs, published on a regular basis, are chockful of info and are useful references in their own right.

Overlook Connection (David Hinchberger, P.O. Box 56, Woodstock, Ga. 30188. 404-926-1762). A favorite watering hole for fans, David's catalog—yo, Dave!—is also a good source of information on what's going on in the horror field. A fan in the best and truest sense of the word, Dave's a happening guy who's way cool!

In his informal, chatty newsletter/catalog, Dave typically offers news on horror writers, excerpts from books to be published, and occasionally coordinates with authors who provide signed bookplates.

Dave publishes supplementary catalogs every four to six weeks, with a big annual catalog. He will send you three free issues, but if you don't order, you're dropped. Fair enough, for if you can't find anything of interest in three issues, you're really not a horror, science-fiction, or fantasy fan, and should go to Waldenbooks for all your purchasing. But if his stuff is your witch's brew, you'll drink deep and hearty here.

Robert and Phyllis Weinberg (15145 Oxford Drive, Oak Forest, Ill. 60452. 312-475-5765). The Weinbergs' monthly book catalog is noteworthy because they don't list anything for sale *unless they've got stock on hand.* Some small presses announce but don't publish on time, but the Weinbergs' policy keeps everyone happy—when you order, you'll not wait for months. Organized by category, their catalog offers horror, calendars, fantasy, mystery, science fiction, and odds and ends.

Time Tunnel (Craig Goden, 313 Beechwood Avenue., Middlesex, N.J. 08846. 908-560-0738). Craig publishes a monthly newsletter that is devoted exclusively to horror fiction. Dealing with new as well as used material, Craig has also issued on occasion a special King catalog.

20
Betts Bookstore
Bangor's Main(e) Place for King Fans
An interview with proprietor Stuart Tinker

In a small town, the opening of a new store is big news.

from *Needful Things*

When in Bangor, a visit to Betts Bookstore is not optional for King fans. It's a must. *The* place to buy King collectibles, Betts Bookstore has become a major presence in the King world. In addition to a brisk walk-in business with locals and tourists, the bookstore mails out its catalog/newsletter to nearly four thousand customers worldwide, who depend on proprietors Stuart and Penny Tinker for their needful King things. (Contact them at Betts Bookstore, 26 Main Street, Bangor, Me. 04401. 207-947-7052.)

One of the best things that has come out of my writing about King is meeting other King fans and sharing our enthusiasms. And among those fans is bookseller Stuart Tinker, whom I am happy to commend to your attention.

In the interview that follows, sandwiched in between a busy schedule that had Stuart making his acting debut in *The Langoliers,* which was being filmed in Bangor, Stuart Tinker takes us behind the scenes and tells us his story.

Q. When did Betts Bookstore open for business?

STUART TINKER: Betts Bookstore opened in 1938. The original owner was Dorothia Betts and she operated out of her home for a couple of years before opening the store in downtown Bangor. She hosted Stephen King book signings with almost each new book, and the store was mentioned in "Letters from Hell" because of that.

We bought Betts in 1991 and moved it to the present location.

Q. What is your relationship with Stephen King?

STUART TINKER: Both Penney and I have always been big readers of most any kind of book. We both have read and enjoyed Stephen's and Tabitha's work from the beginning.

It was nice that they were locals, but the decision to purchase the bookstore was not influenced by the Kings in any way.

After we made the decision to own Betts, we took a hard look at the other eight bookstores in our area to see what they were stocking. The one thing we noticed was that none of them featured King books other than the current title. We then decided to stock all of Stephen's and Tabitha's titles in both hardback and paperback.

The collectible end of bookselling took on a life of its own. Since we were starting out with no experience and no money, we really struggled, and Steve knew it. He agreed to do a book signing—his first locally in six years. Afterward, he came into the store on a regular basis and did what he could to help us get the store up and running.

We probably have been his biggest nuisance in the local area, but he has remained gracious and helpful through it all, even when I called him at home early on a Sunday morning and woke him up!

Stephen King is a one-man industry who has many people counting on him to make their living. The pressure he must be under is something I can only imagine. We try to contribute as little as possible to that pressure, but probably have not done as good a job as we should. We try to protect the Kings' privacy and abide by their wishes. For instance, we had planned to manufacture T-shirts and other salable items, but Steve indicated he was not comfortable with those ideas, so we dropped them.

Our relationship with the Kings is dictated by simple respect, common courtesy, and friendship.

Q. Do you plan on publishing a newsletter on King?

STUART TINKER: We really do not publish a newsletter at this time, but we do publish a sales flyer and catalog with some King news in it a couple times a year. Sometimes we publish quarterly, but it depends on what we have for sale and what's newsworthy.

We will never print the terms of one of Steve's contracts, if we know it, because we feel that it is not anyone's business except Steve and Tabitha's as to how much money they make.

I would not want my personal life held up for everyone and I am quite sure they don't either.

Most everything we print in our flyer is okayed by Steve's office. There have been times when we learned things that they didn't want released at that particular time, and we honored that, which is why you might read some things in other places but never about it from us. [Ed. note: In the past, other publications have reported unconfirmed King news, prompting some fans to complain that they hadn't heard it first in one of Stuart's newsletters. In most cases, the news was prematurely reported, or inaccurate, but when there was hard, confirmed news to report, Stuart dispensed it in due time.]

Q. What is the most frequently requested King collectible?

STUART TINKER: An autographed book.

Q. You've seen virtually every limited edition. What, as to aesthetics and desirability, do you feel are King standouts?

STUART TINKER: Aesthetically, the limited editions of *Insomnia, Firestarter, The Stand* [II], and *Christine*. From a desirability standpoint: the first editions of the Doubleday books are always in demand, as are anything signed, the *Dark Tower* series in hardcover, and, of course, any limited edition.

Q. If someone wants to find a real King bargain, where would you suggest he look?

STUART TINKER: Your local used bookstore is the first place to look. Yard sales, estate sales, and small auctions are all worth your attention.

We have a local customer who bought a first edition of *The Gunslinger* for $1.00 at a yard sale here in Bangor; the dust jacket was gone, but we had brand-new, never-folded jackets, so now she has a valuable book.

Q. What scarce collectibles have you handled?

STUART TINKER: We have sold a number of copies of *The Plant;* because only two hundred were printed, it is quite rare. We also had the original manuscript to *The Napkins,* published as *The Eyes of the Dragon.* We have had props from some of the movies, including the director's chair and all the actors' chairs from *The Langoliers,* as well as most of the small props used in that movie.

Q. The most recent King limited edition is Ziesing's Insomnia. *What do you think of this latest offering?*

STUART TINKER: The Mark Ziesing edition of *Insomnia* is a fantastic book. At 591 pages and a 9.5-by-8-inch trim size, it is a fairly good-sized book. Limited to 1,250 signed and numbered copies, each comes in a maroon leather tray-case with gold lettering—simply great. This edition is signed by Stephen King, artist Phil Hale, and book designer Arnie Fenner. It has a sewn-in bookmarker and is constructed as a book should be.

I think everyone involved in making this book should be very proud of it. We had forty-two copies that were presold at the publisher's price of $175. We purchased several later on the secondary market that retailed for $275 to $300. I think the value of this book will be about $400 by early 1995.

The "gift" edition was limited to 3,750 copies, unsigned. Bound in blue with silver lettering on the slipcase, it is an absolute bargain at $75.

Q. What is the circulation of your catalog?

STUART TINKER: It goes to about four thousand King fans worldwide. We may cut that down a bit, since postage and printing costs are so high, but for now, that's where things stand.

Q. What are your favorite King books?

STUART TINKER: My favorites include *The Stand, Talisman, It,* and *Dolores Claiborne*—in that order. Penny's favorites include *Talisman, Dolores Claiborne, The Tommyknockers,* and *The Stand*—in that order.

Q. Obviously, everyone collects Stephen King, but what kind of market is there for Tabitha King's books?

STUART TINKER: We have many people that collect her books, but we have many other customers who don't realize that she writes or don't know that she's as good as she is.

I think it's a crime that she is so underrated as an author. Her *Nodd's Ridge* series—*Caretakers, Pearl, One on One,* and *Book of Ruben*—are wonderful books: the stories are very well written.

It is unfortunate she is so overshadowed by Steve.

When she hits the best-seller lists, her early books are going to be extremely hard to find in the first editions, and will become quite valuable.

Q. Do the audiotape versions of King's books sell?

STUART TINKER: We have done quite well with them, especially the ones he's read.

We sell but also rent books on tape, and the King books on tape are always coming and going.

Q. There's been a large number of books about King. How do they sell in your store?

STUART TINKER: Books on Steve do okay. By far the best-selling book on Steve is *The Stephen King Companion,* which is the choice of most, even though it's somewhat outdated. *The Stephen King Story* would sell much better with a different cover—people want a visual image.

The revised *Companion* should do very well, if you have a good photo on the cover similar to the current one, and it has some sort of banner proclaiming NEW AND IMPROVED in bold letters.

Stephen King: Master of Horror by Anne Saidman is a great little book about Steve and also sells very well: lots of pictures, inexpensive, with very accurate information.

The other books on King? They sell just so-so.

21
"The Mist"

There was a time when radio ruled, back in the days before television debuted. Before TV, radio dramatizations like Arch Obler's "Lights Out" and "The Shadow" and dozens of others caught the imagination in a way that movies could not. The stories played out in skull cinema—your mind—and you imagined the most horrific images, far more horrific than anything the special-effects wizards in Hollywood could produce.

If you're too young to have experienced those radio shows, you owe it to yourself to see what all the excitement was about.

"The Mist" is a good place to start. Though there may be a movie version from Frank Darabont, the audio version is the ideal format because it plays in skull cinema.

A short novel by King originally commissioned and published in Kirby McCauley's anthology *Dark Forces*, "The Mist" is King at his best. It is a gripping, first-person tale of what happens in a small Maine community when a strange mist rolls in, bringing with it monsters that lurk from within. "The Mist" is ideal for dramatization.

Fortunately, ZBS Foundation did the dramatization, recording in real time on chrome tape. Directed by Bill Raymond, story adaptation by M. Fulton, assistance by Dennis Etchison, an eerie musical score by Tim Clark, "The Mist" comes alive in 3-D sound because of the state-of-the-art recording process used, the Kunstkopf binaural sound.

Best listened to—hell, *experienced*—through headphones, "The Mist" transports you into another world. (At one point, when a door slams, I jumped ten feet, thinking someone had entered my house. But it was only the recording . . . I think.)

No longer available through ZBS, the preferred edition is the digitally remastered compact disc available for $15.

KING ON THE FIDELITY OF HIS WORK

FRANK MULLER: Don't all these different versions of "The Mist" begin to distort the original work?

STEPHEN KING: No. Not a recording, not a computer game, not a movie. In fact, a bad recording would probably hurt me more than anything else, because the recording seems a lot closer to the mind of the writer.

There was a graduate student who came to interview James Cain, who wrote *The Postman Always Rings Twice* and *Double Indemnity* and *Mildred Pierce*; and when the student moaned to Cain about what the movies had done to his books, Cain immediately turned around to the shelf behind him in his study and said, "Didn't do a thing. They're all right up there, so far as I can see."

Illustration for the original ZBS cassette recording of "The Mist" with art by Kevin Brockway.

22

Stephen King Makes a Stand for Independent Booksellers

by Donna Kimura

"James Michener on a Harley. That would be cool."

Stephen King, when asked if other authors might follow his cue and tour the country by motorcycle

✱

When the word went out in early 1995 that King would be promoting Insomnia *with book signings across the country, King fans couldn't believe their good fortune, nor could the independent booksellers. Concerned about the survival of independent bookstores that in recent years have had a tough time holding their own against the chain bookstores with heavy discounting, book superstores, and warehousers like Sam's Club and Price Club, Stephen King made his stand and elected to sign* Insomnia *at independent bookstores only.*

Starting out at the Northshire Bookstore in Manchester Center, Vermont, King worked his way across America: Ithaca, New York; Worthington, Ohio; Lexington, Kentucky; Nashville, Tennessee; St. Louis, Missouri; Manhattan, Kansas; Colorado Springs, Colorado; Sun Valley, Idaho, and finally, Santa Cruz, California.

The following piece, reprinted from the Santa Cruz Sentinel, *was published in its October 25, 1994, edition.*

✱

One of the most popular storytellers of any generation roared into town aboard a Harley-Davidson motorcycle Monday.

With a grin that was more friendly than frightening, the prince of terror found his last stop on a ten-city book tour.

He could have stayed home, watching his latest offering, the 787-page *Insomnia*, rise to the No. 1 best-seller.

Instead, Stephen King hit the road for the first time in a decade for a journey that stretched from his front door in Bangor, Maine, all the way to Santa Cruz—a town once called "Murder Capital of the World."

It was 4,690 miles total, said the man who has terrified millions with a rabid Saint Bernard named Cujo, a lethal automobile called Christine, and a No. 1 fan by the gentle name of Annie Wilkes.

In addition to promoting *Insomnia,* King is rallying to small family-run bookstores, such as Bookshop Santa Cruz, which played host to his local appearance.

"It's more difficult for independent book stores to sell my books," he said, explaining that they have to compete with big "price chopper" stores like Costco. ". . . Independent book stores are a dying breed."

Hard to imagine, but King said his career began with the country's small book dealers.

His first novel, *Carrie,* started with just 2,500 copies in those book stores twenty years ago, he said.

Now he is one of the few writers who can turn a literary event into a rock 'n' roll show. For loyal readers from out of town, tickets to his appearance at the Santa Cruz Civic Auditorium were sold through BASS/Ticketmaster, and the words "Sold Out" were placed prominently on posters advertising his only West Coast appearance.

Adding to the flavor of the whole event, a man drove through town in a van with photos claiming that King was involved in John Lennon's death.

"That's Steven Lightfoot," King said, apparently familiar with the outside agitator.

Santa Cruz police took Lightfoot into custody Monday afternoon on suspicion of trespassing at Bookshop Santa Cruz, where King made a brief stop.

Would King's high-powered road trip make it fashionable for other writers to hit the country's highways?

"James Michener on a Harley," he mused at the store. "That would be cool."

Five hours later, King stepped onto the stage at the Civic to a standing ovation usually reserved for rock impresarios and foreign dignitaries.

"I wish you all a happy Halloween," he began. "I [expletive] hate it."

Thousands of kids, he said, will show up at his door for candy.

The master of the macabre said he is plotting a grid to send bolts of electricity through this year's trick-or-treaters.

Instead of standing behind the podium, King casually paced the stage holding a microphone.

Each time he mentioned one of his books, fans who paid $6 to see him would applaud. King's appearance raised $10,000 for Friends of the Santa Cruz Library—the single largest benefit for the group.

"Maybe I won't talk," he said. "I'll just say book titles. *Christine.*"

He told audience members they were free to leave at any time.

"Just go," he taunted. "But if something happens to you tonight . . ."

King then turned into the storyteller who stopped in the village to tell his latest tales. As the auditorium lights dimmed, he read from *Insomnia,* a story about victims of sleeplessness in Derry, Maine, the setting for another King novel, *It.*

While he has made it his lifework to scare the masses, King also showed that he could see the other side.

Earlier in the day, he said he has learned on his tour that "common good is more common than the press gives it credit."

In Laramie, Wyoming, people gave him instant-heat packs that would warm his hands and feet as he traveled in cold weather.

King said he had visions of riding his motorcycle with his boots on fire.

While traveling on Interstate 80, he stayed at a Ramada Inn. The motel didn't have space to keep his motorcycle out of the rain, but a woman who worked there let him park it in her garage.

Through it all, he remains Stephen King.

"I just want to remind you to check your backseat," he said before leaving town.

Writing

23
Stephen King Helps Spearhead Censorship Referendum Defeat
by Christopher Spruce

It's a scary idea, especially in a society which has been built on the ideas
of free choice and free thought. . . . No book, record, or film should be
banned without a full airing of the issues.

Stephen King, in an op-ed piece for the *Bangor Daily News*

✳

*To every creative person, the subject of censorship hits close to home. In my case, I
wrote about it at length, providing both sides of the issue in* War of Words: The Censorship Debate, *which was published as a trade paperback by Andrews and
McMeel. The book was a critical but not a financial success, nor did anyone, including
my publisher, think it would be. Still, we both thought the book needed to be written, if only to provide a needed resource so that students would know where to look
for more information.*

*Stephen King is no stranger to censorship. Frequently the target of censors who
would bowdlerize every sexual reference, every profanity, and anything else that
smacks of obscenity in their eyes, King has seen his books pulled off the shelves of
school libraries all over the country.*

*In a 1977 interview, published in King's hometown newspaper, King commented
on the Lisbon High School English department's banning by secret vote of Alexander Solzhenitsyn's novel,* One Day in the Life of Ivan Denisovitch. *A powerful anti-
Stalin novel that was instrumental in bringing Solzhenitsyn to the attention of the
world press, as well as the cornerstone of his receiving the Nobel Prize for Literature,* One Day *is a simply told tale of Ivan Denisovitch from the first wake-up call
to lights out—it's Solzhenitsyn at his best. Of the banning, King wrote: "It's repul-
sive to the whole idea of education. I can't believe the dishonor the English depart-*

ment is calling down on the school. And I expect Solzhenitsyn must be confused and upset about having his book banned in the United States of America."

Solzhenitsyn, who in 1994 returned to his homeland after years of exile, after years of seeing his books banned in his own country, would probably have shaken his head. As he has pointed out before, the enemy of government is a free press that will not be muzzled. How curious that in the good ol' U.S. of A. his voice was silenced by the very department that should stand up to celebrate a free press!

In 1986 the censorship infestation grew beyond the isolated bannings of books in schools. While directing Maximum Overdrive *in Wilmington, North Carolina, the home fires back in Maine were burning, as Rev. Jasper Wyman, chairman of the Civic League, decided to lead his Christian soldiers onward and put the issue of obscenity to a statewide vote in a referendum that would ban it. The problem is, who can define the word? Like beauty, obscenity is in the eye of the beholder.*

In the following piece, published in Castle Rock *(July 1986), Christopher Spruce—journalist and editor/publisher of* Castle Rock—*tells the story of how King made his stand in Maine against Rev. Wyman and his followers.*

✳

Claiming the rights of a million Maine residents were being threatened, Stephen King took to the airwaves and newspapers of his home state during May and June to help turn back a referendum on censorship.

The referendum was rejected by Maine voters by a whopping 72 to 28 percent margin in a primary election held June 10.

"I'm against it [the referendum initiative]," King told a radio audience June 6, "because I don't know what it will do."

The referendum was put forth by the Maine Christian League which sought to ban the promotion and sale of pornographic material in Maine. Rev. Jasper (Jack) Wyman, chairman of the Civic League, said the referendum was necessary to establish a law which would protect children from exposure to pornography and to reduce the incidents of child abuse and rape. Wyman, who debated King on a radio talk show prior to the referendum vote on June 10, asserted that scientists had found a direct link between the use of pornography and the commission of sex crimes, particularly those against children.

The central issue in the debate was whether the government should have the right to determine what materials adults should be allowed to read or view. Wyman argued that obscenity was not a protected form of free speech under the Supreme Court's interpretation of the First Amendment, and the Court had defined obscenity in its many rulings over the years. Opponents of the initia-

READ THIS BOOK

an editorial by the *Bangor Daily News*
(March 20, 1992)

In a column on today's op-ed page, author Stephen King has some simple but sound advice for students upset because two of his books have been banned: Hit the public library, read the books, and find out what makes them so horrible that they must be yanked from the school library.

Mr. King has plenty of experience with banned books. At various times around the country his novels *Carrie*, *'Salem's Lot*, *Firestarter*, *Cujo*, and *The Shining* have been banned, and proposed bans have been laid on *The Stand*, *Christine*, and his short story "Children of the Corn" from the collection *Night Shift*. A junior high school in Jacksonville, Florida, now adds *The Dead Zone* and *The Tommyknockers* to the list of those banned.

Banning books creates a dangerous precedent. The intellectual freedom generally assumed to exist in this country will continue only as long as citizens protect the right of authors to place their ideas before the public. That doesn't mean that a pornographic magazine belongs in an elementary school library, but it does mean that novels widely accepted by the public should not be banned.

It's a testimony to the power of the written word that books that describe violent or sexual scenes or contain swear words are kept from teenagers, while television and the movies virtually are left alone. Television, even on the three major networks, guarantees a nightly prime time menu of murder, rape, disfigurements, shootings, stabbings, maulings, and beatings. That's entertainment. Cable TV stations, to which almost all teens have access one way or another, regularly show movie versions of some of the very books by Mr. King that have been banned. No protests here.

Books such as *The Adventures of Huckleberry Finn* and *The Catcher in the Rye* are willfully misinterpreted and banned every few years in some misguided hope that children will be shielded from the realities of the world. The world creeps in anyway, leaving the bans no purpose other than to restrain free speech.

tive, including King, argued that "obscenity" does not have a universally accepted definition when applied to various print and film materials; that something pornographic to Wyman might not be pornographic to thousands of other citizens. Further, opponents said similar laws had been used in other states to remove books from school and public library bookshelves which were considered works of literature by most, but found to be obscene by a few.

King, who had had his books banned from some school libraries, said he didn't know what the law might result in. "Jack," he told Wyman during the radio debate, "you can sit there and say you know what it [the law] will do, but you don't. No one does. And that's why I'm against it. I'm against what I don't know about."

While decrying a television ad run by those against the referendum—the spot depicted a man in a black leather jacket setting fire to several paperbacks, including *Grapes of Wrath* and *Valley of the Horses,* and suggesting that could happen under Wyman's so-called antiporn law—Stephen, nevertheless, allowed that such an exaggeration might someday be possible should the referendum be enacted into law. "I hate that ad," King told Wyman. "I mean, the guy in it looks like a Nazi. But, you know, once you start down that road [to censorship], it might not be that far off. . . ."

Wyman, himself, wasn't above using scare tactics in the campaign. The referendum proponents ran commercials citing alleged evidence connecting child sexual abuse and exposure to pornography by criminals. The slogan used by the Civic League was the highly inflammatory line: "Do it for the children."

Wyman, a former state representative and a veteran of a few nasty political skirmishes, insisted that the referendum's passage would not result in the banning of any works with literary value. He said claims by referendum opponents that a similar law in North Carolina had resulted in the banning of books such as *Little Red Riding Hood, Huckleberry Finn,* and the "R" volume of the *Encyclopedia Britannica* [it had a section on reproduction] were totally false.

King, who spent the summer of 1985 in North Carolina, where he directed the making of *Maximum Overdrive,* said he saw firsthand the chilling effect the North Carolina obscenity statute had on bookstores and magazine dealers:

> When their antiporn statute became the law of the land last July . . . between Tuesday evening and Wednesday morning, all the *Playboys* and *Penthouses* disappeared from the news racks in the little convenience store where I stopped for my morning paper and evening six-pack. They went so fast it was as if the Porn Fairy had visited in the middle of the night.

In another Wilmington store, the "X"-rated section of tape rentals disappeared overnight. In some cases, "R"-rated tapes such as Brian De Palma's *Body*

Double were removed from the shelves. "'I'm not taking any chances,'" King quotes one storeowner. "'They'd love to shut us down.'"

"Pass a law like this and where does it stop?" King asked in a column printed in the *Maine Sunday Telegram* (June 1 edition). He elaborated:

> I think the idea of making it a crime to sell obscene material is a bad one because it takes the responsibility of saying "no" out of the hands of citizens and puts it into those of the police and the courts. I think it's a bad idea because it's undemocratic, high-handed, and frighteningly diffuse.

As a side note, it was only a couple of months ago that a school board in a town near Vancouver, Washington, voted to remove King's *The Shining* from the shelves of its junior high library. The board, accepting arguments from supporters of the ban, agreed that there was too much vulgar language in the book. One woman even claimed she took time to count the incidents of vulgarity— her total, 156.

The banning of the book caused a great stir in the community and prompted editorials and letters to the editor at a number of newspapers in the area. The comments of those opposed to the ban were not a whole lot different in tenor than those made by King during the recent censorship debate in Maine.

King freely admits that censorship scares him because it threatens his livelihood, his "reason for living," as he put it to Jack Wyman. But King also fervently believes in the First Amendment guarantees made by our Constitution and in the idea that people living in a free country ought to be free.

24

Clive Barker: An Interview

conducted by George Beahm and Howard Wornom

Clive Barker is the most important new writer of horror since Peter Straub.
The first true voice of the next generation of horror writers.

Ramsey Campbell

*Clive Barker, an artist, writer, playwright, and filmmaker, looks normal, but you re-
ally can't judge a book by its cover. Born in 1952, he bears an uncanny resemblance
to Paul McCartney, who, depending on your age, either led a band called Wings or
was in a band called The Beatles.*

*Appearances are deceiving. What, asks Barker, is the connection between our
bodies and books? "Every body is a book of blood; wherever we're opened, we're red."
Right.*

*If you were to summarize Barker with one comment, it would be from a line from
a* Nightbreed *movie poster: "There are no limits." Refusing to censor himself for any
reason, Barker takes a long, hard look at taboo subjects and, without flinching, records
what he sees through his private, hellish window.*

*To most horror fans, Barker came to their attention after Stephen King anointed
him the next dark prince of horror. "I have seen the future of horror and it is Clive
Barker," King said. That was enough of a recommendation by the king of blurb-
meisters to check out the Paul McCartney look-alike who had published collections
of short stories back home,* Books of Blood.

*Barker's stories are awful—and I mean that as a compliment. The stories broke
new ground in the horror field, bringing a literate sensibility with a no-holds-barred
attitude that catapulted Barker to the forefront of horror writers, leap-frogging over
older statesmen who have labored long and hard in the horror graveyard, none of
whom had his unmistakable and inimitable talent.*

Naturally, interviewing Barker was a priority for the original version of The
Stephen King Companion, *but his schedule was such that when we finally conducted
the interview—by phone, long distance, from Virginia to London—*The Stephen
King Companion's *contents had been finalized, and the following interview could
not be squeezed in, making an already big book even bigger.*

Photo by Greg Preston, courtesy of Michael Autrey

Clive Barker

Rather than see it go unpublished, I self-published it in 1989 in a small, digest-sized book called Grimoire, *available only in a limited edition, given away as a bonus to customers of my small press.*

Concerned about being misquoted, Barker asked that the transcribed interview be sent to him for review and correction. I agreed, putting the transcript out of my mind after sending it, thinking that it'd be weeks, maybe months, before I'd see it again, but I was wrong. Barker speedily went through the transcript and made numerous corrections—tightening the prose, restoring his voice, smoothing over awkward transitions—and sent it back by Federal Express within the week.

I was, in a word, flabbergasted.

I'm sure Barker's book publishers are pleased to publish him, because he probably is the direct antithesis of the cranky author, who is hell-bent on sowing seeds of self-destruction. In this interview, Barker was a joy to work with, and it's my plea-sure to bring the interview to a larger audience.

Barker, currently directing four films, has moved permanently from London to Los Angeles so that he can concentrate on his film career. (In his spare time, he writes long fantasy novels that have won him a mainstream audience that, frankly, would never read a horror novel if so labeled.)

Conducted in 1989 by myself and Howard "Rusty" Wornom, the interview was transcribed by me, and edited by Barker. Naturally, the subject turned to thoughts of King, who named him as the new dark prince, a writer who certainly belongs—as Benjamin DeCasseres said of Clark Ashton Smith—in the Brotherhood of the Un-earthly Imagination.

✳

Q. The American publishers have taken King's endorsements of you and put them on the covers of your paperback books. What effect did his endorsements have on your career in this country?

CLIVE BARKER: In the beginning, I think it was the thing that made people pick up the books. The books appeared on the shelves along with however many other new titles appeared that month, and to have Steve's comment made a dif-ference in drawing potential readers to them in the first place. Choices have to be made and given the fact that when my books first appeared in the U.S., I was an unknown quantity, it really did make a difference to have Steve's name on the covers.

Q. At that time, Books of Blood *was not available in the U.S. How did he get a copy?*

CLIVE BARKER: I don't know. All I know is that Steve Jones [Barker's biographer] came back from where Steve had been praising some of the stories at, I presume, the World Fantasy Convention in 1984. At that stage, I hadn't been published in America, so inevitably it came as a pleasant surprise.

Q. On what occasion did you finally get to meet King?

CLIVE BARKER: I met Steve in New York for a joint appearance on either "Good Morning, America" or "The Today Show." We had met for dinner be-forehand so we could get our shtick together.

Q. Considering his reputation, did you feel nervous around him since you were the new kid on the block, or did you feel comfortable from the onset?

CLIVE BARKER: I don't feel nervous with people whose reputations are that of being benign individuals, and Steve's reputation is exactly that. I never really feel nervous around talented folks—it's a pleasure to be with them. The only time you feel nervous is if you are dealing with people who have got major ego problems or have reputations for giving people a hard time.

Q. Are there a few of those in the horror field?

CLIVE BARKER: There are, but I won't name names.

Q. As to the U.S. marketplace, where do you think the horror market would be if King were not writing in the field?

CLIVE BARKER: It's impossible to judge, isn't it? That's a purely notional question. One could deal with it hypothetically and say, *Clearly, he's opened the market to a huge number of potential readers.* One would also have to say that his definition of horror is so broad and so populist that whether he's actually opened a market for the very hard-core horror writer is a moot point. I think his great genius is to make horror acceptable, to make it acceptable to read on the train without covering it behind the cover of the new John Updike novel.

Q. And what do you think you bring to horror?

CLIVE BARKER: We should address what may be a larger question here: What do we mean by the word in the first place? It's so open to interpretation, it arguably covers such a large area of literary endeavor in stage work and movie work. I begin to think that the closer you try to analyze it—like the Quest Beast—the more likely it is to flee you. Steve's contribution, I don't think, is as much to horror fiction as to what I would call *fantastique,* fantasy fiction, the fiction of the imagination. Clearly, there are massive overlaps in his fiction between science fiction and horror, between fantasy fiction and horror, and indeed mainstream fiction and horror. It almost becomes redundant to say, *What does Steve offer to the horror genre?* What we should be asking is, *What does he offer to writing, to the business of prose?*

Q. I think we can all agree that King has been pigeonholed as a horror writer for the convenience of his publishers, to help the sales and marketing effort.

CLIVE BARKER: Yes, but I think to some extent in his interviews and in his public pronouncements of various kinds he has played along with that. I don't think he would deny that. When I see him interviewed, he does enjoy . . . there's something quite gleeful about the pleasure he takes in the scare. He will tend not to emphasize the fantasy elements in his work, tend *not* to emphasize the science-fiction elements in his work.

My passion is to break the mold and to be constantly asking people to assess whether this thing called horror fiction is a meaningful genre in the first place; and if it is, whether it isn't so wide that trying to make generalizations of what it is or what it can do becomes redundant.

I think it's very important to keep stressing that these forms of fiction have their roots in fairy tales, folklore, campfire tales, urban tales, and many other forms which would not be characterized as horror fiction.

Q. Which should *be, though . . . some of the horror tales.*

CLIVE BARKER: Well, you could look at it either way. It's a two-way street. But I think one should quickly establish that there's an awful lot of horror fiction that is found in *Grimm's Fairy Tales,* and that's important.

Q. You come from a grand guignol *type of background, don't you?*

CLIVE BARKER: *Grand guignol* is a very specific theatrical tradition. It's a tradition that flourished for twenty years—at most—in one theater in Paris; and when the theater burned down, that was pretty much the end of that. What it's come to stand for is a very hard-core approach to horror—a very vicious, graphic, visceral approach to horror. Certainly there is that stuff in my work, but there certainly is a lot of my work which *isn't* that. It's a term which has to be used carefully, or it becomes another cage to lock a kind of work in, and I think that's dangerous. I'm not being bloody-minded or pedantic; I just think it's important that we who are interested in the genre be more careful than the critics and the academics who all too often are careless with these terms.

Q. What do you see as the future of horror? What direction will horror fiction take?

CLIVE BARKER: I think if you look across the spectrum of material which is being published, you will look in vain for a single type of fiction, a single direction that horror fiction is taking. There's a lot of very subtle, oblique work out there, and there's a lot of very hard-core work out there. Then there are people like myself and Steve who are trying to do a bit of both.

Q. Certainly there are many different voices, but do you see any trends?

CLIVE BARKER: No, in all honesty, I don't. All I see is good work and bad work. The starting places for this kind of fiction remain the same: death, obsession, madness, violent death, sexual dependency—the subjects which preoccupied Victorian writers and writers in the thirties and the forties. The issue isn't whether the future of horror will be about different things, because I don't think it will be, any more than tragedy will be about different things, or comedy will be about different things in thirty years. What is interesting is to see a larger cross-section of approaches at work, because I think that's one of the few ways that we can convince the detractors that this genre is worth the study and acknowledgment which I believe it deserves.

Q. Do you think that will ever happen?

CLIVE BARKER: Yes, I do. I have more faith than some in the fact that critics will notice . . . I mean, critics *do* notice in America. I get large pieces in the *Washington Post,* and so does Steve. There's been a lot of good criticism written about Steve's work; there's been some very good stuff written about mine. I don't feel as if I'm a prophet unheard in my own city.

Q. Who do you think are the important writers in the field today?

CLIVE BARKER: The problem with naming names—I've got to be bloody-minded here—is that either you miss someone and he is offended, or you start to make judgments about an entire body of work when in actual fact you may like a particular book by somebody and not the rest of the work. What we should celebrate is the range of work that is going on. I read widely in every genre. At the moment, in the stack of books beside my bed, there is nothing that was written this century.

Q. When we interviewed Douglas E. Winter at his home in upstate Virginia, he commented that at a public gathering with you, you two were discussing your perceptions of the many people who read Stephen King and your work but who apparently read little else. They have no frame of reference outside your and King's body of work. Theirs is a very self-limiting experience.

CLIVE BARKER: I think that's true, and I regret that. I regret the fact that there is a reluctance to reading widely through the *fantastique;* to looking at books and paintings and films and theater work that may touch on these subjects but not be typical horror fiction. I'm presently doing a piece for the *Daily Telegraph* [a London newspaper] talking about my favorite horror pieces. They get somebody in from each genre to write about what he finds influential and important. I'm using Grimm, I'm using Marlowe's *Dr. Faustus,* I'll probably use a John Webster play like *The White Devil.* It's important to celebrate the fact that these subjects are approached and analyzed and explored in many forms, and have been for hundreds of years.

It distresses me when people ask me what my influences are at a convention, and I say Goya—

Q. —And they say: Who?

CLIVE BARKER: That's distressing because Goya is clearly an artist of the *fantastique,* whose imagination has survived the test of time.

Q. What you find with many recent converts to horror is that they have tunnel vision. They have no frame of reference with the arts in general—for instance, the visual arts—and no sense of history. They may have heard of H. P. Lovecraft, but they've never read anything by him, much less works by lesser known horror writers.

CLIVE BARKER: It's a situation which, whenever I do an interview, I try to do something about. Rather than simply saying, *I love Steve's work and Peter Straub's work and Ramsey Campbell's work,* I mention Hoffman, maybe Machen; Fuseli, Goya, and so on.

Q. And filmmakers, too.

CLIVE BARKER: I generally find that fans are much more savvy about the movies than they are about paintings. They will know about Cronenberg and modern filmmakers. They may not know about Buñuel, Franju, Cocteau, but having mentioned those names in some circumstances, I've had people come back to me, a year later, who've said, "I saw *Les Yeux Sans Visage* and it's the scariest movie I've seen in my life!"

Q. That's true. . . . Have you noticed a difference between your British fans and American fans?

CLIVE BARKER: No. With a couple of notable exceptions, I find them for the most part affable and approachable, accessible and intelligent. I have a good time with my fans. I enjoy their observations, and on occasion learn from them.

Q. How about critical opinions—British compared with American?

CLIVE BARKER: I think the American critics have less of a problem with the idea of popular authors than British. So the genre is given a little bit more credence than it is over here. Our heavyweight newspapers—the equivalent of the *Washington Post*, the *New York Times*, or *Time* magazine—which review me regularly will give me a few lines, but little more than that; and they will tend to be descriptions of the book, rather than any analysis of its content.

Q. Getting back to King. When we talked to Harlan Ellison, we agreed with his notion that when you look at a writer's work, it's as if you were looking at a mountain range with peaks and valleys—a range of work over the years. With that in mind, can you single out two or three novels by King that you think are particularly important?

CLIVE BARKER: I think Harlan's point has validity, but equally I think one's got to be careful with those kinds of assessments. The reason being, very simply, that today's meat is tomorrow's poison. My own view on the books that I valued have changed over the years, not just in Steve's case, but generally—I hated *Moby-Dick* when I was fifteen, but now I think it's a masterpiece. So no view is anything more than—

Q. —Checking in at this point in time, as Ellison has said.

CLIVE BARKER: Right. This is what I think today at this hour with this amount of drink in my system, and maybe it'll all be different tomorrow. For the sake of argument, I would talk about the books which I most admire—*The Dead Zone* and *The Stand,* which I think are his masterpieces, but my views may change. I think the short fiction remains perhaps the most vital of his output, and I regret that there isn't more of it.

Q. Ellison made a comment that I thought was very thought-provoking. He said that when he looked at King's novels, he considered that King's strengths tend to be in the shorter lengths: short stories, then novellas; and the novels—with a few exceptions—could have been condensed to novella length.

CLIVE BARKER: I think Harlan tends to view in extremes, but I think it would be tough even with several people working on the project to condense *The Stand* to a novella.

Q. Our mistake: Harlan cited as exceptions The Stand *and the* Dark Tower *novels. He was thinking in the whole of other King novels.*

CLIVE BARKER: Maybe. The fact is that they were written as novels, and that was the creative judgment Steve chose to make at that particular time; if he had chosen to do it a different way, then I'm sure it would have been just fine. I defer always to the creator—I think you have to. And if the creator chooses to make that judgment, then he will live with the brickbats and the bouquets. I think it's fairly ridiculous to say, *Wouldn't it be better as a short story?* The fact is that it *isn't* a short story. Conceivably, it could have been got down to a haiku, if we tried really hard. I think it's perfectly plausible to say of several of Harlan's short stories that I would like to have seen them as novels, but the fact is that Harlan made them short stories.

Q. You directed Hellraiser 1, *and you've directed* Nightbreed. *Are there any King novels that you think would have translated faithfully to the screen if you had directed them as opposed to other directors?*

CLIVE BARKER: I don't think Steve's had a great time on the screen. I think there's been a lot of movies but too few which have been great pieces of movie making, like *Carrie.* I'm not a fan of *The Shining,* although I know a lot of people whose opinions I respect are fond of it.

Q. It's more Kubrick's The Shining *than King's.*

CLIVE BARKER: It's much more Kubrick's, and it seems to take out the heart of the book in order to make it work in his work. I think that there are stories of

Steve's which I regret have been turned into inferior movies, because I think they are wonderful stories, like "Children of the Corn"—a wonderful story but a terrible movie. *Cujo*, I thought, didn't translate well, either. The dog was nowhere near as terrifying in the flesh as he is on the page.

I think it's been a mixed bag on the whole, and I was rather disappointed that Steve didn't follow up on *Maximum Overdrive*. I know he didn't like the picture or the circumstances under which the picture was made, but nevertheless I would love to see some more of his work. Power to the artist.

Q. I think that after Maximum Overdrive, *which had taken a real beating from the critics and fans, King has been reluctant to get back in the director's chair, which is a shame because it's unrealistic to assume that someone will direct a film perfectly the first time out. King's learning and should go back and give it another shot.*

CLIVE BARKER: Yeah. *Hellraiser* was my first movie, and I think of it as being extremely flawed.

Q. How popular is Stephen King in England? His prose is so colloquial and so distinctly an American voice. What's the reaction to his work back home?

CLIVE BARKER: Steve is very popular. His books regularly hit the best-seller lists. We are a colonized country, and there's a lot of American television and movies here, with the colloquialisms which are so much a part of Steve's life.

Q. King dwells on rural life. Are there a lot of parallels between American rural life and British?

CLIVE BARKER: I think there is something very distinctive about the small Maine towns that Steve describes. I don't think you should find the equivalent here.

Q. One of King's stories, "Crouch End," takes place in London. Have you read that story?

CLIVE BARKER: Yes. I used to live in Crouch End.

Q. What do you think of the story?

CLIVE BARKER: It's a good story. There are hints of Lovecraft in there, right?

Q. Right.

CLIVE BARKER: I'm not a great Lovecraft fan, actually, though for the first time I am treading into that area in *The Great and Secret Show,* in the sense that it is about invasions from other dimensions.

CLIVE BARKER'S SHADOWS IN EDEN

edited by Stephen Jones

A companion book compiled in collaboration with Clive Barker, *Shadows in Eden* is a textual and visual delight—assuming your tastes run a little on the dark side. Published by Underwood–Miller, this 465-page book is profusely illustrated by Barker, whose demons, imps, and hellish souls spring from his pen with the ease with which his stories flow from that same pen.

A phantasmagoric book that won the 1992 Bram Stoker Award, *Clive Barker's Shadows in Eden* is, as *Booklist* pointed out, "A bloodfeast for horror fans. Barker is revealed as an intelligent and genuinely personable writer."

It's a hellish book—there's no other way to describe it—and simply indispensable reading for any Barker fan.

Q. On "The Larry King Show," you said that your work leans more toward literature than toward what we would consider popular fiction.

CLIVE BARKER: I think you opened several cans of worms there. Arguably, literature is what happens when popular fiction gets good. I would certainly consider Raymond Chandler literature, but clearly the traditions he was working in were those of popular fiction. I think it's very important not to get too tied down with these definitions. I would say that part of the issue is to be always looking to assume Chandler or Steve's reader—for the sake of argument—is able to take the obscure reference, is able to interpret a paragraph which is elaborately wrought. The popular reader is in fact much more responsive to nuance than he or she is given credit for.

Q. When you write, do you work with outlines?

CLIVE BARKER: Absolutely.

Q. King doesn't use outlines. He simply sits down to write the story. He's clearly an intuitive writer, capable of shaping the story as it unfolds in his mind's eye.

CLIVE BARKER: I couldn't do that. For one thing, I want to be able to plant in chapter one payoffs that won't happen for four hundred pages. If I am to get that right, it seems to me I have to plan that.

Q. *King mentioned in an interview that there are things he won't write about—for one thing, gratuitous violence. There's also very little explicit sex in his books, for which he's been chided by Peter Straub, though clearly King could write it if he wished. Are there limits to what you would write about?*

CLIVE BARKER: As far as treatment is concerned, I'll do whatever the story needs. If that requires graphic sex, I have been known to turn my attention to that. If it needs graphic violence, I'll do that as well. There are certain subjects I *would* avoid—the concentration camps, for instance. The whole point about horror fiction is that it *does* work as a metaphor. There are still people alive who have survived the camps. I don't want to be writing about that because I feel that would be an invasion of their privacy. I'm still writing popular fiction, which is essentially entertainment. But to turn genuine grief, genuine loss, genuine tragedy into the stuff of popular fiction would seem to me to be in bad taste.

25
Stephen King
A Chautauqua in Pasadena, California

I can't really lecture—I'm not good at that—and I can't speak with any
sense from prepared notes. About the most I can do is *chautauqua,* a fine old
word that means you babble on for a little while about
the things that you do and then you sit down.

Stephen King, introductory comments to a lecture given at
Virginia Beach, Virginia, in 1986

✳

*No matter where he goes to lecture, his fans show up to pepper him with questions.
At a lecture in Virginia Beach in 1986, the procedure was for the audience to write
questions on paper that were stuffed in a box, from which King pulled at random,
answering questions. But after answering several, he abandoned it, saying he
needed the interaction of a live audience. He then started fielding questions from the
podium as a sea of hands went up.*

*In town to do research for a story that would eventually be published as "The Li-
brary Policeman," published in* Different Seasons, *King covered familiar territory,
and new ground, as well, in his question-and-answer session that followed his informal talk in Pasadena, California, in 1989.*

Here, then, are glimpses into his life.

When asked why he came to Pasadena: I'm working on *The Library Policeman.* The main character is a woman who is a vampire and a sexual psy-
chopath. This story came about as a result of something my twelve-year-old
son Owen said at the breakfast table one morning. He said something only a
child would say, and I think that only somebody who writes imaginative fiction both as a vocation and avocation would want to carry the step through.

On being a latchkey kid: When we were kids, my brother and I were on our
own a lot because my father was gone and my mother was working all the time.

So we grew up, and in and out of school we were with kids who were older than us and knew stuff.

On lobsters: For a lot of my childhood, I grew up where I live now, which is Maine. We used to eat a lot of lobster—a poor man's steak. We always used to get seconds, particularly in the summer: Whatever was left over at the end of the day you could buy for a dollar a pound.

And some kid told me that if you bought a lobster and cracked open the tail, there's a nerve dangling down its back, and if you eat that, you'd be paralyzed. I know it's not true, but I can't bring myself to eat that black thread.

On fear and imagination: I relate to the kid who is afraid because he's heard his father talking about the twilight double-header, a monster that he thinks is in his closet.

On his fan mail: You'd be surprised at some of the letters I get. There are strange people out there—present company excepted, of course.

On his most frequently asked question, "Where do you get your ideas?" The answer is Utica, New York. There's a used idea shop . . .

On where his ideas really come from: Ideas come from everyplace, and they strike at the most odd moments.

On the symbolism in horror fiction and movies: They are unreal symbols of very real fears. I don't think that horror fiction works unless you are talking in two voices: on one level, in a very loud voice, you are screaming at your audience about ghosts, werewolves, shape-changers, whatever; and in another, very low voice—a whisper—you are talking about *real* fears, so that in the best cases, you are trying to achieve that nightmarish feeling we've all had: We know it's not real, but that doesn't matter anymore. When I can get that, I know I've got people right where I want them.

On Roger Corman's horror flicks of the fifties: This is not high culture.

On why he writes horror fiction: I like to scare people.

On whether or not he's ever going to write anything "serious": I'm serious-minded whenever I sit down, regardless of what I'm writing about.

On whom he knew that got him started in the business: [Tongue firmly planted in cheek] I use Satan.

Has he ever seen a ghost? I have seen a ghost. It's a real ghost story but not a Stephen King story. [At a 1984 Democratic fund-raiser, Stephen King goes upstairs to retrieve coats for himself and his wife, after a fifteen-minute appearance.] I realized there was a man sitting by the window across the room, so I raised my head slightly to bring him into sight. Through my glasses, I saw a bald seventy-year-old man with round glasses; he was wearing a blue pinstripe suit. I began to feel very strongly that this man thought I was looking through the coats to see what I could steal, and because I was feeling more and more uncomfortable, I finally said, "Gee, it sure is hard to find coats when people come in." And as soon as those words came out of my mouth, I realized that the chair was totally empty—nobody was sitting there. My reaction to this was to get our coats and say nothing whatsoever about it.

We got halfway to the restaurant where we were going to eat dinner and, inside my mind, I stopped and said to myself: *Now wait a minute, the guy was there—you saw him. Why are you pushing this away? You never took your eyes off him.*

My guess is that's about as exciting as most psychic phenomena get.

On his influences: Don Robertson, Richard Matheson, and a thousand bad horror movies.

When asked if evil exists: The question is whether or not there's some kind of outside evil. I'm haunted by the idea that there's some kind of outside evil—something that almost floats free. I worry about guys like Ted Bundy. Whatever it was that was in him was gone when they put him in the electric chair—they fried a shell. Maybe whatever it was it blew away.

On why he's never finished *The Plant*: After I saw *The Little Shop of Horrors* between the second and third installment, I realized *that* was what I was writing, so I decided to stop right away.

On his writing speed: I write very fast.

On the storytelling process: I usually know where I'm going, and I usually have an idea about what the end is going to be. I think some of you who have read my books would be surprised to find out how many of them were intended to be much bleaker than they turned out to be. For instance, I expected everybody to die at the end of *'Salem's Lot;* I expected everybody to die at the end of *The Shining.*

I think that for me, the most important thing—once you have the idea—is to play fair and, whether it's a make-believe idea or a fantasy, if you're going to use real people in a story, the characters dictate events. You have to let the characters do what they have to do. I don't think events dictate character.

On his favorite work: "The Body."

On what he reads: I read a lot of novels. I have a tendency to enjoy crime novels, suspense novels, some horror novels, although I don't read as many horror novels as I used to. If I had to name a book that's made an impression on me lately, it would be Larry McMurtry's *Lonesome Dove,* which I liked very much. . . . I just got around to reading for the first time *Look Homeward, Angel* by Thomas Wolfe. I loved that book. That guy didn't know how to say quit; he would turn on his typewriter and everything would vomit out. I can relate to that.

On whether or not *Misery* was autobiographical: It's pretty accurate in terms of emotional feeling. I sometimes don't know what people want. . . . People really like what I do, or at least some people do, but some of them are quite crackers. I have not met Annie Wilkes yet, but I've met all sorts of people who call themselves my "number-one fan" and, boy, some of these guys don't have six cans in a six-pack.

On selling his work to the movies: When you sell something to the movies—and I love the movies; it's immensely flattering to have somebody want to turn your book into a movie—there's two ways to go about it. Get involved all the way, or part of the way, and stand up and take the blame or criticism for everyone else; or to say, *I'm going to sell it and take the money.* John Updike used to say that it's the best of all possible worlds when they pay you a lot of money but don't make the money. But when you don't get involved, you are in a no-lose situation because if it's good, you can say "It's based on my work," but if it's bad, you can say "I didn't have anything to do with that."

On the problem with movies: I've done good work, I've done bad work; I've done work that I'm proud of, I've done work that I'm ashamed of. But once you get into a team effort, the bullshit seems to float to the top.

On whether or not writing *The Dark Tower* or the Bachman books was a departure for King because they didn't "seem to fall into your usual horror kind of thing—they don't seem to quite fit in. Are they like vacations to you?" All I can say is: I'm a horror writer if you *want* me to be one; you can call me anything you want to—I don't care.

In America, everybody's got to have a brand name. You've got your generic game-show host; you've got your generic Western writer; you've got your generic bad-guy actor; and you've got your generic horror writer.

I just write stories, but I *tend* to write horror stories.

I mentioned this before. A few years ago, I tried very hard to write a Western, because it's a form I like. I wrote about 160 pages, but the only scene that really had any power was when the old guy got drunk outside a farmhouse and fell into the pigsty—and the pigs ate him. . . . That one scene had some real drive and punch. That is what turned on my lights, for some reason I don't understand.

KING ON BREAKING INTO PRINT

I'm not sure what you do about it. My own success . . . I was lucky enough to have a book that was adapted into a successful film. I've always wondered what would have happened if *Carrie* the film had been a failure—would I be anywhere near where I am today? I like to think so, but who knows?

It think it's something of a crapshoot, but I'll tell you one thing I *do* believe: talent almost always finds the light, even today. If you need proof of that, look at Amy Tan, who is a fantastic success story and deserves every bit of it. I just wish as many people as know Amy Tan knew Katherine Dunne, who wrote *Geek Love*.

On the Grant editions of *The Dark Tower [I]: The Gunslinger:* The book was published at $20, and I was a little bit horrified by what happened afterward when the book became a collector's item and the price jumped. It hadn't been my intention to see these books climb from $20 to $50 to $70 to whatever. I wanted to do something about it, and Don Grant, who was upset, wanted to do something about it. We talked on the phone one night and I said, "What if you publish another five hundred or five thousand?" Don sighed. And I said, "That would be like pissing on a forest fire, wouldn't it?" Don agreed. Eventually, we issued it in trade paperback, which seemed like a nice compromise between a hardback and a mass market paperback.

On his writing schedule and rock and roll: I write two, three hours in the morning. I crank the music up as high as I can. It keeps people away when you turn the music up loud because it poisons the air—AC/DC and Judas Priest. . . . I've discovered new guys like Metallica and Anthrax—nobody comes near when those guys are playing.

On whether or not he was planning a break from writing: I'd go crazy. I'm a creature of habit.

On why he wrote *The Talisman:* I've known Peter Straub since, I think, 1974, when my wife and I lived in England. Peter's a really cool guy. We wanted to do a book together and we stumbled around and finally came up with an idea. We got modems and finally did the book. We had a great time.

Asked if King's perennial antagonist would make another appearance:
Randall Flagg never goes away.

On whether or not he's ever suffered from writer's block: I've had it twice.
Shortly after *Carrie,* I went through a writer's block that was about a year long.
And after I finished *The Tommyknockers,* I went through a year of hell that I
would never want to go through again: Nothing would seem to come up; I
would write and it would fall apart, like wet tissue paper. I don't know how
to describe it, except to say that it's the most impotent, nasty, awful feeling. You
feel like a batter in a slump. Finally, what happened was that I wrote a little
story called "Rainy Season" and, all at once, everything opened up and
flooded out. I've been writing horror ever since.

On whether or not he'd ever write a sequel to *'Salem's Lot:* I don't think
now there will be one. I'd have to go back into the past.

Part 3

A Chronological Look at the Books

by Michael R. Collings

King criticism has generally fallen into one of two camps: fanboy burblings that amount to a personal response to King's novels (the reviewer either liked it or didn't), or an academic approach that is written in prose so turgid it requires an advanced degree to decipher.

This section is a chronological look at each major King book, which is discussed in its own right, related to its literary traditions, and, finally, viewed as part of a growing canon of work.

I wanted a single voice in this section (but not mine), so I asked Dr. Michael R. Collings if he would provide that voice. When he agreed, I knew that King and his work could not have been better served. For Collings, unlike many of his colleagues, does not consider fantasy, science fiction, and horror to be bastard children of literature, the shantytowns across the railroad tracks that separate True Literature from Shock/Shlock.

Carefully, analytically, and with a great respect for King's canon, Collings's literary fruits of labor follow.

My original plan, by the way, was to follow up each of his pieces with background information, quotes from King about the work in question and other miscellanies. But since I had covered those well-trod grounds in *The Stephen King Story,* I decided not to repeat myself. Besides, to read Collings's pieces, in order, is to see a rich tapestry emerge—King's weaveworld, as it were, composed of many diverse elements. When you pull back far enough, distancing yourself from the works in question, you see through Collings's eyes major themes interconnecting, forming a whole.

26
Michael R. Collings
An Interview

If you have any interest in Stephen King beyond reading the books and seeing the movies, you'll inevitably run across Michael R. Collings's six books on Stephen King: The Annotated Guide to Stephen King *(a bibliography),* The Many Facets of Stephen King, The Films of Stephen King, The Shorter Works of Stephen King *(with David Engebretson),* Stephen King as Richard Bachman, *and* The Stephen King Phenomenon. *You will also find Collings's ideas on King, King's novels, and his place in the American literary heritage in articles in* Gauntlet, The Stephen King Story *and* Demon-Driven: Stephen King and the Art of Writing.

✳

Q. What are your academic credentials?

MICHAEL COLLINGS: I am a tenured full professor of English in the Humanities Division at Pepperdine University, as well as the director of the Creative Writing program in the Communication Division. I received my Ph.D. in Milton and the Renaissance from the University of California, Riverside, in 1977, with an emphasis in epic theory. My interest in modern manifestations of the epic impulse in literature led me first to science fiction, and from there to novels such as King's *The Stand.*

I have presented papers on King, horror, and related topics at a number of academic conferences (often to the accompaniment of raised eyebrows from more conservative colleagues), including several annual meetings of the International Conference on the Fantastic in the Arts, the Lloyd J. Eaton Conference on Science Fiction and Fantasy at UC Riverside, the Philological Association of the Pacific Coast, Brigham Young University's annual Symposium on Science Fiction and Fantasy, and Horrorfest '89. In fact, for the past two years, I have had the honor of serving as Poetry Guest at Brigham Young University's annual Symposium on Science Fiction and Fantasy (and resident King-expert on panels), with an invitation to return in February 1995. And in July 1995 I am slated to serve as Academic Guest of Honor for Mythcon XXVI, at Berkeley, and present an address on fantasy and realism in Orson Scott Card and C. S. Lewis.

Q. How many books have you published?

MICHAEL COLLINGS: At last count, the total had hit fifty-five books and chapbooks. That includes the six studies of Stephen King as well as *Piers Anthony* (1983), *Naked to the Sun: Dark Visions of Apocalypse* (poetry, 1985), *Brian W. Aldiss* (1986), *Reflections on the Fantastic* (as editor for this collection of scholarly essays, 1986), *Card Catalogue: The Science Fiction and Fantasy of Orson Scott Card* (1987), *Dark Transformations: Deadly Visions of Change* (horror poetry and fiction, 1990), *In the Image of God: Theme, Characterization, and Landscape in the Fiction of Orson Scott Card* (1990), and nearly two dozen poetry chapbooks, the latest of which is *A Vapor of Vampires,* a collection of vampire poetry. In addition I have published a cookbook, a collection of hymn variations for the organ, over ninety articles in scholarly and popular publications, almost three hundred reviews (primarily science fiction, horror, and mystery, including reviews of many of King's later works), and well over four hundred poems.

Q. What are you currently working on?

MICHAEL COLLINGS: I've become more and more interested in contemporary poetry, particularly in the way the poets have for the most part moved away from their audiences and internalized their ideas, images, symbols, and structures so completely that many of what are considered the major poems of our time are unintelligible even to careful readers. I am working on a textbook for writing poetry, and at the same time exploring how writers such as King, Dean R. Koontz, Robert McCammon, and Orson Scott Card use story as a means of defining and welding a community identity among their readers . . . then trying to apply those techniques to SF, horror, and mainstream poetry.

Q. What is your background in science fiction and horror?

MICHAEL COLLINGS: I have held memberships in the Science Fiction Research Association, the Science Fiction Poetry Association, and the International Association for the Fantastic in the Arts . . . and am a recent member of the UnDead Poets Society. I have reviewed for the *SFRA Book Review, Fantasy Review, Extrapolation*, the *Science Fiction & Fantasy Book Review Annual,* and most recently as featured reviewer for Ed Gorman's *Mystery Scene* (which, in spite of its name, has been interested in King, Koontz, and other cross-genre authors).

Q. Your teaching credentials?

MICHAEL COLLINGS: Well, I have been known to introduce William Shakespeare to my classes as "the sixteenth century Stephen King." As far as straight SF/F/H goes, I teach a course titled "Myth, Fantasy, and Science Fiction" that frequently includes King materials and approaches them as modern technological mythologies. The year *It* appeared in paperback, I assigned my students a twenty-five-page critical essay on the novel, knowing full well that at the time there were only two articles and a handful of reviews available as research materials (and several of those by me). It forced the students to fall back on their own reading, critical, and scholarly skills . . . and the result was one student paper that was later published in *Castle Rock* and that earned the student a personal letter from King.

I also incorporate references to contemporary works in nearly all of my literature courses, trying to show how the literature of the present can affect readers in the same ways as the literatures of the past originally did. Some students are bothered by the allusions; others find them exciting and stimulating, often moving from my offhand comments into further studies of their own. Several students in a recent graduate seminar on the Epic in English, for example, chose to do their final oral presentations on epic in science fiction, fantasy, and horror, including again *The Stand*.

Q. When did you first read a King book?

MICHAEL COLLINGS: One of my students, David Engebretson, urged me to read *The Dead Zone* after a discussion in a creative writing class. I did—and then everything else I could lay my hands on by King. In fact, during the next summer break, I read all of King then available, as well as most of the novels by Koontz, Ramsey Campbell, and several others. I was intrigued initially by the sheer power and internal consistency of King's storytelling ability; later, as I reread the novels and stories, I began to enjoy them as much for their connections with and critiques of the world around me as for their evocations of terror and horror. (David, by the way, later cowrote *The Shorter Works of Stephen King* while he was still an undergraduate student at Pepperdine.)

Q. How did you come to publish six books on King at Starmont House?

MICHAEL COLLINGS: In early 1985—just after I sent Ted Dikty and Roger Schlobin the typescript for my second Starmont book *(Brian W. Aldiss)*—Ted called to say that King had publicly admitted to being Richard Bachman. Since Douglas Winter's excellent volume on King for the *Starmont Reader's Guides* series had been sold to New American Library as *The Art of Darkness*, Ted did not have a King volume anymore. He asked me to do one on the Bachman books—and have it camera-ready within two months. I said yes.

A week later, he called again and asked me to consider doing a replacement volume for the Winter book—an overview of King's primary works. Again, I said yes.

A few days after that, he called a third time and proposed a seven-volume series, including a collection of essays to be edited by Darrell Schweitzer and books by me on the Bachman novels, King's novels (*The Many Facets of Stephen King*), collected and uncollected short fiction (*The Shorter Works of Stephen King*), King's films (*The Films of Stephen King*); an annotated bibliography (*The Annotated Guide to Stephen King*); and a concordance. Since preliminary work on a concordance to *Carrie*—including only proper names, place names, and important themes, etc.—suggested that a similar treatment of all of King's works would take several years to complete and at least a thousand-page book to publish, Dikty decided to discontinue that part of the project.

A little over a year after the initial telephone call, the entire series was in print. Since then, *The Films of Stephen King* has been translated into German and sold quite well as *Stephen King und seine Filme*. The *Annotated Guide* is currently out of print; the rights were transferred from Starmont to Rob Reginald's Borgo Press, where a massive (three-thousand-plus entries) revision updating primary and secondary bibliographic materials to about 1991 is awaiting publication.

Q. What is the current status of criticism on King?

MICHAEL COLLINGS: Shortly after Ted Dikty's death several years ago, Starmont House ceased publication. His plans to issue casebooks on every King novel had already led to a collection of essays on *The Shining*, but as with his other projects, that one has been seriously disrupted.

Even so, the past few years have seen a number of strong works dealing with King from multiple perspectives. Carroll Terrell's *Stephen King: Man and Artist* gives a part scholarly, part impressionistic view of King from Terrell's unique position as authority on several key modern mainstream writers, and as one of King's professors at UMO two decades ago. The Twayne series has published two volumes on King, covering his first two decades as a novelist; both provide strong introductions to King and his works. And other books, chapters, and articles continue to appear regularly, suggesting that in some areas at least, King is now considered an important figure in American literature.

Q. What dealings have you had with Stephen King?

MICHAEL COLLINGS: King was generous and open in all my dealings with him. I sent him an initial letter outlining the series and assuring him that, however critical individual sentences might be, the thrust of all the books would be positive—I do not believe in wasting my time writing studies of people whose works I do not think have value.

Over the several years of the Starmont project, he responded to my questions, occasionally writing long, informative letters that provided valuable insight into his stories. His secretary was equally responsive and supplied me with copies of several key stories, reviews, etc. I could not have asked for a more professional or more sustaining relationship between author and critic.

Q. What about the recent works?

MICHAEL COLLINGS: King has always had the strength of being a storyteller. Whatever else scholars and critics might find lurking in his texts (and subtexts, and probably sub-subtexts), he has always given his readers the sense of a fair payback for the time spent in reading. This has led him into taking real risks: the length and narrative complexity of *It,* for example, or the even greater length and scope of the unexpurgated *Stand.*

To some extent, his latest works turn away from the intensive awareness of storytelling. *Misery* is compelling, but in a sense is more self-directed than most of what readers might call "classic" King. It is introverted, the story of a writer struggling with writing. Instead of children versus monsters—the formula that he used so successfully in novel after novel, while at the same time offering devastating critiques of contemporary American society—he seems to be focusing on the writer as writer. *The Dark Half* carries this theme further, succeeding in spite of its preoccupation with the internal *angst* of the author.

With *Gerald's Game,* King almost discards the elements that made him one of the most popular writers of the past two decades, substituting political and social agenda for the sheer power of storytelling that characterizes his best work. He has *always* written novels with political and social overtones—from *Carrie* on he has tackled issues including education, parenting, socialization and maturation, religion, politics. He has campaigned for women, for children, for minorities . . . but always in the context of a story in which strong women, strong children, strong characters have demonstrated strength. In *Gerald's Game,* for the first time, he bluntly asserts rather than demonstrates, and the novel is the weaker for it. *Dolores Claiborne* pulls back a little. Still overtly programmatic, it again has the strength of King's storytelling power behind it, a tour de force exercise in narrative art that consists of a single, uninterrupted monologue, spoken by a powerful character.

When King tells stories—and they are often *important* stories—he simply cannot be touched. When his message shouts louder than his narrative voice, the techniques that make his best works strong seem to act against him, making him seem strident, aggressive, and assertive.

Q. Where would you rank King as a literary writer?

MICHAEL COLLINGS: I think some of King's works have a strong chance to last. *'Salem's Lot, The Shining, The Dead Zone* (in spite of its sometimes dated historical setting), *It, The Stand* (unexpurgated version)—all of these are remarkable narratives told with authenticity and truth. All of them lend themselves well to both the classroom and scholarly/academic study. All of them repay the reader/critic with new insights into life, society, literature, and art. And all of them are unique artifacts of the movement of American life in the final quarter of the twentieth century, chronicled by an unblinking and highly perceptive eye. I think that at least these—and probably several others—should have a long, long literary life.

27

Of Books and Reputations
The Confusing Cases of King, Koontz, and Others
by Michael R. Collings

In academic circles, the phrase "publish or perish" takes on special meaning. In order to get ahead, professors must publish on a regular basis, writing on approved subjects that will satisfy the requirement. And he who does not publish . . . will perish.

In the case of Dr. Michael R. Collings, a professor at Pepperdine University, "publish and perish" seems more apt, since he's chosen the road less traveled: writing criticism about—horrors!—science fiction, fantasy, and horror fiction. Applying the rigorous tools of academic criticism to the field, Collings broke new ground in the field of King criticism, lifting it far above the fanboy burblings of self-appointed critics whose criterion was, simply, whether or not they liked the story. (That's personal opinion, not criticism.)

In the case of Dr. Collings, "publish or perish" means that his mainstay publisher, Starmont House, folded up a few years after the death of its founder, Ted Dikty, who said that he "saw a need to publish reference books in the fantasy and science-fiction field." A longtime publisher and fan, Ted was the founder of Carcosa House and a partner in Shasta House (a leading small press in the fifties), which gave him the background to publish successfully a line of critical books in the field.

Typically published in small print runs, mostly in trade paperback, with "on demand" printing, the books became staples at college libraries, and private collectors, finally, had a line of well-written and authoritative books that took that "sci-fi stuff" seriously.

Starmont's best-selling title was Starmont Reader's Guide #16, *written by Douglas E. Winter, and was about—you guessed it—Stephen King. (Later, Doug scoped out this book into his groundbreaking work,* Stephen King: The Art of Darkness, *which is the only major book about King written in cooperation with the subject.)*

A quiet, soft-spoken gentleman who doesn't mince words when it comes to what he likes, and doesn't like, about King's work, Dr. Collings is the real thing: the ideal, genuine critic. (He's also a poet, a bibliographer, and a book reviewer.)

In this piece, originally published in Demon-Driven: Stephen King and the Art of Writing (1994), *Collings takes to task a high school English teacher who, like so many others, can't or won't allow fantasy, science fiction, or horror to be taught in her class, the traditional response among teachers.*

*

Several weeks ago, my teenage son came home from high school chuckling— itself an odd enough circumstance to merit remembering. But the reason for his laughter was even more intriguing than the fact of it, particularly as it bore directly on my own efforts in science fiction, fantasy, and horror criticism.

His junior English class is preparing to face the great unmentionable, the horror of the year—the dreaded TERM PAPER. His teacher had handed out a long list of possible topics, all American authors, and the students were required to submit proposals for a paper that would discuss at least three works by a single author, or one work by three authors, combining the students' perceptions with relevant outside sources.

During the discussion, one student noted that Stephen King, his favorite author, was not included on the list. No, the teacher answered solemnly, King was not included. Another student noted that several other contemporary popular authors were also missing from the list and asked why.

In response the teacher said that such writers were only of interest to readers unable to handle the sophisticated expression of the "classics."

"In other words," the second student shot back, defending himself and his friends who read King and others, "we read them because we're too *stupid* to understand the classics?"

"Uh, no," the teacher answered, obviously backpedaling. She continued to talk in generalities about the lack of sophistication in contemporary popular writers, noting in passing that most students hadn't even considered using King as a topic for the paper until a few years before, when a professor from Pepperdine began publishing books about him.

At this point, my son sat up and began paying more attention.

Then, the teacher continued, the professor made things worse by holding discussion groups at the local library, actually talking with groups of high school students about King and his works, as if they had literary merit.

Now my son was *really* paying attention, wondering if he should raise his hand and say "That's my father," or wait it out and see what else the teacher would say.

He decided to wait it out.

And discovered that in spite of such odd behavior (fortunately isolated) in a college professor, there really wasn't enough criticism on Stephen King or writers like him to merit including them on the list of possibilities for the TERM PAPER.

End of discussion.

When my son reported this experience—grinning the whole while and (I'm sure) wondering how I would take this implied slur on my reputation (such as it is)—I was struck again by the short-sightedness of academic establishments that continue to exclude King, Koontz, and others like them from the lists of "approved" materials.

While Hawthorne and *The Scarlet Letter,* Melville and *Moby-Dick,* and Dickens and *A Tale of Two Cities* are certainly central literary achievements in our culture, even fascinating topics for further research and discussion by adult readers, I am even less convinced now than I was as a high school student that they are necessarily appropriate for freshmen, sophomores, and juniors in high school, many of whom are barely beyond being functionally literate, many of whom lack even the barest backgrounds or historical perspectives for assessing such novels, and many of whom are explicitly more interested in Poe, Bradbury, and King. Yet instructors are forced in turn to force high school students to read works that probably even most teachers would be unlikely to read for pleasure.

On the other hand, the opposite approach seems to be requiring texts that are themselves less literary than exercises in political correctness, sociological conditioning, and artificially induced diversity. Either way, the established programs often simply ignore the fact that kids like to read (and watch) things by Stephen King.

There are, of course, strong arguments against allowing King into curriculums, even as tangentially as letting students use his work for an out-of-class term paper.

His writing is often violent. It is often gross and explicit, both sexually and linguistically. It is often fantastic. It is often highly critical of accepted institutions, including home, family, politics, and education.

But the kids *read* him. Based on my experiences leading discussion groups about his books, high-school-age readers often *devour* his books, memorize his books, know more about what he has written than I do.

And then they are told by teachers that he is too unsophisticated, too peripheral to what is really important in the universe, too *common* for students to waste their time on, when it would seem that teachers would welcome the opportunity to confront a writer who perhaps more than any other is molding the imaginations and minds of contemporary adolescents. After all, if so many students read him, and he is so awful, so damaging to the social fabric, so utterly without redeeming social value, it would seem even more important to discover what it is that draws young readers to him. To refer back to my son's experience, the teacher stated to the class that anyone who read more than two or three King novels had to be warped, perverted, highly disturbed. At that point my son couldn't help laughing out loud—and was tempted to put the teacher even more on the spot by noting that he had read about thirty King novels and that his father had read *everything* that King had published. If two or three relegated a reader to warp-dom, where would thirty, forty, or fifty books put someone? Perhaps wisely, my son restrained his impulse, and the teacher was free to continue her defense of the status quo reading list.

No, King is not sufficiently elevated, not sufficiently elegant, not sufficiently a part of the teachers' own university backgrounds—implying that they might actually have to read him and study him themselves in order to lecture to classes—that he is simply inappropriate as the subject for a research project.

And to prove their point, they pound the final nail into the coffin of any would-be term paperist: *There's just not enough criticism written about him to make the effort worthwhile.*

Again and again I have heard this comment and am stunned by the ignorance it betrays. Certainly for many science-fiction, fantasy, and horror writers, the claim is accurate. Even some of the finest writers in the genres have been ignored by traditional critics and scholars, to the point that accurate bibliographies are not even available for many, if not most. In spite of the valiant efforts of publishers like the late Ted Dikty of Starmont House and his series editor, Roger Schlobin, who between them saw the publication of several dozen introductory monographs, or Rob Reginald at Borgo Press, with his continuing series of definitive bibliographies—in spite of the work of dozens of scholars and critics approaching such monumental tasks as the lifeworks of Isaac Asimov and Robert A. Heinlein and others almost as prolific and as central to our reading heritage—in spite of all this effort, it is still to easy for teachers to issue lists of term-paper topics that ignore some of the most popular and influential writers of our times.

But to make that claim for Stephen King?

I glance at the bookshelf and see the three-inch-thick manuscript that represents my work on a Stephen King bibliography, scheduled for publication by Borgo Press, and I wonder. Woefully out of date since its completion in 1991, the manuscript nevertheless includes over *three thousand* items, both primary and secondary, including titles of several dozen books exclusively about King (a number of them from prestigious university presses), more dozens of articles in scholarly and popular journals and magazines, and hundreds of reviews ranging from the *New York Times Book Review* to localized fan presses—but this is not enough to allow students sufficient exercise in the fine and ancient art of literary research.

Granted, not all of the criticism and scholarship available on King is first class. I think of one article that discovers Vietnam allegories in a King story, when King himself has stated publicly that he sees (or intended) no such subtext himself. Or another critic who, after publishing three very expensive specialty editions of interviews and criticism, notes that he considers King little more than a literary hack (although presumably a source of no little income).

Nevertheless, it seems important to recognize that much of the criticism is solid and, more important yet, that horror writers are an intrinsic and essential part of understanding late-twentieth-century American culture. Writers like Stephen King, Dean R. Koontz, Robert McCammon, Dan Simmons, and others have written works that transcend narrow genre classifications, that have grappled with the fundamental social problems we face today, and have explored them through the *metaphor* of the monstrous and the horrific—as if AIDS, molestation, homelessness, and *-isms* of various sorts were not already monstrous and horrific enough. These writers have described *us* in the clearest and broadest of terms—not pessimistically or nihilistically but often with an undercurrent of true hope. On the surface, their images may be frightening, but then so is our world. The "premillennial cotillion" that Koontz depicts graphically in *Dragon Tears* is not just a figment of his imagination. The worldwide plague that wipes out most of humanity in King's *The Stand* is only a few degrees beyond the plagues—diseases, social unrest, political threats—that we presently face. The fictional disintegration of society in McCammon's *Swan Song* or *Mine* or *Stinger* reflects the real disintegrations we see around us. Their unique visions of what it is to live here, to live now, is captured in these and other novels and stories in ways that no alternative form can legitimately duplicate.

And our children read those novels and stories.

Our children see the world in terms of the visions these novels and stories create.

Our children need to understand more completely what it is that these writers are struggling to achieve.

Stephen King and the Critics
A Personal Perspective
by Michael R. Collings

I am not so much scholar or critic as facilitator.

Michael R. Collings

Most of my attitudes toward criticism, scholarship, fans, and King are implicit in my article in *The Stephen King Phenomenon* and in the introduction to *The Many Facets of Stephen King*. I firmly believe that King speaks for our times; he touches on elements of American culture that are keystrokes to understanding ourselves. He is enormously popular—and scholars hate that. He writes for a popular audience—and academicians hate that. He tells stories for the sake of stories—and theorists hate that. On the other hand, he is being increasingly dissected by academics, many of whom seem spurred more by the "publish or perish" syndrome than by any real desire to understand the nature of horror—and fans hate that. But . . . kids read him.

I moderated a panel earlier this year with Ray Bradbury, who argued that the ultimate value of his fiction was that it made kids want to read. The kids start there and then perhaps move on to better things. At the least, this is true with King. I have led several teenage book discussion groups for the local library. Generally, the groups muster twenty or so students to discuss an assigned book. When I came to talk about *Firestarter* or *Christine,* there were more than sixty students. And last fall, when I spoke at a special session of the group to which parents and teachers were invited, there were over eighty present. I was to suggest what I saw as important in King, and the parents and teachers were free to explain what why they did *not* want their children reading King. None of the parents or teachers voiced any criticism. King is not for all children, of course; but he can help them into the world of imagination.

On the other hand, working with King has hampered my own career and the careers of others who have seriously tried to add to the body of knowledge. Some universities simply do not count any work of science fiction, fantasy, or horror as a legitimate publication when professors are up for promotion. In my own case, I was turned down for a merit increase—in spite of having over three hundred published works in the past ten years—for two reasons: first, the Starmont books were printed from camera-ready copy rather than typeset, and therefore were obviously hackwork to be dismissed (I never did get any substantive criticism of the *quality* of my work); and second, it was felt that I was wasting my time in the field as a whole—I should be working on yet another scholarly interpretation of Milton, or something similar. I have had colleagues introduce literature courses by noting that in that class, the students would read literature, "not that Stephen King stuff." I have had colleagues tell my students that they should never come into a university professor's office carrying a Stephen King novel. And I have had colleagues disparage my work without ever having read either my criticism or King's novels.

Still, the climate may be changing. My division chairmen in Humanities and Communication have both been more than supportive. Both divisions have organized specific courses on science fiction and fantasy, including courses that use King's books as base texts. Both chairmen encouraged me in my work. The Seaver College Reassigned Time Committee has given me released time from teaching assignments to work on the King books, on a science-fiction novel, and on projects on Orson Scott Card and C. S. Lewis.

So my experiences have encapsulated the ambiguity that surrounds King himself: accepted and rejected—often fanatically—and with few sound reasons.

My own belief remains unaltered: I try to stand midway between the academics who are surrounded by their dusty tomes and who seem interested in literature-as-artifact (new criticism) rather than literature as a reflection of the living experience—and the unthinking fan who knows what he likes but has no idea *why* he likes it. I try to suggest that contemporary literature can meet the standards of academia; and at the same time the standards of academia can help fan readers understand the books better. I try to make suggestions about things in King—and anyone else I work with—that I found exciting and stimulating, then urge my readers to *return to the work and find out for themselves* if what I say is true. I am not so much scholar or critic as facilitator. Nevertheless, I remain true to the need for scholarship, academics (in the best sense of the word), and clarity.

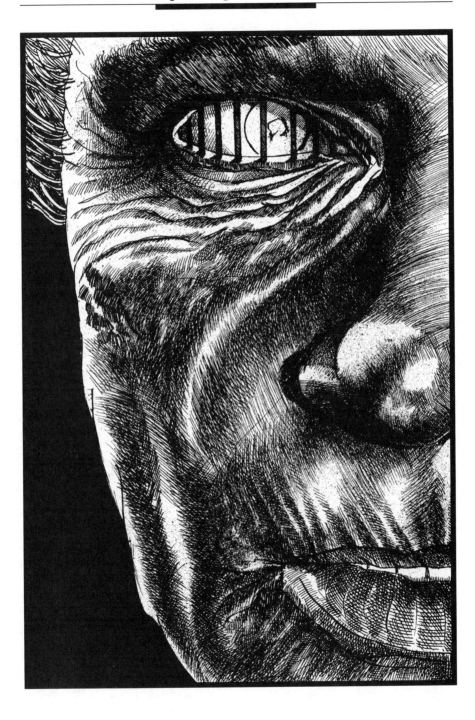

29

Carrie

(1974)

Carrie probably remains one of King's best known but least read novels. Since its publication two decades ago, and more specifically since its first appearance on the best-sellers' charts in December 1976 (where it remained for fourteen weeks), it has provided an icon for specific elements in American culture. Although perhaps not as enormously popular with readers as *The Shining, The Stand, Misery,* and other later novels (particularly with the newer generation of readers, for whom the 1970s are the stuff of myth and legend), it is nevertheless among the most recognizable of King's works, with the single word "Carrie" sufficient to suggest the whole range of King's subsequent novels. The novel and its lead character had been alluded to in other horror novels (including King's own, as in *The Dead Zone,* where a distraught character accuses Johnny Smith of setting a building on fire "with his mind, just like in that book *Carrie*") as well as in comic strips, in parodies, and on television sitcoms. With the possible exceptions of *Cujo* and *Christine,* probably no other single King work has attained to such a level of popular culture, mass name recognition.

To use King's own term, *Carrie* has become a "brand-name" novel.

In fact, it is appropriate that King's first novel receive such treatment. Rereading it after twenty years, and with the experience of the intervening forty-odd novels and collections, dozens of short stories, decades of film versions, and constant streams of imitators and parodists, it may be rather surprising to see how well the novel holds up, particularly since it is a "first novel."

That last comment is, of course, only partially true. *Carrie* was in fact King's first *published* novel, but by the time it appeared, he had written five complete novel manuscripts—a rigid apprenticeship in anyone's terms. And King's commitment already shows. *Carrie* is a precise, focused, controlled exercise in narrative, as compelling for its story as for its brutal images of death and wholesale destruction and its examination of wild-card psychic talents as metaphors and symbols for things deeply wrong with American society and life. In its stark portrayal of the bleakness, the terror, the emptiness of the life of an adolescent outsider, it is difficult to surpass. And given the fact that one of King's primary audiences consists of precisely that age group that the novel anatomizes and in part pillories (that is, high school students), it is almost perfect in its ambitions and its effects. It presents the world of its characters—and of a large group of its readers—with clarity, skill, and appropriate brutality.

At another level, *Carrie* is important since it introduces what readers should immediately recognize as many of King's standard images. The story focuses on an outsider—an early version of Johnny Smith, or Arnie Cunningham, or the seven children in *It,* or any number of others. This outsider is set apart by a specific trait; in this case, of course, it is Carrie White's telekinetic and pyrotechnic talents. The outsider remains the focus of both sympathy and threat; readers are invited to penetrate and understand the mind of the character, yet at the same time, there is a sense of danger inherent in the character. With Carrie or Arnie, the danger becomes overt as the character becomes a prime mover in climactic struggles; with Johnny Smith and others like him, the danger is controlled and the wild-card talent used to preserve rather than to destroy. But in either case, the mere existence of the outsider and the preternatural talent is sufficient to cause, directly or indirectly, suffering, disruption, destruction, and death.

Set against the outsider are peer groups. In *Carrie,* those she should have been able to bond with (to use eighties jargon) represent the most immediate enemy. Isolated from parent and family, from the entire adult world (as all of King's children ultimately are), from those whose job it is to guide and protect— the assistant principal cannot remember her name, even after it is repeated to him twice—she is left to discover her own nature and try to reshape her own reality while constantly struggling against the opposition, fear, contempt, and outright hatred of her own age group. And the result, in this novel and elsewhere, is tragedy.

Sue Snell's attempt at integrating the outsider stems from good intentions, but Snell's ignorance of how rigid the barriers determining acceptance and behavior in high school are, is great enough that she unknowingly impels Carrie into horror. Tommy Ross's equally goodhearted attempt at bringing Carrie into the charmed circle leads directly to his death. And Christine Hargensen, Billy Nolan, and the others actively seek her embarrassment, her discomfiture, and ultimately her death.

Adults in *Carrie* also set the stage for adults to come. Without exception, they are distanced, vague, or dangerous. Mr. Morton's job is to understand and aid students; but while he can lecture Billy deLois and Henry Trennant from rote memory, he is entirely incapable of grasping even the smallest truth about Carrie. Miss Desjardin approaches the level of sympathy, but her first response to Carrie's initial terror in the shower is an almost overwhelming desire to shake some sense into the girl. And King's deft touch of detailed description—Miss Desjardin is "slim, nonbreasted," wearing "a silver whistle, won in college archery competition" and white gym shorts—gives her a mythic Diana-like aura; she is somehow not really a functional part of Carrie's life, but as distanced as the classical goddess Diana, forever chaste and untouched.

More central, perhaps, is King's portrait of Carrie's mother. Herself an outsider and the victim of lifelong terror stemming from emotional instability, Margaret White (her name means "pearl," an ironic counterpart to her internal and external darkness) stands at the head of a long line of parents whose sole purpose becomes to destroy their own children . . . literally as well as figuratively. Margaret White's religious fanaticism, John Hargensen's obnoxious power-plays (ultimately as destructive to his own daughter as they are to Carrie), Jack Torrance's madness, Donna Trenton's numbing fears of life itself, Regina Cunningham's narrow vision of who her son is—again and again King will return to the motif of the destructive parent, archetypally represented in the single figure of Margaret White.

And finally, there is the monster. In *Carrie,* as in several other of King's novels, including *The Dead Zone, Firestarter,* and more recently *The Dark Half,* the monster is part of the central character. But whether King works with potentially destructive psychic powers, or with the sudden intrusion of the uncanny into an ordered society, as in *Cycle of the Werewolf,* or with a truly mythic level of evil and darkness, as in *The Stand* and the *Dark Tower* stories, King's monsters are dynamic, vital, fascinating . . . and most often deadly. In fact, of course, his monsters are the element in his fiction that nonreaders and casual readers first pick up on; *Carrie* is, after all, "just" a novel about a girl who can move things with her mind, start fires at will, and generally destroy an entire town. To read *Carrie* at only that level, however, is to miss King's trenchant criticism of American life: home and family as threatening rather than nurturing, friendship as distorted social status, education as horror that ignores essential elements of becoming both mature and human. In *Carrie* as in almost every other King novel, the "monster" either stands for or is subsumed within the greater "monsters" of contemporary life—cancer, brain tumors, and other wasting diseases; fanaticism of any sort that leads to self-destructive and socially destructive actions; self-centered materialism that manifests itself in social and political programs designed to benefit the few at the expense of the many, and so on.

As King's first public statement of what he intends to do in his novels, then, *Carrie* provides readers not only with a strong story in its own right, but also with a paradigm by which to read, assess, and enjoy most of what King will subsequently write. In fact, the first page of the novel provides an unmistakable key to understanding King's techniques.

Carrie is a dual novel, as are most of King's novels with the possible exception of clear fantasies such as *The Eyes of the Dragon* or complex multigeneric works such as the mythic-epic-Western-action/adventure-thriller-horror-science-fictional tales that make up the *Dark Tower* saga to date. *Carrie* re-creates the "real," using King's trademark techniques of meticulous observation, careful detail, and incorporation of name brands to create the illusion that the world being presented is truly the reader's own. *Carrie* emphasizes this almost immediately, when the initial news item about odd events in Chamberlain, Maine, begins with the phrase, "It was reliably reported . . . that." From here on, King's stories will be invariably "reliably reported"—worded, structured, and developed in ways that convince readers that what occurs is in some important senses plausible, if not possible. In *Carrie,* King constantly interrupts his own fantastic tale with bits and pieces from "documented" sources, counterpointing one narrative with what is in effect a second, sometimes contradictory one. As soon as the reader is confronted with an incontrovertibly paranormal event, King follows up with an excerpt from a scholarly study, an eyewitness account, or a popular article that sets the event into the context of a rational, logical, scientifically verifiable world. The fact that King incorporated much of the documentary apparatus in order to bring his terse story up to novel length is largely irrelevant; it merely makes obvious what King had intended all along, that Carrie's story has to be judged against the "realities" his readers know, understand, and expect.

And yet . . . and yet in the next paragraph King identifies the second elemental source of his storytelling power: his consistent penetration into the "subconscious level where savage things grow." This phrase is central to *Carrie* and to the novels and stories that will follow. Aware of his reputation as "horrormeister," "shockmeister" (some critics might respell that *schlockmeister*), and purveyor of thrills, chills, and shudders, King lives up to expectations here and elsewhere. He sets out to create horror; failing that, he is willing to work for terror; and if all else fails, there is always the physiological disgust of the "gross out." Against the crispness of a "real" world, he juxtaposes the dark places that lie beneath the intellect, beneath reason and logic, beneath coherence and motivation and probability—these are the areas King has taken for his own and begins to map in *Carrie.*

30

'Salem's Lot

(1975)

'Salem's Lot stands today as one of the finest treatments of the traditional vampire since Bram Stoker's *Dracula* (1897) and one of the last serious treatments of the mythos surrounding the vampire that had developed over the course of the preceding century. In a period when vampire lore was already moving from source of horror to fodder for parody, and when most conventional vampire stories looked to the past not only for inspiration but also for settings and characters, *'Salem's Lot* infuses vitality into a tired tradition while simultaneously attempting to re-create in a contemporary American idiom the atmosphere of evil that characterizes Stoker's *Dracula*. Just as Stoker's tale of the walking undead was set in then-contemporary late Victorian England, so King's tale unfolds in a small New England American community, at once typical and unique. Yet even here there are the analogues to Stoker's massive and intimidating castle of Count Dracula and his shadowy Carfax Abbey—looming above a typical American town stands the Marsten House, King's symbol throughout the story for the degenerating, enervating, and ultimately terrifying effects of evil unleashed (foreshadowing other of King's archetypal "Bad Places," including the Overlook Hotel in *The Shining*, the Mansion on Dutch Hill in *The Wastelands*).

Similarly, just as Stoker's tale depends for its effect upon fragmentation of the small group of people dedicated to fighting the incursive evil of Dracula (the story is in fact told in letters and journal entries, and far too often one or more characters miss crucial pieces of information that leads to further complications and ultimately death), so King's story depends ultimately for its effect on fragmentation and isolation. Neighbors do not speak to neighbors, except on the surface level of gossip. Parents prove remarkably incapable of protecting their children, while in several other cases child-victims actively prey on their parents (both recurring symbolic motifs throughout King's fictions). The dividing line between adult's world and child's world is clear and decisive, and only those few characters capable of believing like children and accepting adult responsibility for their actions survive. To this extent, *'Salem's Lot*, then, is an ambitious project—an updating of, a transformation of, and an application to King's own world of the themes, images, and motifs codified by Bram Stoker three quarters of a century before.

To understand King's mastery of materials, his ability to make the incursion of the supernatural into a rational world seem not only possible but plausible, is to penetrate to the center of 'Salem's Lot. Following Stoker's artistic lead, King does not suddenly thrust the fact of vampire upon his readers. Even though the opening chapters suggest something seriously wrong back home in Jerusalem's Lot, and Ben Mears's initial experiences in the Lot confirm that there is mystery aplenty to be found there, King carefully allows the readers at first to assume a "rational" horror—after all, Hubie Marsten's sexual and psychological aberrations are frightening enough to compete with the most sensational of today's newspaper headlines; and the petty grievances and grudges of character after character give the Lot a distinctly unhealthy air.

But at the crucial moment, when Barlow manifests himself for the first time and takes a victim, the reader's sense of appropriateness is total. Peter Straub—a perceptive reader and an equally perceptive writer of horror fiction in his own right—comments in "Meeting Stevie" on his own sense of startlement: "My God! I thought: a vampire! Nearly everything about this moment took my breath away . . ." (Fear Itself).

Straub's shock is indeed justified. King's revitalization of a tired set of conventions and clichés simultaneously culminated the progression of vampire lore following Stoker's masterpiece and made it virtually impossible for subsequent writers merely to re-create the vampire. In the two decades since 'Salem's Lot appeared, vampire tales have been forced to take one of three directions.

First, if writers choose simply to follow Stoker's lead and imitate his traditions, they are forced to write in the shadow of 'Salem's Lot, tacitly acknowledging King's artistry. The results are the eminently forgettable volumes with glossy black and red covers that haunt the paperback shelves for a month or so before disappearing forever . . . to say nothing of the two largely unsuccessful attempts at transforming the magic of 'Salem's Lot to film.

Second, they may choose to parody the entire tradition (generally a strong indication that a literary tradition has reached its apex and can move no further in the directions it has followed—much as Milton's summation of epic tradition in Paradise Lost is followed by the mock-epic and mock-heroic poems of Dryden, Pope, Byron, and others, but not by a single serious successful attempt at verse epic in the original sense). Stan Dragoti's 1979 film Love at First Bite shows how successfully the most horrifying vampiric images and themes can be transformed into parody and humor.

King signs *'Salem's Lot* at a Maine bookstore.

And third, they may attempt to restructure the entire tradition, to jettison what in the hands of lesser artists remain tired clichés and exhausted conventions and make of the vampire something unique to their own time and place. One measure of King's achievement in *'Salem's Lot,* in fact, is to note the extent to which the major horror writers of the past two decades have *avoided* working within the traditional framework of vampire lore. In almost every instance, King's mastery of the motifs that constitute vampire fictions seems implicitly to underpin the radical re-imagining of the tradition. Consider such examples as:

- F. Paul Wilson's startlingly inventive and striking masterpiece, *The Keep* (1981), in which traditional vampire materials are used to misdirect both characters and readers, disguising the face so that what seems to be a vampire story is in reality a tale of cosmic powers on the scale of Lovecraftian Great Old Ones;

- Whitley Strieber's *The Hunger* (1981), which creates essentially science-fictional rather than horror vampires, with the vampire/lamia historically, psychologically, and genetically a separate species from human, coexisting with humans throughout history, and capable of transforming humans through blood transfusions;

- S. P. Somtow's *Vampire Junction* (1984), with its public, rock-star vampire, making explicit the connections between the symbolic vampire of literature and quasi-vampiric nature of the rock phenomenon at its most extreme, to create what Edward Bryant recognized as "the first ambitious attempt at post-King dark fantasy";

- Robert McCammon's *They Thirst* (1988), in which vampires literally take over Hollywood. McCammon's vision of a Los Angeles darkened by vampires until rescued—paradoxically—by the "Big One," the granddaddy of all earthquakes that Californians are taught to expect and to fear, is in some sense diametrically opposite of King's small-town, claustrophobic infestation; McCammon in fact says as much when he writes that he "wanted a vampire novel with a huge cast, set in a city where anything was possible." But at base their visions reflect their perceptions of modern society transformed into symbolic forms;

- Dan Simmon's ambitious *Carrion Comfort* (1989), which elevates the traditional bloodsuckers of lore to etiolated psychic vampires, linked to the horrors of Nazism and living off excesses of violence in contemporary American society;

- Brian Lumley's necroscope series, which features extraterrestrial SF/fantasy eroticized vampires engaged in power-plays that span the world;

- Anne Rice's multivolume *Vampire Lestat* series, with its lushly luxuriant, undisciplined eroticism, its covert sexuality disguised as traditional vampire imagery, and its seemingly never-ending supply of new vampires to be resurrected, new stories-within-stories-within-stories to be told. With Rice, the vampire has moved as far from King's careful, controlled treatment of a recognized subgenre as possible; in the *Lestat* novels, the symbolic value of the vampire becomes almost lost as she concentrates exclusively on the vampire's worldview, with humanity diminished to little more than fodder.

That such novels as these were even published is due in no small part to King's demonstration that the vampire may be unDead but is not necessarily dead—at least not to the reading public entranced by King's blend of old and new, his transformation of everything familiar into something new and strange and awesome.

Following the quiet success of *Carrie, 'Salem's Lot* (which remains one of King's favorites among his works) demonstrates his ability to write complex, multileveled narratives; to create extraordinary but ultimately believable, memorable characters; to make full use of his increasingly symbolic landscape, eventually building from the rough blueprints for the Lot his own private landscape for horror in Castle Rock and its haunted environs; and to write fictions that, while making full use of horror motifs, nonetheless touch readers on levels transcending mere horror.

In this, his second published novel, King confirms his status as a master of contemporary dark fantasy.

31
The Shining
(1977)

The Shining is the second of King's "Big Three"—three novels completed during his first decade as a published novelist that to this day still largely define his role in American letters and that provide an internal standard against which almost all of his subsequent books have been judged: *'Salem's Lot, The Shining,* and *The Stand.* Each of them shows King stretching his talents and abilities, each shows him exploring different variations on fear, terror, and horror, and each of them shows his awareness of the importance of "place." *'Salem's Lot* has the Marsten House; *The Stand* has the more expansive polarity of Boulder, Colorado, and Las Vegas, Nevada (with minor foci along the way); but *The Shining* has arguably the most immediately recognized Bad Place in all of King's fiction, an image so intense that it nearly overwhelms everything else in the novel—the Overlook Hotel.

Based loosely on the physical layout of the Stanley Hotel in Estes Park (which hosted a King-oriented Horrorfest, during which one participant changed almost all of the room numbers to 217), the Overlook Hotel is a core of evil power trapping anyone it can, but especially those visitors who "shine," who have an uncanny ability to see beyond the visible and to speak their thoughts to others who "shine." Danny Torrance not only "shines," but shines more brightly than any visitor the hotel has known throughout its long, acquisitive, and merciless history. And the Overlook understands that the way to harvest Danny's talent is simple—through his father, Jack. Jack's struggle for sanity and Danny's for survival form the heart of *The Shining,* one of King's most definitive masterpieces.

A prevailing theme throughout most of King's work between *Carrie* in 1974 and *It* in 1986 is the breakdown of the family. Children often have no functional parents at all (for example, Mark Petrie in *'Salem's Lot* or Ray Garraty in *The Long Walk*), and when parents are present they are just as likely to be destructive as constructive—witness Margaret White in *Carrie* or Regina Cunningham in *Christine.* In *The Shining,* King amplifies on this theme until it becomes almost obsessive. Jack, Wendy, and Danny Torrance are not merely a family facing the triple threat of alcoholism, divorce, and possibly madness, they are such a family isolated from almost any other human contact by miles of mountain and forest and snow—and they are living inside a haunted hotel that wants nothing more than to destroy all three of them. King's careful treatment of Jack's disintegration, of Wendy's gradual awareness of their plight, and of Danny's incremental terror as the hotel reveals itself more and more directly, generates an energy and movement unmatched in any of his other novels. From the first scene through the last, the story moves inexorably to its devastating conclusion, and nothing Jack, Wendy, or Danny can do will stop the Overlook from altering their lives forever.

The Shining also represents one of King's few narrative excursions beyond New England. To this extent, his story of greed, moral corruption, and haunting fear represents a transfer of the darker elements of King's New England—and Hawthorne's, and Poe's, and Lovecraft's—to the newly opened West. King amplifies this sense of transplanted literary heritage with multiple allusions to mainstream writers (Frank Norris, Shirley Jackson, and others), horror writers (it is almost impossible to read the novel without recalling again and again Poe's "The Mask of the Red Death," or missing offhand allusions to Ray Bradbury), modern dramatists (the novel is structured like a five-act play, with its own prologue in the separately published original introduction, "Before the Play"), and others. In fact, *The Shining* is one of King's most teachable novels simply because in it he consciously incorporates so much of his own reading background, while at the same time using those references to create unique sequences of symbolic images. *The Shining* functions throughout on several levels—literal, symbolic, metaphorical—often with characters themselves pointing out the connections the readers should be making, as in Jack Torrance's elaborate meditations on the meaning of wasps. The novel provides a casebook example of literary nurturing, owing much of its power to King's articulate manipulation of others' words and images in the process of creating his own. This is not to suggest that *The Shining* is limited by its literary connections; on the contrary, here King demonstrates an unusual skill in controlling outside references, in matching his style to meet the needs both of his story and of his literary texture.

In addition, because *The Shining* has a relatively limited cast of characters (for a King novel, at least) and such an intensely focused setting, it allows King to examine new depths of characterization and of image. Hallorann, for example, rapidly and smoothly emerges from the backdrop, giving Danny his first true understanding of "the shine" and setting up key actions realized in the final pages of the novel; and not coincidentally, he will play a role in another novel almost a decade later, King's *It*. But what are most memorable about *The Shin-*

ing, perhaps, are its images: The mysterious word "Redrum." Danny's dream-vision friend, Tony. The hedge animals coming to life (replaced in Kubrick's film version with a maze that became almost as powerful an image as the novel's original one). The blood-filled clockwork in the main ballroom. The concrete rings in the snow-filled playground. Jack Torrance in the empty bar. The Presidential Suite, its walls stained with brain matter, its window exploding with the force of the Overlook's destruction. The mantalike shadow that may or may not have escaped from the final flames to being its infestation elsewhere.

Memorable because evil (at least in the earlier King novels) never truly dies.

One final note. Stanley Kubrick's reimagining of the novel, while shifting emphasis from the hotel's inherent evil to Jack's incipient madness, nevertheless helped in establishing King's name recognition. Released in 1980, shortly after Brian de Palma's convincing *Carrie* (1976) and Richard Kobritz and Tobe Hooper's notably less successful television miniseries *'Salem's Lot* (1979), *The Shining* demonstrated that even King's longer, more complex novels could be brought to the screen. It also began a flood of film versions of King properties that range from the ridiculous (*Children of the Corn,* with its unforgettable line, "Outlander, we have your woman!") to the sublime (Rob Reiner's superlative *Stand by Me*) and continues well into the mid-1990s.

32
Rage
(1977)

King's fourth published novel represents one of his earliest attempts at full-length narrative. One of five novel manuscripts completed before King wrote *Carrie, Rage* was begun in 1966 under the title *Getting It On,* when King was a senior in high school. Left unfinished for several years, it was completed in 1971 and published six years later when, as King says in the introduction to *The Bachman Books,* it "occurred to [him] that [he] ought to publish *Getting It On* . . . which Doubleday *almost* published two years before they published *Carrie.*"

Had the novel been published under King's name in 1977, following the increasing maturity and complexity of *Carrie, 'Salem's Lot,* and *The Shining,* it might well have been seen as a disappointment by his growing numbers of fans—by March 1977, all three novels had appeared on the best-seller lists, with *The Shining* marking King's hardcover debut. It seems unlikely that at that time even the coattails of King's name would have been sufficient to propel *Rage* to best-seller status; a solid work, it is also far more restricted in scope, in characterization, in theme, and in achievement than the first three "King" novels, as is to be expected from what is essentially juvenilia.

As a "Richard Bachman" novel, however, *Rage* was forced to make its own way, and until King's public acknowledgment of his pseudonym in February 1985 and the near hysteria that erupted among segments of King's reading public, the novel was not subjected to comparison to King's later, more sophisticated works. That is perhaps as it should be. The Bachman novels are, in general, unlike most of the works published under King's own name—tauter in structure, less dependent upon external horrors, more closely connected to mainstream fiction . . . or at least the illusion of "reality" propounded by mainstream fiction.

Rage is an extended study in adolescent *angst,* beginning with its first-person killer/protagonist, Charlie Dekker, and spreading like an infection throughout the high school class he holds hostage. The action is direct and brutal: Dekker meets with the principal for disciplinary action after Dekker nearly killed the shop teacher. He is expelled and told to leave school immediately. He stops at his locker, takes out a pistol, returns to class, shoots the teacher and intimidates the students until it is too late for them to escape. For the next several hours, he invites them to "get it on" with him—to examine their own lives and motives, their frustrations and fears. After systematically making fools of school and police officials, Charlie lets the class go and fakes the police into shooting him.

Oh, and along the way, he just as systematically destroys the mind of the one student who represents the adults' idealized view of normal childhood, and does so with the active aid of everyone else in the class.

The novel is not based on action, as King himself recognizes, but on psychology and penetration, primarily into the illusions held by adults about their roles in parenting and educating children, and the illusions held by children about their roles as subordinates to their parents. By placing his story of childhood memories revisited, examined, and finally exorcised (by some of the students, at least) among a classroom full of high school seniors about to be thrust into adult responsibility whether they like it or not, King provides an ideal fulcrum for assessing the deficiencies of parenting and socialization. Charlie Dekker is not the only member of the class tottering on the edge of sanity, and he is not the only one to tip the balance during the course of the novel.

There are weaknesses in the novel. It is preachy. It presupposes certain 1960s Freudian truisms that are less rigidly accepted today. It reduces adults to hollow, posturing fools incapable of dealing with Charlie's manic cleverness. It breaks its own narrative mode at the conclusion with the intrusion of court documents, memos, and letters of the same sort that strengthened *Carrie;* here they seem almost anticlimactic. The first-person narrative places a greater burden on Charlie Dekker than he is able to bear, since at times he seems more abstract image of rebellious teen than concrete person.

On the other hand, there are also strengths, many paradoxically growing out of the weaknesses. Charlie's obsession with his own interior processes gives him the momentary authority to set the entire class-sized encounter session in progress and to draw the darkest secrets from each of his classmates. And more than the horror of Charlie's murders, more than the terror of being in a locked classroom with a killer, more than watching the adult world stand by, bumbling and helpless, those secrets define the purging effects of "getting it on" for characters willing to reach inside, reveal the darkness, and accept it.

Compared with *It, The Stand,* or *The Shining, Rage* is certainly a weaker novel and a lesser achievement. On its own terms, however, with its narrowly defined characters, perhaps the most limited time span of any King novel or story, strictly focused themes and development, and idiosyncratic narrative voice, it nevertheless manages to hold its own as a document of a past time and as a novel examining ongoing human crises and resolutions.

33

The Stand

Following closely upon King's best-selling performances with *Carrie, 'Salem's Lot,* and *The Shining,* as well as Brian de Palma's film version of *Carrie* (1976), the 1978 appearance of *The Stand* confirmed King's preeminent position among the ranks of contemporary horror writers. His most ambitious novel to that point, even with substantial portions deleted before publication, *The Stand* provided a backdrop for the full array of King's talents in characterization, plotting, theme, and development.

An extension far beyond an earlier story called "Night Surf" (first published in *Cavalier,* 1974), *The Stand* is a tale of worldwide apocalypse caused by the accidental release of a superflu virus that kills most of the world's population. Then, when the survivors have begun adjusting to the realities of life *as* survivors, they are thrust into a far more complex, ultimately more frightening and paradoxically meaningful struggle between the elemental forces of the White and the Dark. Each individual must choose sides in the oncoming struggle for supremacy, climaxing in the detonation of an atomic warhead—precisely the end-of-the-world scenario envisioned by the military minds who created the superflu precisely to forestall such an event.

At well over eight hundred pages in the Doubleday hardcover edition, *The Stand* allows King the leeway to develop his ideas, in many cases in intricate details. Minor characters take on almost as much life as major ones. And the major characters in turn number among King's most memorable creations: Stu Redman, as solid and stable as the earth itself; Frannie Goldsmith, who, like a goldsmith creating beauty out of precious metals, will bear one of the first children in the new world the superflu and the Dark Man have created; Abagail Freemantle, with her evocatively symbolic, almost biblically intense surname; Harold Lauder and Nadine Cross, whose names also provide important hints as to their characters and their roles; Trashcan man, with his obsession with fire that inadvertently triggers the destruction of this round of the Dark Man's warfare against the Light; Tom Cullen, whose mental deficiencies make him a perfect foil to the Dark Man's intricate scheming; and the mysterious and threatening Randall Flagg, the Dark Man himself.

As early as 1969 King had begun working on his vision of a mysterious dark man, an embodiment of evil who comes and goes at will, leaving disruption and turmoil in his wake. In the same issue of UMO's student magazine, *Ubris,* that contained "Stud City" (later incorporated into *The Body*), King published a short poem called simply "The Dark Man." The figure in that poem may become one of the most important icons in assessing King's fictions, since in various guises and under various names (although frequently using the initials "RF") this quasi-mythic figure appears in novels as apparently disparate as *The Stand* (with an even more heightened role in the 1990 unexpurgated edition), the three volumes to date of the *Dark Tower* series, *The Eyes of the Dragon, The Talisman,* and *Needful Things. The Stand,* then, becomes important not merely as one of King's acknowledged masterpieces and one of the handful of postapocalypse novels with the potential of becoming an American classic, but also as the first full-scale introduction of a figure that will be more fully developed in subsequent works, and that links a novel as close to mainstream fiction as *The Stand* with the overt children's fantasy of *The Eyes of the Dragon,* the epic quest of the *Dark Tower* novels, and the moral allegory of *Needful Things.* Through Randall Flagg, *The Stand* becomes a cornerstone for what seems to be developing as a cosmic vision on the scale of Lovecraft's Great Old Ones and their accompanying mythos, but here embodying a tighter narrative focus and ultimately a more definitive moral base. Randall Flagg, in all of his guises, represents the Dark—against him are arrayed the various forces of the Light, beginning with Mother Abagail and continuing on to include Roland of Gilead, Jack Sawyer, the rather mundane Alan Pangborn, and others. Taken as a whole, the Dark Man stories suggest a universe interlinked through alternate worlds and alternate realities, in which elemental good and evil are locked in perpetual struggle.

To place *The Stand* thus in the context of a larger body of interrelated works is not to diminish its impact as a story. Although long, it is one of the three or four best novels to read for an introduction to King's style, techniques, and sheer storytelling ability. Its cast of characters is enormous, as befits a work about the end of things and about new beginnings. Unusual for a King novel, its settings range from New England to Los Angeles, with multiple stops at key places throughout the Midwest, finally focusing on Boulder, Colorado (where King lived for a short time in the mid-1970s), and Las Vegas, Nevada.

Its genre is equally all-inclusive. The story begins as a straightforward science-fictional extrapolation: what if there were a superflu that destroyed almost every human alive (along with most of the larger land mammals)? How would the survivors deal with such pragmatic questions as what to do with the bodies, how to re-create an orderly society, how to bear up under almost unimaginable burdens of guilt, loneliness, and despair? Within a few chapters, however, King adroitly shifts genres, as the survivors begin dreaming true dreams and feeling the call of the Dark or the Light. He moves almost seamlessly from SF into high fantasy, with theological, moral, allegorical, and philosophical overtones that highlight even more the commonplace personalities and actions of his characters as they struggle against nearly insuperable odds. As the dreams and visions intensify, so do biblical allusions—and suddenly the reader discovers that the novel had become an apocalyptic vision dealing with the End of Things and the physical revelation of Evil. Without relying on elevated tone, self-consciously heroic personages, or other traditional elements of epic, *The Stand* nevertheless takes on epic qualities of breadth and scope, magnitude and significance (again amplified in the restored 1990 edition).

To support such an ambitious undertaking, King builds on the literature of quest-epic, apocalypse, high fantasy, and horror. He amplifies his already expansive vision with specific references to Herman Melville's *Moby-Dick*; H. P. Lovecraft's mythos of the Great Old Ones; John Milton's epic *Paradise Lost* (especially through oxymorons such as "dark life and hideous good cheer"); J. R. R. Tolkien's *The Lord of the Rings*; H. G. Wells's end-of-the-world nightmare, *The Time Machine*; George Orwell's classic tale of the bureaucratic Dark regime, *1984*; Bram Stoker's archetypal conflict between good and evil, *Dracula*; Edgar Allan Poe's "The Raven," as well as his tales of madness and mystery; William Golding's allegorical apocalypse, *The Lord of the Flies;* Richard Adams's equally allegorical beast-fable, *Watership Down;* and others. Along the way, King invites into his novel W. B. Yeats, Robert Frost, Ernest Hemingway, William Faulkner, William Shakespeare, Bob Dylan, "The Who," Cary Grant, and *Charlotte's Web,* as well as a handful of his own novels and stories. The result is a richly embroidered tapestry that is simultaneously an extraordinary story on its own merits and a perceptive anatomy of late-twentieth-century, technologically-oriented, morally confused American society on the brink of destroying itself.

In many ways, *The Stand* marks the end of the first phase of King's development as a novelist. Ambitious, long, complex, multileveled, it is the culmination of King's increasingly wide scope, moving from *Carrie* through *'Salem's Lot* to *The Shining*. The sequence of novels following *The Stand* will be more tightly focused on individuals, on specific suggestions of horror or the supernatural: *The Dark Zone, Firestarter, Cujo, Christine,* and *Pet Sematary.* Only with *The Eyes of the Dragon* and *The Talisman* (both 1984) and the continuing episodes of the *Dark Tower,* will King return to such a huge canvas and resume tracing the movements of the Dark Man through worlds and times.

34

Night Shift

(1978)

Night Shift is among the few books King has published that have not enjoyed a stint on the hardcover best-seller lists. Missing the lists is not unusual for a collection of short fiction, which typically do not sell as well as individual novels. On the other hand, the paperback edition of *Night Shift* did appear on the lists for thirteen weeks following its release in February 1979, an achievement that foreshadowed the remarkable success of King's subsequent short-story collections—*Different Seasons* appeared on both hardcover and paperback lists in 1983; and *Skeleton Crew* not only appeared on both but was the number-one hardcover best-seller for nine consecutive weeks and the number one best-selling paperback for seven (it remained on the hardcover lists for twenty-two weeks more, incidentally, and on the paperback lists for an additional month).

The success of these and subsequent collections of King's short fiction is due in part to the strength of *Night Shift*. This first selection of twenty stories whetted his readers' appetites for more and demonstrated at the same time King's virtuosity in handling a wide range of subjects, styles, and types. In addition, many of the stories included are among his best known, in part because the collection has provided a rich vein of film possibilities that has been assiduously mined over the past two decades. Of the twenty tales, half have appeared as films, television episodes, and videocassette presentations, including "Graveyard Shift" (a stronger story than the film version by far), "The Mangler," "The Boogeyman" (a student film, one of the earliest attempts at filming King), "Trucks" (the source for King's directorial debut, *Maximum Overdrive*), "Sometimes They Come Back," "The Ledge," "The Lawnmower Man" (although the only connections between the resulting film and King's story are the title and the fact that someone mows a lawn somewhere), "Quitters, Inc.," "Children of the Corn" (two film versions tried to capture the essence of this one, both unsuccessfully), and "The Woman in the Room," which remains one of the most powerful film adaptations of a King property to date.

The contents of *Night Shift* provide a solid introduction to many of King's themes, images, and interests during the years from 1970 through 1976, when a number of the stories originally appeared in *Cavalier, Penthouse,* and *Gallery,* which in spite of the focus of their pictorial spreads, were among the few markets that paid well for horror fiction. Other stories appeared in *Maine* and *Cosmopolitan.* Among the tales are several continuations of earlier novels, or early sketches for motifs that would be important in later works, such as "Jerusalem's Lot," a mood-piece meditation (one of the last written, in fact, among the tales in the collection) that provides historical backgrounds for King's vampire novel, *'Salem's Lot,* revisited later in the collection in the penultimate story, "One for the Road." "Night Surf" provides a compressed view of one moment in the tapestry of *The Stand;* and "The Mangler" takes place in the Blue Ribbon Laundry, a detail that links this story, King's *Carrie,* Richard Bachman's *Roadwork,* and others. "The Boogeyman" develops the monster-in-the-closet motif that King will later build into *Cujo* in transforming that novel from a "Bachman" to a "King"—as well as touching on one of the oldest fears of childhood, the shadowy thing that lies just out of our vision

On a more allusive front, "Graveyard Shift" and "Gray Matter" evoke King's reading of Lovecraft and Poe, putting new spins on old story-types and demonstrating that modern readers may still be attracted to older forms of horror. (Unfortunately, the film version of "Graveyard Shift," while well advertised and eagerly anticipated before its Halloween release, was among the weaker adaptations of a King story, overly long and ultimately more tedious than terrifying.)

Just as it glances at the past, *Night Shift* also considers the present and the future as sources for horror. "I Am the Doorway," along with "Beachworld" from *Skeleton Crew,* represents one of King's few excursions into "mainstream" science fiction, although even here elements of horror emerge (literally) to transform both the story and its genre. "Battleground" and "Trucks" similarly tackle an area of horror particularly applicable to the twentieth century, the technological horror of machines rising against their makers, based fundamentally on but far transcending what some consider the first true work of science fiction *and* of horror, Mary Shelley's *Frankenstein.*

"Strawberry Spring" moves the reader to an internal, psychological landscape, with the story of a serial murderer's gradual discovery of his own madness. King's handling of the subject in *Night Shift* is particularly interesting since it radically revises a story King first published in the UMO literary magazine, *Ubris,* in 1968. The transformation of the original from a prose tone-poem to a fully developed narrative of discovery and horror illustrates King's own transition from neophyte to master in his chosen genre (for a fuller discussion of the changes, see Collings and Engebretson, *The Shorter Works of Stephen King*). King's use of myth as source for internal and external landscapes is equally evident in "The Lawnmower Man," which remains one of his more evocative tales.

"The Ledge," "Quitters, Inc.," "I Know What You Need," and "The Man Who Loves Flowers" are interesting in part for their strong characterization of individuals caught in circumstances for which no previous experiences could quite prepare them. Each of the stories touches as well upon key elements in contemporary life—isolation, frustration, obsession, fear of violence.

The capstone of *Night Shift* is arguably its strongest story (just as "The Reach" will bring *Skeleton Crew* to an emotional climax). "The Woman in the Room" is partly autobiographical, fictionalizing the death of King's mother. A story without any monsters or supernatural intrusions into everyday life (except, appropriately enough, as metaphors—images of death and decay), it is nonetheless a chilling story about life and death and about the choices that inevitably link the two. It is finely crafted, each word working toward a final understated theme, never working too obviously on the readers' emotions yet moving them nevertheless with its starkness and simplicity. "The Woman in the Room" is an appropriate conclusion for *Night Shift,* a collection of stories about darkness and fear and ultimate transformations.

Anyone involved with King scholarship or criticism is invariably asked two questions: "What is his best work?" and "If I haven't read anything by Stephen King, where should I start?"

Answers to either question are bound to include *The Dead Zone*. Because of the breadth his novels cover, it is almost impossible to isolate a single work as his "best," simply because a number of novels are superlatives, each in different ways. However, a consensus might include *'Salem's Lot, The Shining, The Stand* (oddly enough, both the 1978 and the 1990 versions could legitimately be listed), *It,* perhaps the cumulative *Dark Tower* novels . . . and *The Dead Zone.* As to where to start if one has never read a King novel, *The Dead Zone* comes almost immediately to mind as one of King's most restrained and controlled, most nearly mainstream, and least "horrific" novels, especially among those published during his first decade as a writer.

Although dated by period references to the mid-1970s, *The Dead Zone* nevertheless reads well, even for 1990s audiences. Unlike many of King's other works (and even unlike the Bachman novels), this story of prescience and its devastating consequences on one individual and those nearest to him does not focus on a strong central character, an almost superhuman "hero" who, like Roland of Gilead, for example, clearly differs from the common run of humanity. King deftly defines his protagonist with his name—Johnny Smith. It is an ordinary name, a literary "Everyman" kind of name that urges readers to see Smith less as exception than as type. And in almost every respect, Johnny Smith *is* an ordinary man: he has goals and dreams, he loves and hopes, he must confront problems of both life and death.

Of course, since he is in fact the central character in a King novel, he is *not* quite that ordinary. There are the dual facts of his four-year-long coma and his emergent "dead zone," a place in his mind that has lost certain of its normal functions but gained frightening new ones. As the novel progresses, King systematically places his protagonist in contexts that require more and more of him, that force him to explore the shadowy areas of his dead zone—a process that leads finally to Johnny Smith's decision to sacrifice his life to save a nation, perhaps a world. And in the end, Johnny Smith, whose name makes him an "Everyman," turns out in fact to be heroic in ways not even he could have imagined.

Bearing up under the burden of an unusual talent/skill/curse forces Johnny Smith into becoming a public figure. King structures the novel around three episodes. First Johnny Smith must deal with the private and personal ramifications of the dead zone. His touch initially brings gratitude as he saves a woman's home from burning and reassures another woman that her son will recover from a dangerous surgery. Eventually, however, as his notoriety spreads, his touch becomes ambivalent—it brings answers, but not necessarily the answers the questioners want. In all other ways "normal," Johnny Smith becomes perceived as a monster for doing precisely what his questioners insist of him . . . and then for *not* performing on demand. King touches upon issues of public versus private, of responsibility versus self-protection, of individual versus society. Throughout, however, he never loses sight of Johnny Smith as a feeling, caring person, aware of his connections to humanity at large.

In the second section, Johnny Smith's wild-card talent becomes public. In order to save the life of a young student, he must assert his talent as a mode of knowing more valid than science, experience, and observation. He must force events to change, and in the process he again places himself in an ambivalent position. He is hailed as a savior by the parents whose children he kept alive; and excoriated as a monster by the segments of the same public he has served. In a moment of conscious irony, King even allows one of the children to accuse Johnny Smith of *causing* the disastrous fire by foreknowing it: "It's his fault, that guy there! He made it happen! He set it on fire by his mind, just like in that book *Carrie*. You murderer! Killer!" King knows full well the essential differences between Carrie White and Johnny Smith; but as will happen with so many of his cross-references to his earlier novels, the speaker sees only simplistic, surface similarities.

The third section moves the story to an overtly public level. Johnny Smith knows (along with the readers) that Greg Stilson is mad, that he is potentially dangerous, and that if he gets elected to the U.S. presidency he will perform some insane act that will plunge the world into warfare and devastation. At this point, King forces Johnny Smith to confront the ultimate responsibility his prescience implies. Again and again, Smith asks those around him a key question: If you could go back in time, knowing what you do now, and kill Hitler, would you? Johnny Smith's conviction that he must act, paralleling his discovery that the dead zone in his brain is in the process of killing him, propels the story to its logical and powerful climax, in which King adroitly allows his character to act on his knowledge in the only way possible . . . and still to avoid the stigma of murder. The novel's gentle, hauntingly ghostly conclusion returns Johnny Smith and his treacherous gift to the realm of the private; his final touch is reserved for the woman he loved.

Throughout, King preserves a sense of balance in treatment. Johnny Smith is a quiet, reserved character who merits a quiet, reserved novel—and for the most part, this is what King provides (this characterization is brilliantly captured in David Cronenberg's film version, with Christopher Walken capturing the essence both of character and of story). If one is looking for a starting place in "things King," *The Dead Zone* is indeed an ideal choice.

36
The Long Walk
(1979)

The Long Walk is among the earliest published examples of King's novel-writing talent, written during the school year 1966–67, when King was a freshman at the University of Maine at Orono. More controlled, perhaps, than *Rage,* and with a more complex cast of characters, *The Long Walk* also represents a long stride forward in King's novelistic techniques, including his control of tone, pacing, and mood as the story progresses from its almost lighthearted beginnings through a systematic and inevitable descent into darkness. As does each of the other Bachman novels, *The Long Walk* demonstrates a countdown to obsession and madness based on the simplest of narrative threads; in this case, in a near-future riff on Selective Service, King gives us a world in which each year one hundred young men around the age of eighteen start out from upstate Maine and walk south. The winner of the Long Walk will receive anything he wants for the rest of his life. The rules of the walk are simple: no interfering with another walker, no veering from the designated path . . . and no stopping.

Walkers who stop once are warned.

Walkers can receive three warnings.

Then they are shot . . . even if they are already dead from exhaustion, despair, heartbreak, or sheer physical breakdown.

The result is a novel that in an oddly positive way is as fatiguing to the readers as the Long Walk is to the boys walking. Readers are invited into the mind of Ray Garraty as he works through level after level of intellectual, physical, spiritual, and psychological engagement, testing the limits of human motivation, frustration, fear, loneliness, terror, exhaustion, and finally compassion, desperation, and the ultimate horror of madness. Since Garraty is from the outset the principal point-of-view character (as well as the local odds-on favorite to win the walk, being "Maine's Own"), there is little surprise at the ending. There is surprise, however, at how compelling and devastating that ending is, and how the young King manages to rivet readers' attention on the undeviating progress of a dwindling group of human scarecrows staggering raggedly, ever southward, toward Boston. Initially, time is carefully counted; Garraty's watch is consulted frequently, and miles and hours passed are central concerns for the walkers. As the book nears its end, however, time itself seems to warp; day and night become indistinguishably bleak. One boy's identity merges into that of another, and another; and the crowd becomes a single monstrous entity, a screaming throat surrounding Garraty and the pitiable handful who survive into the final pages.

There are, of course, brief flurries of action to break the ongoing stasis of the walk. One boy runs to the crowd to embrace a tauntingly beautiful girl—and for his sexual impetuosity earns three warnings and nearly loses his life. Another attacks the half-truck accompanying the walkers and is gutshot as a warning to the rest. Garraty himself almost dies when he receives his third warning as he reaches out desperately for his girlfriend's hand in the crowd. And so it goes. Walk. Talk. Walk more. Walk. And die.

Within this taut narrative scheme, however, King has exploited a mine of opportunity for characterization. Some of the walkers remain unchanged from their introductions to their deaths; even these minor figures, shadowy as they might be, show King polishing his hand at deft creation of strikingly individual characters, often within a sentence or two that describe habitual actions, clothing, language, movements. As does Garraty, readers may at times confuse the *names* of characters, but rarely their essences, their true nature. The handful of central walkers that form Garraty's unofficial company—Peter McVries, the closest Garraty comes to a friend among the walkers; the inscrutable and obnoxious Stebbins; Olson, Baker, and the others—open themselves even more completely as we see them walk, hear them talk about life and death and love and hope and emptiness.

The Long Walk is, in its own way, as preachy as *Rage*. It differs from the earlier novel, however, in that King carefully connects his long passages of internal monologue to the increasing dissociation from reality Garraty and the others experience, as every part of normal life and normal memory falls away leaving nothing but the exposed souls of the boys—children sacrificed (as so often in both the "Bachman" novels and the "King" novels) to the unfathomable and apparently insatiable needs of the adult world.

Central to the walk and hence to the story, but paradoxically missing through most of its length, is the Major, the leader in this future dystopia, who passes in and out of the walkers' consciousness, appearing in his military jeep and military clothing and military sunglasses to urge them on to greater effort. The father-figure that seems absent from every life touched on in the novel, he represents precisely the kind of rarely seen, never understood, shadowy authority that King pillories in *Rage* and *Christine* and *It* and elsewhere, his face "kind but unreadable behind the mirror sunglasses" (*Bachman Books*).

But even beyond him, there is the other figure, hinted at in the final pages of *The Long Walk* (and in a poem written at about the same time) and developed in *The Stand, The Eyes of the Dragon,* the *Dark Tower* series, and *Needful Things*—the dark figure, "up ahead, not far, beckoning . . . for him to come and walk, to come and play the game." And the game is insanity and death.

With the intrusion of that figure, we know that there can be no winner to *The Long Walk.* In an imaginary science-fictional world that is really *our* world stripped to its essential needs, without resorting to techno-jargon or high-tech surfaces, King compels readers on long walks that take them to the heart of living and dying . . . and one step beyond.

At the end, it is hard to forget the grim irony implicit in King's opening quotation from John Kennedy: "I would encourage every American to walk as often as possible. It's more than healthy; it's fun."

```
┌─────────────────────────────────────────┐
│ ┌─────────────────────────────────────┐ │
│ │                                     │ │
│ │                 37                  │ │
│ │            *Firestarter*            │ │
│ │              (1980)                 │ │
│ │                                     │ │
│ └─────────────────────────────────────┘ │
└─────────────────────────────────────────┘
```

Firestarter is a midrange King novel, certainly an interesting read, but representative neither of his strongest nor of his weakest works. It lacks the breadth of plot and setting that elevate earlier novels such as *The Shining* or *The Stand* to the level of masterworks and potential classics of contemporary American letters; and it equally lacks the cosmic scope of later works, including *It, The Talisman,* and *Insomnia,* that expand readers' horizons and expectations to something approaching epic intensity.

Like *The Dead Zone* and *Cujo,* which bracket it in order of publication, *Firestarter* focuses on a single individual and her struggle against a specific intrusion into her life. At the same time, those intrusions are less overtly supernatural and horror-oriented than vampires, haunted hotels, quests for the nexus of worlds, and centuries-old space-alien monsters that rise periodically to feed off the psychic energy and fear of children; at times, the horror rises more from King's mode of telling than from the story itself.

Also like *The Dead Zone* and *Cujo,* it seems more distinctly a product of its time than many of the other novels. Johnny Smith's story is linked inextricably to events in the late 1970s in that the political and social issues he faces seem unique to that decade; *Cujo* is likewise in part a critique of the single-minded consumerism developing during the same time. *Firestarter*—with its story of two young people undergoing scientific experimentation with drugs, and the unforeseen consequences of those experiments for themselves and for their only child—draws on an increasing paranoia about government manipulation of, control of, and interference in the lives of citizens growing out of the drug culture of the 1960s.

The Shop, represented by Cap Hollister and the amoral assassin Rainbird, appears here as a principal antagonist to Charlie McGee and her nascent talent as a firestarter. It is not accidental that *Firestarter* alludes to works such as Orwell's dystopic *1984,* with its "unpersons" and its absolute governmental control of all elements of each person's life, or to Franz Kafka's nightmare visions of surrealistic and unquestionable authority. Less horror than science fiction, with its central departure from consensus reality based on at least pseudoscientific premises, *Firestarter* moves closer than most of King's works to novels of direct social criticism, to mainstream attacks on the unbridled power of secret agencies, and to examinations of "realistic" characters in conflict.

With his typical flair for the telling detail, King peoples *Firestarter* with powerful figures, however, capable of lingering in the readers' imaginations. Charlie McGee and her increasingly impotent father, Andy; Irv and Norma Manders, who become surrogate grandparents for Charlie and provide a moral norm for the novel; Cap Hollister and his obsession for secrecy and power; and above all, the renegade Rainbird, with his equally strong obsession for understanding, controlling, and ultimately killing Charlie McGee—all work together to create a taut story of a child standing almost alone against an immense, unseen, virtually unnamed power that first created her and now sets out to destroy her. In the great genetic game of chance, she has been handed a wild-card talent; as Johnny Smith discovers, to use such a talent may at first open worlds of possibility, but eventually it becomes lethal. Throw into this narrative mix a persistent thread of anti-establishment fear that gradually shifts toward paranoia as the CIA and the FBI step in to support the Shop's terror tactics, and one has a reasonably clear sense of the novel. (In this respect, it is no accident that the final scene takes place in the offices of the countercultural *Rolling Stone* magazine.)

A straight-line narrative of the same sort as *The Dead Zone* and *Cujo*, *Firestarter* was an obvious choice for film adaptation. It became one of the spate of films released in 1983 and 1984: Lewis Teague's happy-ending *Cujo*, Cronenberg's superlative *Dead Zone*, John Carpenter's *Christine*, Fritz Kiersch's abortive *Children of the Corn*, Mark Lester's *Firestarter*, and Lewis Teague's *Cat's Eye*, from King's screenplay version of three short stories. While Lester's version, based on Stanley Mann's screenplay, is among the most literally faithful adaptations of a King story to film, it also illustrates a persistent difficulty in transferring King's words to visual images. In spite of a strong cast (including Art Carney, Martin Sheen, and George C. Scott) and enough pyrotechnics to destroy half a dozen CIA compounds, the film remains oddly static. Without the magic of King's words—his stylistic mannerisms, his brusque interruptions of narrative with parenthetical exclamation, and his storyteller's eye for the precise detail in the precise place—the images transferred to screen do not come fully alive.

38
Cujo
(1981)

Early in *Pet Sematary,* Judson Crandall explains to Louis Creed that keeping wild animals as pets is dangerous because there are "Lots of rabies in Maine now. There was a big old St. Bernard that went rabid downstate a couple of years ago and killed four people. That was a hell of a thing. Dog hadn't had his shots. If those foolish people had seen that dog had had its shots, it never would have happened." Crandall's words not only provide one of King's frequent cross-references to his earlier novels, but also pinpoint one of the reasons that *Cujo* is a disquieting novel, generally considered among King's weaker works, the sense that almost everything that happens results from foolishness or—worse—is simply accidental, including the death of Tad Trenton.

In King's stronger pieces, there is frequently an underlying current of purposefulness approaching tragedy. Characters make important decisions and then must accept the consequences of those decisions. The soil of the heart is stony, Crandall also says in *Pet Sematary,* and you must live with what you grow there. Ben Mears's decision to write about the Marsten House and follow its mystery to the horrifying end, Jack Torrance's decision to take the job as caretaker of the isolated Overlook Hotel, Arnie Cunningham's wholehearted submission to whatever force controls Christine—all of these are willful acts that the characters at some level embrace. The characters might not know the full truth when they chose, but the *act* of choosing allows King to tell their stories.

In *Cujo,* almost every key event seems accidental. Early in the novel Vic Trenton considers the element of chance in human affairs: "If a man is crossing a darkened room with a deep, open hole in the middle of it, and if he passes within inches of it, he doesn't need to know he almost fell in. There is no need for fear. Not if the lights are off." In *Cujo* the lights may be off most of the time, but nearly without exception characters simply fall into the holes they cannot see. Even more disquieting, those key choices that alter lives and lead to disruption and death do not seem weighty enough to warrant the devastation that results. Vic Trenton should have been more aware of Donna's need for fulfillment—but he is not particularly obsessed with success. His business is at a crisis point and he must be away from home; the fact that a malformulated dye in a breakfast cereal has put his livelihood in jeopardy is completely outside his control. Even beyond that, the formula that makes children seem to vomit blood is itself not only a small mistake, but a totally harmless one. Even more significantly, Donna Trenton's affair is less a matter of self-conscious decision making than of tumbling into a mistake, which she rectifies almost immediately. Even her decision to take the car out to the Camber farm for repairs is innocuous in itself.

Only in conjunction with Cujo's purely accidental rabies do any of these decisions combine to establish a framework for death, and although the novel tries to suggest from the opening pages that the forces at work are related to those that subverted Frank Dodd in *The Dead Zone,* the thrust of the novel paradoxically works against a supernatural explanation for events. Dogs get rabies. Adults have affairs. Business arrangements suddenly go sour. Cars stall at inopportune moments. And children die. If the catchphrase of the novel becomes "Nope, nothing wrong here," the story forces readers to add: "except perhaps life itself." What we perceive as evil may just be part of reality in a harsh world where otherwise good men have marital and sexual problems, where otherwise good mothers allow their frustrations to force them into unwise decisions, and where good dogs fall ill and turn into killers. The monster in the closet, about which Tad Trenton makes such an issue, is more strictly metaphorical in *Cujo* than in any of King's major horror novels. If there is a monster, it is an ambivalent one, formulated by passages of what become verbal (and hence, in the context of the story, false) horror—the monster is *asserted* by the language King uses, not by the internal logic of the narrative. And indeed, the final pages of *Cujo* reinforce the fact that while there may be terror and horror in the novel, both are ultimately explicable. After all, as the last page of the novel tells us, Cujo "had never wanted to kill anybody. He had been struck by something, possible destiny, or fate, or only a degenerative nerve disease called rabies."

King has noted that originally he conceived of *Thinner* as a "King" novel and *Cujo* as a "Bachman" novel. The overlay of horror added to *Cujo's* base narrative when he changed his mind is insufficient to create out of a tale of mainstream, real-life horror something supernatural, something on the order of a haunted hotel or a haunted car or a haunted town called Jerusalem's Lot. *Cujo* remains a "tweener," a novel captured between two opposing states of storytelling, and as a result, it is weakened.

39

Danse Macabre

(1981)

To date, *Danse Macabre* is King's only full-length foray into nonfiction, academic criticism, or scholarship. Although he has amassed enough wordage for several accumulations of criticism in the frequent (and frequently lengthy) introductions and afterwords to his novels and collections, as well as in reviews and interviews, his primary statements concerning horror as genre appear here. The result of a brief teaching stint at the University of Maine at Orono in 1978 and 1979, and based on his Themes in Supernatural Literature course, *Danse Macabre* is doubly valuable as an insider's history of horror in literature, film, and television over several decades, and as a guide to King's own personal vision within that genre.

Anyone associating the terms "critical," "academic," and "scholarly" with a book claiming to be the results of a series of university courses or a disquisition on the development of a literary genre will be pleasantly relieved to discover, early in *Danse Macabre,* that just because King is writing nonfiction he has not left behind the distinctive narrative voice that had already become his trademark. Although the book is a cogent and concise study of dark fantasy, it is also clearly from the mind and pen of Stephen King, replete with personal reminiscences that in turn set the stage for conclusions about the functions, nature, and purposes of horror.

Danse Macabre covers the field from the release of *Earth vs. the Flying Saucers* through John Carpenter's *Halloween* and David Lynch's *Eraserhead* (both released in 1978). Along the way King discusses key films and novels that contributed to the development of contemporary horror. As an added bonus, he includes alphabetical lists of one hundred films and one hundred novels particularly important to horror (giving title, director, and year of release). These lists, coupled with a full index, contribute to the book's value as a research tool. Within the text, he discusses such seminal writers as Peter Straub, Anne River Siddons, Shirley Jackson, Ira Levin, Jack Finney, Ray Bradbury, Richard Matheson, Ramsey Campbell, and James Herbert; and such films as Romero's *Night of the Living Dead,* and Don Siegel's and Philip Kaufman's versions of

Invasion of the Body Snatchers, on his list of the twenty scariest films ever. Many of the observations about these and other cultural artifacts are King's own; others are citations from academic and popular-culture critics that help bolster King's personal comments.

Besides films and novels, King examines television series, including *The Twilight Zone, Thriller,* and *The Outer Limits,* providing readers with a number of useful keys in understanding the frequent cinematic quality of King's stories. Many of his own narratives depend for their effects upon childhood memories of specific television episodes and filmic images. And, lest he be criticized for dealing exclusively with what have evolved as classics, he also tackles the long list of less successful ventures into television horror: Darren McGavin as the unforgettable (because so awful) *Kolchak, the Night Stalker* and Irwin Allen's *Voyage to the Bottom of the Sea.* Even the failures are notable in their ambitiousness; as King notes about the *Kolchak* series, "there is something childlike and unsophisticated in its very awfulness."

In the final chapters, King defines essential connections between the dark fantasy of page and stage and screen (silver or small), and the darker realism of the world around us . . . as mediated by the "dreamy eyes of [the] child" one perceives in a Ray Bradbury or a Jack Finney or an H. P. Lovecraft or a Harlan Ellison. For King—and presumably for the readers and fans who consume his words—horror is not merely a dance of death, a *danse macabre;* much less is it simplistic escapist literature to be enjoyed by the unsophisticated and the unlettered and then discarded. Instead, it is "at bottom a dance of dreams. It's a way of awakening the chld inside, who never dies but only sleeps ever more deeply. If the horror story is our rehearsal for death, then its strict moralities make it also a reaffirmation of life and good will and simple imagination—just one more pipeline to the infinite."

Perhaps more than any other single critical remark, King's own evaluations of his chosen genre in *Danse Macabre* provide its ultimate rationale and justification. Indirectly, his text concentrates on the strict morality of almost all of King's own tales, on their ultimate affirmations, and on their essential positioning, clearly on the side of the Light.

40
Roadwork
(1981)

Perhaps the best introduction to *Roadwork,* the third published Bachman novel, is King's own tag-quotation:

> I don't know why. You don't know why. Most likely God don't know why, either. It's just Government business, that's all. [Man-in-the-street interview concerning Vietnam circa 1967]

King's Barton George Dawes is trapped in the same conundrum as the man in the street. Dawes does not know why—why his son Charlie died of a brain tumor; why he and his wife had no more children; why the government decided to build a freeway extension that would destroy the home where Charlie died; why the roadwork would also destroy the Blue Ribbon Laundry where Dawes has worked his entire adult life; why he finds it impossible to look for a new home, even when the government has offered him more than fair market value for the old one; why his ties with his wife and to his marriage are slowly disintegrating; why his whole life, in fact, is disintegrating; why *he* is disintegrating.

There are no true answers to any of these questions, but Dawes's search for at least some illusion of understanding makes up most of *Roadwork,* arguably the closest to a strictly mainstream novel King would write until well into the 1990s and *Gerald's Game* and *Dolores Claiborne.* Here, however, King does not allow one specific social or political agenda to distort the coloring of his tale, as he will in *Gerald's Game;* instead he uses a complex of public issues central to the mid-1970s as periphery to his primary story of a man driven to obsession, insanity, and death by his inordinate need for answers. While there are horrors in *Roadwork,* they are the "real" horrors of gas shortages (whether genuine or artificially induced is irrelevant), small businesses being gobbled up by conglomerates for whom the "bottom line" is indeed the bottom line, increasing suburban isolation and alienation, disruption of social and family ties by devastating economic pressures, and always the specter of death by cancer, by accident, by suicide.

In *Roadwork,* King follows the same basic pattern as the other Bachman novels. His central character is thrust onto a road to obsession from which there is no deviating and no turning back. He understands that death or madness waits at the end but has no choice but to continue. The countdown to the final chapter, "January 20, 1974," continues as inexorably as Charlie Dekker's confrontation with the cops, as Ray Garraty's eternal Long Walk, as Ben Richard's rigged run, and as Billy Halleck's implacable weight loss (to say nothing of Roland of Gilead's quest for the Dark Tower, or the gravitation of seven children/adults to a hidden den in the sewers beneath the streets of Derry).

At the same time, there is a strong sense of King moving beyond the limits of his straight-line narrative. Literary allusions to Hemingway's Nick Adams stories surface at oddly disquieting moments and demonstrate King's awareness of and attempts to incorporate mainstream literature into his text. *Roadwork* also breaks with King's frequently transparent narrative voice as King suggests the tensions building in Dawes not only through the character's words and actions, but also through the narrative style itself. Virtually every sign, every written word noted by Dawes in the novel (and there are quite a few, from construction signs to digital clocks) is introduced with a minor variation on the static phrase "And it said:"—as if the acts of *saying* and of *meaning* are somehow alienated from each other and the fact that signs "say" must constantly be underscored in order to have some control over meaning and reality. The phrase becomes a mantra for Dawes, who seems to keep his tenuous hold on sanity by repeating habitual actions as frequently as King's narrator repeats "And it said: . . ."

The sense of tension building to an explosion point in a novel with the prosaic title *Roadwork* emphasizes King's achievement in creating his own unique sense of terror and horror without any fantastic or overtly supernatural elements. His consistent awareness of larger social and political themes that can be interwoven throughout his story and transformed into vehicles for modern horror is here highlighted, as are several of his equally consistent characters. We see the Italian-American mobster who, while not having anything approaching a heart of gold is nevertheless oddly attractive to and attracted by a wholly unlikely protagonist—a figure increasingly important in *Thinner* and transformed to threat in *The Drawing of the Three.* We also have the father-figure/son-figure relationship of Ben Mears and Mark Petrie in *'Salem's Lot,* and Roland and Jake in the *Dark Tower,* but here developed in the connections between Dawes's alter-ego George and the shadowy memory of his dead child, which transforms what should be a healthy exchange into one fraught with peril. We have the husband and wife divorced by insanity long before the courts can legally separate them, as in *The Shining.* And worse, at least from Dawes's point of view, we see the wife blooming in unexpected ways after she separates her identity from that of her husband's wife. Finally, we have a wash of minor characters whose sole purpose is to expose and heighten our awareness of Dawes's instability, yet who take on a vigor and an individuality that are one of the hallmarks of King's prose.

In the final analysis, *Roadwork* is weakened by being a one-note novel . . . and the pitch of that single note is undeviatingly hysterical. Dawes's inability to adapt to new contexts remains consistent throughout, and each of his incrementally more devastating confrontations with coworkers, employers, wife, friends, and finally civil authorities is essentially the same scene, emotionally and psychologically. Even so, however, *Roadwork* maintains a solidity of pacing and development, a sense of inevitability that even Dawes in his greatest extremity would have recognized . . . and perhaps admired.

41
The Running Man
(1982)

With the words "Minus 100 and Counting," King opens a novel that follows an inexorable countdown to the cataclysmic scene in the final chapter, "Minus Zero and Counting." The countdown motif provides continuity and structure to a novel that might otherwise fragment into separate episodes loosely linked by the presence of Ben Richards, King's protagonist. But the ever-present chapter titles, with their metronomic countdown, constantly remind us that the novel is a game show, that the hero is a contestant, and that the time on the clock is running out. And as with any successful game show, the task to be completed is designed to elicit maximum suspense as clock and participant move closer and closer to the final seconds.

King's story is, like those of the other "Bachman" novels, relatively uncomplicated. Ben Richards lives in a near-future America controlled by the Network. Public opinion is shaped by Free-Vee, now mandatory in every home (but it is still legal to turn it off occasionally). The dividing line between "haves" and "have-nots" is both economic and physical, with the lowest classes living in squalor in huge tracts of antiquated, disintegrating, filthy apartments, killed by the very air they breathe and the hazards of the few jobs available to them. They have no hope of decent jobs, decent conditions, decent lives, even decent deaths.

Except the Games.

In order to buy medicine for his dying child and to save his wife from a lifetime of prostitution that earns barely enough for black market food and ineffective medications, Richards volunteers for the Games and is selected as a contestant on "The Running Man." His task—to survive for as long as he can. If he is spotted before a month is up, he can be killed, and his killer will receive a cash prize from the Network. Worse, he is subjected to the humiliation of seeing his life and loves distorted on the Free-Vee until he becomes not simply a contestant but a despised public enemy to be hunted down and destroyed like a beast. He must film himself twice a day, both as evidence he is still alive and as fodder for the masses who seem to live only to watch the routine degradation of fellow human beings.

225

Richards runs. Through four key episodes, he runs: first, mindlessly holing up in a Boston YMCA before realizing that the hunters are already on his trail; then more cannily linking with an underground of fellow sufferers dedicated to breaking the Network's monopoly on information; then desperately taking a wealthy woman hostage, introducing her to the grim realities of life; and finally, aggressively taking the hunt back to the Network itself, hoping to destroy the entity that has so offhandedly manipulated and destroyed himself, his family, and his world.

The Running Man is King's major foray into strict science fiction, complete with an assumed jargon to indicate that as close as Ben Richards's world might be to ours, the two are nevertheless fundamentally different (the SF overlay in *The Long Walk* becomes less and less critical once the novel begins, and the SF elements in the *Dark Tower* saga are so intertwined with other genre patterns that Roland's quest really ceases to be science fiction in any precise sense). The genre allows him to develop a focused sequence of images, motifs, and themes while continuing the underlying pattern of *Rage, The Long Walk,* and *Roadwork.* Charlie Dekker balks at the oppression of parents, friends, and society, and decides to "get it on"; Ben Richards stands up to the pressures of the media, never accepting their attempts to humiliate him, increasingly able to counter their attempts at manipulating him. Ray Garraty walks; Ben Richards runs—but the results are virtually identical. Barton Dawes has lost his child and is in the process of losing his wife; in a very real sense, Ben Richards has already lost his family psychologically the moment he enters the Games building, and as a direct, tragic, and ironic result of his becoming the Running Man, he loses them physically as well.

King has noted that *The Running Man* was written in seventy-two hours over one weekend and later published with essentially no changes. The speed of composition might have led to some moments of excessive melodrama (the description of Richards's escape in the tunnel beneath the YMCA, for example) and some largely stereotypic characters (hip, rebellious, dialect-ridden, streetwise young blacks; an overweight, nerdy, white technical genius out of touch with realities of life; a monstrous mother whose life is her child and who destroys him as a consequence). But it also adds a sense of compression to the action itself. As in *The Long Walk,* the reader is never allowed to rest until the game is finished; the movement propels, impels, and compels without a break. The tensions might be physical or psychological, or emotional, but from "Minus 100 and Counting" the novel shows King's ability to control pacing, character, and story.

To date *The Running Man* is the only Bachman novel to be released as a film—and perhaps may remain so, especially in the case of *Thinner,* for which the weight-loss special effects would be so demanding as to verge on the impossible. In spite of what seems on the surface an obvious miscasting of Arnold Schwarzenegger as Ben Richards, and the happy-ever-after ending required by film audiences, it is surprising how much of the tone and feel of King's story remain. The massive rewrites that transformed surface events into essentially a new story altogether still do not destroy the sense of desperate motion that King works to portray in the novel. And for many readers coming to the novel *after* seeing the film, the persistent image of dingy backgrounds and high-tech, slick running costumes superimposed over King's words and story may lead to heightened involvement with *The Running Man*.

42
Creepshow
(1982)

In retrospect, 1982's *Creepshow* seems little more than a *jeu d'esprit,* a game of wit in reproducing a long-dead subgenre of horror. Certainly it is the only comic book format collection King has published, and in his choice of stories and treatments, he is clearly attempting to recapture the feel of the 1950s EC comic books—specifically, the level of horror that he refers to in *Danse Macabre* as the "gross-out." Each of the five stories in *Creepshow* might ultimately reach the higher level, what King refers to as a "dance—a moving, rhythmic search. And what it's looking for is the place where you, the viewer or the reader, live at your most primitive levels." But even if they do not attain to that refinement, they nevertheless concretely define the essence of contemporary horror.

As illustrated by Berni Wrightson, King's tales of terror take on the period effect of the EC comics—stark outlines that emphasize rather than mute the visceral effects of horror . . . and that simultaneously assert the fundamental moralism of such stories. In the world of EC comics and of *Creepshow,* good and evil are distinctly different, and evil merits its just and immediate rewards. In the first tale, "Father's Day," the revenant Nathan Grantham takes appropriate revenge on the woman who killed him. Every element of the tale, from setting to characterization to final overstated and unsubtle irony, contributes to the comic book effect King is trying for.

"The Lonesome Death of Jordy Verrill" and "The Crate" are the only reprints in the collection, the first appearing as "Weeds" in *Cavalier* (May 1976) and *Nugget* (April 1979), and the second initially published in *Gallery* (July 1979). "Jordy Verrill" is most memorable for King's performance in the title role for the film version of *Creepshow,* and in both versions owes much to the atmospheric tale of the unnamable thing from outer space perfected by H. P. Lovecraft in *The Colour out of Space.* "The Crate" is equally archetypal in its story of a horror hidden away for decades that, when released, begins its preordained task of consuming human flesh. While there are touches of the Tasmanian devil in King's descriptions and Wrightson's illustrations for the monster, "The Crate" actually focuses more on fear of the unknown—and an eminently justifiable fear, at that.

Revenge without any supernatural paraphernalia is the initial theme of "Something to Tide You Over"—hinging on the punning title as a clue to how to deal with an adulterous wife and her lover. But when the two victims return, the story turns a wicked 180 degrees and becomes a classic permutation on the "biter bit" motif. Even more bluntly, "They're Creeping Up on You" incorporates one of King's top-ten horrors—fear of insects—and orchestrates an even more neatly realized story of revenge, this time on an ecological level.

Interesting, predictable, and fun, *Creepshow* simply does not attempt the seriousness of the novels produced within the next few years: *The Talisman, It,* and others. High seriousness, high art, even the elevated states of horror (as opposed to the "gross-out") are not its goals. Instead, King attempts to re-create a long-lost tone, a well-remembered atmosphere, and revive it through his own words and Wrightson's meticulous artwork.

As a film, *Creepshow* did well enough to inspire and justify a second anthology film, appropriately entitled *Creepshow II*—with one episode based on "The Raft," one of King's most frightening short stories, and two original episodes written for the film. It inspired no comic book version, however—a form King has not yet returned to this extensively.

43
Different Seasons
(1982)

King's second collection of short fiction, *Different Seasons,* appeared on the hard-cover best-seller lists during its first week of publication and remained there without interruption for thirty-four weeks, until the end of March 1983. Then after a five-month hiatus, the book reappeared, this time on the paper-back lists, where it remained for an additional ten weeks. This kind of response to short fiction was not typical, but then the stories that compose *Different Seasons* are not typical, either.

In the author's "Afterword," King notes that each of the four tales followed im-mediately upon his completing a novel: "The Body" came after *'Salem's Lot,* "Apt Pupil" after *The Shining,* "Rita Hayworth and Shawshank Redemption" after *The Dead Zone,* and "The Breathing Method" after *Firestarter.* It is, he notes, as if he "finished the big job with just enough gas left in the tank to blow off one good-sized novella." More intriguing, perhaps, is the sense that each of these stories continues in some way a major theme developed in the companion novel.

The oldest story, "The Body," is a meditation on death told through the eyes of a boy on the verge of growing up, a boy similar to Mark Petrie in that he has figuratively lost his family—or rather, that because of the death of his older brother, his parents have closed themselves off to him so completely that they might as well be as dead as the Petries. Isolated, an outsider, a younger boy often preyed upon by a cadre of older, vicious boys, and approaching his first con-frontation with death, Gordon Lachance suggests Mark Petrie in a world which is without vampires but in which death can be as sudden and as treacherous and as life-altering.

"Apt Pupil" is as appropriate as a companion piece to *The Shining.* In both stories, innocence is corrupted by pervasive evil. Jack Torrance's alcoholism is as destructive as Todd Bowden's obsession with the "gooshy" parts of Kurt Dus-sander's Nazi past, and both aberrations lead the characters to insanity and mur-der, either potential or actual.

Similarly, both "Rita Hayworth and Shawshank Redemption" and *The Dead Zone* deal with an innocent trapped within circumstances beyond his control yet still able to preserve the essence of that innocence and even a fairly strong element of hope. Johnny Smith and Andy Dufresne have both been dealt a raw deal by life, fate, God . . . whoever or whatever controls human experience. Both have lost an important part of their lives, yet both are determined to make whatever remains as valuable as possible. Both seem physically and emotionally fragile to outsiders, but that external fragility disguises an admirable resilience and inner strength. As with the other pairings, the novel incorporates the supernatural to some degree while the novella is more strictly realistic. In both instances, however, the emphasis is on survival and hope.

"The Breathing Method" is not as closely connected to *Firestarter*. In a sense, King has in fact reversed the relationship, so that while *Firestarter* is marginally tied to scientific experimentation and logical cause-effect patterning, "The Breathing Method" is a traditional "winter's tale," a fireside story of single-minded determination (an internal connection among the four stories of *Different Seasons*, by the way) that results in a fracturing of what one assumes to be natural law. In its closing paragraphs, in fact, "The Breathing Method" expands until it comments elliptically, and with more than a touch of horror, on the nature of fiction and storytelling itself.

These connectives between novella and preceding novel are not so intricate as to reduce the stories to little more than glosses on the major works. In fact, the stories in *Different Seasons* are among King's most powerful midlength works. Lacking the depth and breadth of the novels, they nevertheless allow King more scope than the short stories. As a result, he is able to concentrate his attention on remarkable characters in equally remarkable settings, and, through the conscious use of the yearly cycle year as metaphor, arrange the four tales in an increasingly dark and threatening sequence of moral change.

In spite of its horrific setting—Shawshank Prison, with its concrete walls and cruel, sometimes stupid wardens and guards, and its bands of "Sisters" whose lives are devoted to viciousness, rape, and violence—"Rita Hayworth and Shawshank Redemption" paradoxically comes across not as an exercise in gritty realism but almost as an attempt at idealism. As seen through the eyes of a hardened inmate (and three of the four stories in *Different Seasons* have a first-person narrator, a rarity in King's fiction), Andy Dufresne brings light to the darkness, a strong gentleness that opposes the stone walls surrounding him. His ultimate escape becomes not only a justified consequence of his patient endurance of a judicial injustice, but also a tribute to the indomitable human spirit.

The second section, "Summer of Corruption," emphasizes the collection's thematic links as "Apt Pupil" moves from that idealism and strength to a story about systematic corruption. Todd Bowden (whose name is, appropriately enough, cognate to the German *Tod*, meaning "death") begins as a typical thirteen-year-old; his story ends when a very different Todd Bowden, now a high school senior and a murderer, aims his .30-.30 toward a southern California freeway and begins firing. In between, he has been altered by his relationship with Dussander, onetime commandant of a Nazi death camp; but in turn, he has also contributed to Dussander's further moral degradation. By the final pages, it is not clear who has most corrupted whom.

Of the four stories, the most resonant is "The Body," perhaps because it is more familiar to recent readers through Rob Reiner's superlative film adaptation, *Stand by Me*. Again told without any substantive recourse to supernatural horror, "The Body" is a semiautobiographical story of a young would-be author finding in himself and his experiences the stuff of true storytelling. Gordon Lachance is in many ways a Stephen King alter-ego, not the least in the fact that "The Body" includes two of Lachance's stories, both published earlier by King under his own name. "Stud City" appeared in UMO's *Ubris* in the fall of 1969, and a fuller version of "The Revenge of Lardass Hogan" in the *Maine Review* for July 1975. In both cases, Lachance critiques the stories-within-the-story, giving King an opportunity to comment on strengths and weaknesses in his own early fiction while at the same time writing a story about the education of a storyteller. Restrained, symbolic, even apocalyptic in the etymological sense of "uncovering that which is hidden," "The Body" is a remarkable achievement. With only minimal plotting, it nevertheless provides riveting portraits of boys on the verge of becoming men, of children confronting adult realities, and of the necessary transition from innocence into experience.

"The Breathing Method" is a first-person story-within-a-story, a framed narrative on the order of Conrad's *Heart of Darkness*. Set in an oddly disquieting men's club, where the traditional Christmas fare is a story with elements of the supernatural, "The Breathing Method" is both a story about the narrator's own acquiescence to encroaching age and the inevitability of death, and a story told by one of the club's members about youth and a desperate attempt to forestall that inevitability. Moving back and forth from first-person narrative to recounted tales, "The Breathing Method" also suggests the complexity of the storyteller's art. The club meets in an old brownstone at 249B East Thirty-fifth Street in New York. But like the story itself, the building seems to contain far more than its exterior suggests. Throughout the tale, David Adley intuits rooms beyond rooms, some of them perhaps containing things best not seen directly. He discovers that the butler, Stevens, is as odd as the building itself, and that in the end, "there are *always* more tales."

As a collection, *Different Seasons* seems remarkably coherent, its stories independent but related sufficiently to make it seem less a random gathering of stories than something approaching the intensity of a novel. The success of *Different Season* made possible a second such collection, *Four Past Midnight* (1990), similarly composed of four novellas written following the completion of major novels, all organized according to the time-related theme indicated in the title.

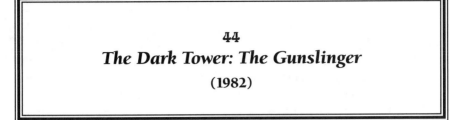

44

The Dark Tower: The Gunslinger

(1982)

"The man in black fled across the desert, and the gunslinger followed."

These sparse words begin the most atypical and in some ways the most imaginative narrative yet to come from King's pen, the opening volume in what promises to be the longest, most complex story from an author whose trademark has become long, complex tales.

As with so many King texts, the basic story of *The Dark Tower: The Gunslinger* is simplicity itself. The gunslinger, Roland of Gilead, has been, is, and (so far as the readers can tell at the beginning) always will be pursuing the dark man, a shadowy, quasi-mythic figure that holds the secrets to Roland's ultimate quest, the Dark Tower, an even more darkly shadowed, more vaguely mythic nexus of worlds, universes, and ultimate possibilities. The quest for the dark man has led Roland from the ruins of his own country—where the world has irrevocably "moved on"—into a vast desert near the far edge of the world. Crossing the desert, he undergoes sore trials and temptations, meeting eventually with Jake, a mysterious young boy from another world, who helps Roland survive and whom Roland in turn grows to love. But he cannot love Jake as much as he loves (or is obsessed with) the Dark Tower. When the brutal choice between Jake's life and his quest forces itself upon him, Roland barely hesitates before sacrificing Jake in order to confront the dark man. At the end of this first installment of the story, Roland has gleaned secret knowledge from the dark man and sits beside the western sea, awaiting dreams of the Dark Tower and the time of the drawing of the three.

The "Afterword" to *The Dark Tower: The Gunslinger* explains that the projected plot outline for the remainder of the story would take nearly three thousand pages to complete . . . and, given the time it took to complete the first volume, King "would have to live approximately three hundred years to complete the tale of the Tower . . ." It also apologizes for the fact that the *Dark Tower* series is not exactly what King's readers have come to expect from him.

In many ways, however, that is precisely the strength of the series, especially this first volume. Coming from the pen of a writer whose popular image is of a single-minded purveyor of cheap horror and the even cheaper "gross-out," whose style is often condemned as wooden and workmanlike at best, whose books are condemned as overwritten and underedited, *The Dark Tower: The Gunslinger* is a pleasant surprise. There are certainly elements of King's trademark horror; the Slow Mutants, for example, resemble strongly similar characters in *The Talisman* and are described in terms familiar to King's readers, while Roland's first response to them is the equally familiar "atavistic crawl in his intestines and privates" often associated with moments of horror in King's novels. And, of course, there is the sense that this volume is merely the beginning of the longest novel yet, one whose ending is so far distant as to be lost in the mists that obscure the Dark Tower itself.

But as an individual work, *The Dark Tower: The Gunslinger* undercuts many readers' presuppositions about King. It is written in unusually spare diction, ranging from typically coarse colloquialisms to carefully constructed analogues of the refined language of high fantasy. There are few narrative digressions in the novel, and few lines and phrases that do not move the story forward. It is, in fact, the shortest of the *Dark Tower* series thus far, and among King's shorter novels.

Beyond the level of style, however, is the larger issue of genre. While King occasionally blends horror with other genres—with mainstream pseudodocumentary fiction in *Carrie,* or with science fiction in *The Long Walk*—in the *Dark Tower* series, he sets himself the ambitious task of combining horror with the Western (Roland is, after all, the last gunslinger), the action-adventure thriller, touches of the romance in both the contemporary and the medieval senses, alternate-universe and multiple-universe extrapolative speculations, philosophical *debât,* heroic saga, apocalyptic fantasy, and above all, the epic quest. Browning's "Childe Roland to the Dark Tower Came" provides a character and a focus for the quest, but King's imagination fills out the spare outlines into a rich tapestry of worlds, some dying, others (ours included) not yet fully aware of an unnamed threat to the Dark Tower itself. Browning also supplies the epic form, but King's imagination again transforms it into prose narrative of a sort rarely attempted.

The epic impulse itself is almost as old as literature, extending at least as far back as *The Epic of Gilgamesh,* inscribed in clay tables with cuneiform script some four thousand years ago. During much of western history, the epic stood at a pinnacle of human achievement, with works such as Homer's *Iliad* and *Odyssey,* Virgil's *Aeneid,* the Anglo-Saxon *Beowulf,* Ludovico Ariosto's *Orlando Furioso,* Luis de Camoens's *Lusiad,* Edmund Spenser's *The Faerie Queene,* and Sir Philip Sidney's prose *Arcadia* continuously transforming the genre to meet new requirements of new audiences. Until its culmination in John Milton's *Paradise Lost,* the epic reigned virtually unchallenged as the highest literary form, at least for Renaissance audiences; after Milton's superlative achievement, however, verse epic almost disappeared, except for such inverted, mock-epic masterpieces as Alexander Pope's *The Rape of the Lock* and *The Dunciad,* and Lord Byron's *Don Juan.* Serious verse epic simply could not force language, structure, and theme beyond the point to which Milton developed them; to all appearances, verse epic ceased to be a viable literary form.

The need for epic itself did not disappear, however, but reappeared in a startling new eighteenth-century genre, the novel. Until the end of the nineteenth century and the novel's descent into realism, naturalism, and the antiheroic, the quest for a hero found its outlet in long prose narratives; and in the twentieth century that impulse was rapidly transferred from the mainstream novel to the science-fiction/fantasy novel, in works as disparate as J. R. R. Tolkien's *Lord of the Rings* trilogy and Frank Herbert's *Dune,* in which the actions of a single individual could in fact make a difference, could even save the world, the solar system, or the universe itself.

It is this literary heritage that lies behind the *Dark Tower* novels, beginning with *The Gunslinger.* King has created an archetypal epic personage, whose past lies hidden in myth and legend and whose future is wedded completely to the object of his quest. King's fable resonates with epic scope and grandeur, particularly in Roland's dream-vision of the Tower and its causal relation to all things. In good epic fashion, King expands the vision of his tale until it potentially represents an encyclopedia of the culture in which it is written; and in *The Drawing of the Three* and *The Wastelands,* volumes 2 and 3 of the saga, that potential becomes actual as King anatomizes the strengths and weaknesses of American society over the past three decades, thrusting Roland into contact with the 1960s, the 1970s, and the 1980s. Through Roland, King examines our obsessions and our frustrations, our hopes and our dreams, our successes and our failures, all from the perspective of an epic character out of this time and out of this place. Roland's perspectives on our world transform the everyday into the alien, giving readers continuing glimpses into who and what we are.

That King intends most of this, and that the saga is important to him in ways that many of his novels may not be, is indicated by the publishing history of *The Gunslinger.* The volume is unique among King's works in that it was first published serially in *The Magazine of Fantasy and Science Fiction* as "The Gunslinger" (1978), "The Way Station" (1980), "The Oracle and the Mountain" (1981), "The Slow Mutants" (1981), and "The Gunslinger and the Dark Man" (1981). The fact of magazine publication may have had an influence on the tautness of style and focus of story; it certainly allowed for King to receive readers' responses to the stories before they appeared in a single volume. When *The Dark Tower: The Gunslinger* finally appeared in a limited edition of ten thousand, it immediately sold out; a second edition of ten thousand also sold out, and by late 1986 collectors might pay as high as $325 for a $20 first edition and $600 for one of five hundred numbered copies. Even second editions were running well over $100. By 1988, however, King had bowed to the pressure of his fans (and to a highly lucrative reprint-rights contract) and agreed to publish mass market paperback editions.

For the first time, King's extraordinary version of epic quest was readily available—and well received. Readers enmeshed in the complex past and present of Roland of Gilead could now only wait with Roland on the distant westering beaches for the next installment of his future, *The Drawing of the Three.*

45
Christine
(1983)

Although now considered by many readers and critics one of King's weaker novels, *Christine* was welcomed in 1983 by rave reviews from the *Los Angeles Times*, *Library Journal*, and other outlets. In the interim, more seasoned responses have pointed to the melodramatic plot that moves beyond extremes into absurdity, the ambivalence of its supernatural intrusions, and characterization that verges on stereotype. Even King has noted that, while writing the novel he firmly believed in what he was saying, he knew even then that he was having difficulties. One of his few first-person novels, *Christine* abruptly shifts to third person when Dennis Guilder suffers a severe football injury (inevitably, given Dennis's characterization) and is hospitalized for weeks—during which time, of course, he not only has no way of knowing what is happening between Arnie Cunningham and Christine. In fact, for much of the early portion of his stay he is so heavily medicated he doesn't even know what is happening in his own hospital room. Then, when Dennis is finally released, the story shifts back to first person and continues to its conclusion.

While the interruption of narrative flow may contribute to a sense that the story is somehow flawed, the fact remains that *Christine* can still offer a good read, especially for younger fans first discovering this story of a deadly, haunted car. One of King's most obviously symbolic novels, *Christine* is both a coming-of-age novel and an indictment of late 1970s and early 1980s society. Built in fall 1957 but a 1958 model, Christine is just turning twenty-one when the story begins. She has reached her majority, as it were, and is about to become an adult, a stage looming frighteningly close for Dennis, Arnie, and the third member of King's distorted romantic triangle (at times almost a quadrangle), Leigh Cabot. And in a real sense, an equivalent moment of adult-style reckoning is looming just ahead for the car-oriented, highly mobile culture of the late seventies, when the story is set—a time of gasoline shortages when behemoths like 1958 Plymouth Furies carry conspicuous consumption to socially unacceptable extremes.

One of the series of novels extending from *The Dead Zone* through *Pet Sem-*

atary that deal primarily with individuals and their responses to the uncanny and the supernatural, *Christine* is a ghost story. Here, however, the Bad Place is not a house like the Marsten House or the Overlook Hotel, and the Bad Thing is embodied not as vampire or werewolf or monster but as a rust-ridden old car that catches the eye and the fancy of a passing teenager. A young novel in the sense that most of the central characters are in their teens, *Christine* explores ghostly possession with King's characteristic energy and verve. If the basic story approaches absurdity on one level—a haunted *Plymouth* no less!—it at least partially redeems itself by the sheer force of its narrative movement. *Christine* creates a kaleidoscope of cars, rock music (the copyright page lists credits for over forty-five songs quoted in the text), archetypal teenage rebellion against equally archetypal overbearing parents (mostly Arnie Cunningham's, since Dennis's and Leigh's parents hardly figure in the novel), fast-food joints, incipient sexuality explored in front- and backseats—all overlying the frightening insecurities and frustrations of adolescence.

Peer groups are threatening. Hoods-in-training like Buddy Reperton recur throughout King's fictions (most notably, perhaps, in another "young" novel, *Carrie*), but in *Christine* they come directly to center stage, cruel and cowardly, getting their limited pleasures through drinking endless cans of beer (often wedged provocatively and symbolically in their crotches as they drive), resisting all authority, and generally raising hell. Adults are equally threatening. Regina and Michael Cunningham have spent Arnie's lifetime giving him conflicting messages, vaunting their liberal agendas, and insisting that Arnie and his friends call them by their first names in order to eliminate the barrier between parent and child; but as Arnie says savagely, the true business of parents is to kill their children, the symbols of their own mortality. King's exposé of the self-deception, hypocrisy, and ultimate destructiveness of parents like Regina cuts deeply and truly. Regina not only symbolically smothers Arnie, but literally causes his physical death as well. Other adults like Will Darnell weave less intimate but just as deadly traps for children. Again and again, *Christine* argues, peers are to be distrusted and adults avoided; the exceptions, including Mr. Casey, the shop teacher, merely support the rule.

Rage without a classroom held hostage or a teenaged terrorist as narrator, *Carrie* without telekinesis, *The Long Walk* without even the release valve of a socially sanctioned way to kill young people (although drivers licenses come close, as *Christine* ultimately suggests)—*Christine* is an anatomy of the ambivalences of adolescence. Perhaps not one of King's "great" novels, it nevertheless has garnered its own following and performs well enough according to its own standards.

46
Cycle of the Werewolf
(1983)

King's first extended treatment of the werewolf motif began with a simple proposal from specialty publisher Christopher Zavisa in 1979. What about a story-calendar, Zavisa suggested, with King writing vignettes to accompany appropriate illustrations by Berni Wrightson. King agreed, although before he was finished with the project, the five-hundred-word vignettes had expanded to a twelve-month novella, entitled *Cycle of the Werewolf*. In 1983 Zavisa's Land of Enchantment published a limited-edition hardcover edition of some 7,500 copies, along with various states of even more limited collectors editions (including one state that was accompanied by a portfolio of Wrightson's artwork). In April 1985 the entire text, including Wrightson's illustrations, was reproduced in trade paperback by NAL, making available to King's fans a unique—and overall quite pleasing—reading/viewing experience. From May to June of that year, *Cycle* found a steady place on the best-seller lists for trade paper—a remarkable achievement, considering that the thin volume actually contains little to suggest best-seller status . . . except Stephen King's name on the title page. Since it appeared at perhaps the height of King's popularity—and collectibility—during the mid-1980s, even this relative lightweight joined the crowd of King's enormously successful titles. (The full text of *Cycle,* along with a foreword by King, King's complete screenplay of the film adaptation *Silver Bullet,* and stills from the film appeared six months later as a trade paperback under the title *Silver Bullet.*)

Thin though it might be—and at 127 pages *Cycle* vies with the hardcover *Carrie* as among King's most compressed tales—*Cycle of the Werewolf* does not disappoint. The words are vintage King through and through, and the basic story of a wheelchair-bound boy who first understands the nature of, then confronts, and finally defeats the werewolf. Tarker's Mills fits neatly into the children-in-jeopardy theme that preoccupied King throughout the decade-plus from *Carrie* in 1974 to *It* in late 1986. Although King seems to have little affinity with the werewolf as monster (with the exception of his rather special treatment of them in *The Talisman*), *Cycle* deals fully and fairly with traditional

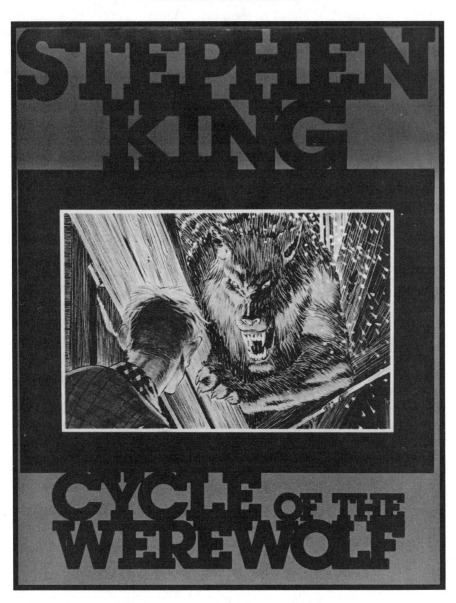

Dust jacket for Land of Enchantment limited edition.

werewolf lore. While a full moon seems at times optional as a trigger for transformation, a silver bullet is more than sufficient to destroy the monster. Typically, the monster walks unknown among the townspeople by day, part of the community upon which his monster-self preys. The suspense in *Cycle* lies in watching how young Marty Coslaw first convinces himself, then his sister, and then his uncle that there is a werewolf in Tarker's Mills and that it must be stopped.

Wrightson's illustrations are a perfect match for King's unusually sparse text. The month illustrations, serving as chapter headings, are exercises in heavy black-and-white patterning, starkly linear and yet at times haunting in their evocation of landscapes—both physical and spiritual. There seems to be much of Maine in them, and of darkness and light, reflecting the constant shift of emotion in the stories themselves. The color illustrations embedded within the chapters, on the other hand, relinquish black-and-white severity for a richness of primary colors that suggests blood and death, and at the same time remind readers of the horror comic book heritage of this sort of story. The werewolf appears directly in none of the black-and-whites; it and/or its victims are center-stage in all of the color illustrations. The balance between black-and-white and color, between absence and presence, between atmosphere and grisly, concrete representation neatly parallels King's gradual revelations of identity and purpose in the text: "There is nothing of God or Light" in the werewolf, King tells readers at the end of the January segment, "it is all black winter and dark ice."

Unlike many of King's longer novels, *Cycle* remains morally ambivalent. The werewolf simply appears—there is no logical or rational explanation, no working out of the inevitable consequences of evil choices. As the human vessel for the werewolf says in November of that fatal year, "This—whatever it is—is nothing I asked for. I wasn't bitten by a wolf or cursed by a gypsy. It just . . . happened." The werewolf may be evil; the man beneath the werewolf's flesh is not necessarily so. Yet when the compulsion to kill rises, the good man must give way to the darker, evil impulses. At heart, this seems to be the metaphorical significance of the werewolf in any of its many guises—evil sometimes simply asserts itself, and then its workings must continue until their inevitable and bloody conclusion. As a consequence, while there is a "happy" ending, and the werewolf is appropriately dispatched by a single silver bullet, *Cycle* lingers in the memory as a fundamentally disquieting, dark, foreboding tale.

47
Pet Sematary
(1983)

Before *Pet Sematary* appeared on the bookstore shelves, the novel had already garnered a word-of-mouth reputation as a story that was too horrifying even for Stephen King. As word filtered through the ranks of his readers and fans of a forthcoming novel about which King had made few public statements, augmented by rumors that he had kept it in the drawer for years before finally releasing it, the immediate implication drawn was that this new tale would define new limits of literary horror.

When King did indeed prove unusually reticent about discussing the new novel after its publication in late 1983, the undercurrents of supposition grew. At an academic conference in early 1984, the moderator of a question-and-answer session with King prefaced his introductory remarks by noting simply that King would entertain no questions about *Pet Sematary*—nor did he. The sense increased that here was something that surpassed even King's stomach for horror. *Publishers Weekly* emphasized this sense by including in its review of the novel that *Pet Sematary* was "the most frightening book Stephen King has ever written." Even taking into account typical book dealers' hyperbole, critical responses such as this one and the hardcover dust jacket's rhetorical question—"Can Stephen King scare even *himself?*"—immediately placed the novel in a special class.

As it turned out, there was good reason for seeing *Pet Sematary* as occupying a unique place among King's fictions.

King's decision to do little to advertise the book after its release (and to hold onto the manuscript for some time before allowing it to be published) had to do more with contractual arrangements with Doubleday than with his concerns about releasing the quintessential horror story on an unsuspecting (but nevertheless eager) populace. In spite of the pragmatic considerations involved, however, *Pet Sematary* did turn out to be undoubtedly King's darkest novel— a fact that only reveals itself in the second half, when events put in motion earlier in the novel take on the weight and inexorability of a moral and physical juggernaut.

The first half moves relatively slowly, never becoming tedious but also never venturing beyond the merest hints of the devastation to follow. In typical fashion, King carefully establishes characters and defines settings, particularly the disquieting Pet Sematary itself and foreshadowings of the deeper, darker Micmac Indian burial ground that the Pet Sematary guards. Characters such as Louis and Rachel Creed and Jud Crandall receive fully empathetic treatment; well before the first critical action—Louis's burial of the family cat in the Micmac burial ground—readers feel comfortable with the Creed family, with their circumstances, with the love that clearly binds them and the secret fears that will force Creed into catastrophic decisions.

In the second portion, King's characters descend into an ever-tightening spiral of grief, loss, tragedy, madness, and death, unrelieved by even the faintest glimmer of hope or optimism. The descent quickly becomes inevitable and irrevocable; even ostensibly generous impulses (such as Jud Crandall's introducing Louis to the burial ground in the first place) are revealed as subterfuge, as efforts by an increasing and increasingly malevolent power to force its way into the Creeds' lives. When Louis Creed absently sketches a spiral in the dirt of his son's fresh grave, he unconsciously acknowledges the depth of his obsession and gives symbolic identity to the final focused, strangling effects of the novel—a downward spiral drawing tighter and tighter upon itself . . . and upon the characters. When the reader arrives at what must be the single most horrifying closing sentence in any of King's novels—"'*Darling,*' it said"—the utter simplicity of the phrasing, coupled with the implications of what Louis Creed has done and of what must yet happen is starkly stunning.

Pet Sematary is King's darkest novel in part because of the underlying theme that there *are* things worse than death, and in part because he has spent so much time in the first half lovingly creating an intense relationship between Louis Creed and his son, Gage. Gage's death—which actually is handled with extraordinary indirection and subtlety for a horror novel—becomes readily acceptable as the trigger for the bloodbath that is to follow. But even beyond the purely personal motivation Louis Creed would accountably feel, King provides him with a recurring leitmotiv for human obduracy in the face of disaster. Again and again, Creed or Crandall repeats the mantra that defines *Pet Sematary*: "*The soil of a man's heart is stonier. . . . A man grows what he can . . . and tends it.*" Fatal decisions and their consequences lie at the center of the novel, as when Louis understands that by burying the cat in the Micmac grounds and thus bringing the cat back to a kind of life, he has become responsible for the cat's subsequent actions—he *owns* not only the cat, with its stink of death and its often venomous temper, but also the ravaged mice and birds the cat begins killing.

As if this were not sufficient foundation for the story, King makes explicit his intention to explore as yet unimagined (and perhaps unimaginable) depths. The opening paragraph of Part 2, "The Micmac Burial Ground," states:

> It's probably wrong to believe there can be any limit to the horror the human mind can experience. On the contrary, it seems that some exponential effect begins to obtain as deeper and deeper darkness falls—as little as one may like to admit it, human experience tends, in a good many ways, to support the idea that when the nightmare grows black enough, horror spawns horror, one coincidental evil begets other, often more deliberate evils, until finally blackness seems to cover everything. And the most terrifying question of all may be just how much horror the human mind can stand and still maintain a wakeful, staring, unrelenting sanity. . . .

With these words, King telegraphs the structural principle of the final portions of *Pet Sematary:* one unrelenting horror following immediately upon, and in fact initiated by, another. Without an emotional or narrative break, the novel penetrates darkness within darkness within darkness, until all that remains is madness or death . . . or both. The result is one of the few King narratives that move unrelievedly into obsessive pessimism. The cautious optimism of *The Shining, The Stand, The Talisman,* or *It* has no place in the world of *Pet Sematary,* where, in the final moments, midnight darkness reigns as undisputed monarch over all.

48
The Eyes of the Dragon
(1984)

The major event of 1984 for King collectors was the publication of a new novel, *The Eyes of the Dragon,* by King's publishing house, Philtrum Press. Announced as a limited run of 1,250 copies (one thousand numbered in black ink, 250 in red ink), at a time when King's hardcovers were routinely selling in the hundreds of thousands to millions range, the book was initially priced at $120 and distributed through a complex lottery system. Demand obviously outstripped supply, and within a year, prices through collectors ranged from $650 to $800, with at least one owner asking $1,200 for a copy—a tenfold increase over the initial price. A large-format book richly illustrated by Kenneth R. Linkhaüser, *The Eyes of the Dragon* achieved almost mythic status among readers and fans over the next three years; just to have *seen* a copy was a mark of status.

The pressure to read the story was eased in February 1987, however, when Viking issued a hardcover edition (the paperback appeared a year later). There were some alterations in the text, and the new edition was illustrated by David Palladini, whose pencil-and-ink sketches lent an oddly appropriate softness to this story of high fantasy, dragons, kings and princes, and evil magicians. Viking clearly understood the drawing power of King's name, even on a nonhorror novel that could with some justification be categorized as a children's story. The initial print run exceeded one million copies; 525,000 had sold by the end of 1987, making *Eyes of the Dragon* one of the top-ten hardcover bestsellers for the year.

Its popularity was well grounded. Emerging momentarily from his public personas as the King of Horror and Master of the Macabre, King here offers a fantasy that is unusually restrained in content and in style. Often criticized for his use of rough street language, King demonstrates in *Eyes of the Dragon* that he can follow the verbal decorum of fantasy as ably as that of contemporary horror. In a narrative voice that suggests the lyricism and deceptively simple-seeming power of folk epic and the oral traditions of storytelling, he weaves a tale originally designed for a listening audience—his own children (the novel is dedicated to his daughter and Peter Straub's son). From the opening sentence, a variation upon the time-honored "Once upon a time," King rapidly settles into the timeless no-time of fantasy, introducing readers to old King Roland, young and beautiful Queen Sasha (like many queens of fabled lands, she dies early and tragically . . . in childbirth), the two princes Peter and Thomas, and the archetypally evil magician Flagg (the fact that his name is the same as the Dark Man's in *The Stand* is no coincidence). All of the major characters reflect the centuries-old conventions of fairy tale, both in personality and in actions. The good queen, for example, is almost too good to live; the evil magician, on the other hand, is almost too evil to live. In many ways, the land of Delain is a land of physical and moral extremes; the climactic storm, we are told, is the worst in the history of Delain. Certainly Flagg is the most maleficent king's adviser in its history. Through it all, the storyteller-narrator mediates among these extremes, weaving order out of chaos and stability out of disruption.

As with any good fairy tale, the social conventions asserted at the beginning are almost immediately disturbed. Sasha dies, Roland dies, and the true heir, Peter, is treacherously imprisoned through the machinations of Flagg. The more pliant Thomas is made king, and becomes little more than a figurehead under Flagg. And also as in any good fairy tale in which the true king is set aside and a false king is elevated in his stead, the land of Delain suffers. Eventually, of course, truth and right triumph. Thomas recognizes and repudiates Flagg's evil, Peter escapes from the tower in which he has been imprisoned, and Flagg's villainy is discovered just in time to forestall wholesale destruction.

Throughout, King displays his considerable powers as a storyteller, with few episodes that do not relate directly to his primary plot. Each action has repercussions; something as simple as the way the imprisoned Peter's meals are delivered ultimately becomes a key to restoring the true monarch (not coincidentally, King's working title was *The Napkins,* acknowledging the centrality of what at times seems a minor point).

The story deals with appearance and illusion, with self-deception as well as deeper, more threatening levels of political, social, and moral deceit. It also becomes an important episode in King's ongoing saga of Roland of Gilead and the quest for the Dark Tower. Clearly connected to *The Stand* (even in the expurgated 1978 version, but far more intimately in the restored 1990 edition), *The Eyes of the Dragon* transports readers beyond the world of science fiction and apocalyptic horror explored in *The Stand* to other worlds. King as narrator cross-references connections between these worlds, explaining, for example, that the "featherex" is Delain's analogue to our "Phoenix." Yet on a larger scale, *The Eyes of the Dragon* and the vicissitudes suffered in a Delain under Flagg's control suggest that just as Peter's world impinges in important ways upon ours—that is, shares some essential "reality"—so even more alien worlds may impinge upon Peter's.

In *The Wastelands,* King makes those connections explicit. While in the city of Lud, Roland and Jake hear the story of a dark magician who had passed through long before, pursued by two young men named Thomas and Dennis. The closing pages of *The Eyes of the Dragon* show a repentant Thomas relinquishing the throne in favor of the rightful king, thus restoring true order. With his friend, Dennis, he sets out on a quest to find Flagg—in his world or others—and take vengeance upon the magician; the narrator assures readers in the final paragraphs that "Peter ruled long and well, and that Thomas and Dennis had many and strange adventures, and that they did see Flagg again, and confronted him."

Given this comment and the reference in *The Wastelands,* and the noncoincidental appearance of a number of "dark men" with the initials "RF" in other stories, it seems clear that *The Eyes of the Dragon* is not simply an anomalous children's fantasy that somehow emerged from among the tales of terror and horror for which King is best known. It is, instead, one more element in the intricate saga of the Dark Tower that incorporates *The Stand, The Dark Tower: The Gunslinger, The Eyes of the Dragon, The Talisman, The Drawing of the Three, The Wastelands,* and, most recently, *Insomnia.* It thus becomes part of an ambitious epic quest-fable that ranges over multiple worlds and through multiple times; and the fairy tale of Peter, Thomas, and Niner the Dragon forms a critical part of that quest. Order has been restored in Delain, but the true Story has not yet been completed.

As the narrator concludes: "But now the hour is late, and all of that is another tale, for another day."

49
The Talisman
(with Peter Straub; 1984)

In a 1985 essay addressing the relationship between commercial success and artistic integrity in King's novels, Alan Warren argued that of all of King's novels published under his own name over the preceding eleven years, Warren "would nominate only two—*The Dark Tower* and *The Talisman*—for oblivion" (*Discovering Stephen King*).

His assessment of *The Talisman* in particular seemed in line with equally strong sentiments expressed by reviewers in trade and popular publications. *Newsweek* attacked the book for its overt commercialism, epitomized by the fact that the 600,000 first-edition hardcover copies set a new publishing record; the review further takes on the novel for defects in plotting, style, characterization, pacing, and narrative effect (Charles Leerhsen, "The Titans of Terror," December 24, 1984). *People* magazine's "Worst of Pages" for December 24–31, 1984, warned that "in horror fiction, two heads are better than one only if they're on the same body."

In essence, *The Talisman* initially suffered the consequences of extremes of both reputation and anticipation. By 1984 King had established himself firmly as the premier writer of contemporary horror; following at some distance but still figures to be reckoned with were such writers as Dean R. Koontz, Ramsey Campbell, Clive Barker, Robert McCammon . . . and Peter Straub. Of the perceived "heirs" to King's throne, Straub enjoyed perhaps the highest standing, in part because of the literary style he brought to such novels as *Ghost Story* (1979), *Shadowland* (1980), and his own apocalyptic version of an escaped virus and its aftermath, *Floating Dragon* (1982). The fact that he had also published an elegant volume of mainstream poetry, *Leeson Park and Belsize Square: Poems 1970–1975* (1983), only enhanced the expectation that his fluid style would rub off on King, that King's storyteller's energy and unbridled imagination would in turn energize Straub, and that their collaboration would almost necessarily result in the greatest horror novel ever written.

Such anticipations seem doomed by their nature to disappointment. Perhaps no novel could have lived up to the publicity hype, or up to the expectations of fans of both writers (King would experience the same kind of critical drubbing with the release of *Maximum Overdrive,* his directorial debut that had been promoted as the ultimate horror movie, scripted and directed by the ultimate horror writer). Certainly most readers looked forward to something like an extension of *The Stand* and *Floating Dragon,* straightforward horror capitalizing on the strengths of both King and Straub.

What they received, however, was an intricately interlaced combination of horror and fantasy, of real-world terror and alternate-universe science fantasy, in which atomic testing in our world can create the vast expanses of the wastelands in the Territories (and, perhaps, in the world of Roland of Gilead as well). Instead of allusions to Poe and Lovecraft, *The Talisman* echoes Tolkien and C. S. Lewis, Mark Twain and *The Wizard of Oz.* Its structure echoes the immensely popular Xanth and Proton/Phase novels of Piers Anthony—both ultimately amalgams of science fiction and fantasy, of "this world" and "others." Instead of King's vividly colloquial prose, or Straub's coolly ironic academic tone, a third, almost wholly unexpected voice emerged, one appropriate not to the ultimate in horror but to an extended narrative that takes on a pacing and movement of its own. And instead of a single-minded quest to destroy (or at least incapacitate) a monster, there is the open-ended epic quest for the Talisman, the mystic nexus of possible worlds—an image as ethereal and powerful as Jake's vision of the Dark Tower itself in *The Wastelands.* Even given the length of *The Talisman,* it would be nearly impossible to do justice to the mythic echoes the Talisman evokes, or to the multiple landscapes in this world and in the Territories that lead to the Black Hotel and the confrontation between light and darkness.

That King and Straub also incorporated critiques of contemporary politicians and writers, of social and economic conditions, of education, of parenting—all of this made *The Talisman* more difficult to approach, and hence seemed to justify the cavils of reviewers and critics.

It did not, however, keep the novel from reaching literally millions of readers. In an unprecedented distribution decision, Viking kept *The Talisman* out of stores until the actual day of publication. This entailed storing nearly 600,000 copies in warehouses, then distributing them overnight. On the first day of sales, with bookstore walls visual seas of black and red and gold, *The Talisman* recouped all of Viking's publicity budget. Less than two months later, by the end of 1984, over 880,000 copies had been sold. The hardcover edition remained on the best-seller lists for twenty-eight weeks, with the paperback adding an additional fourteen to the total; for almost a quarter of that time, the novel was in the number one position. Within three years, *The Talisman* had appeared in Spanish, Dutch, German, Italian, French, and Swedish translations, attesting not only to King's growing international popularity, but, in light of multiple reprints in those languages, to the novel's as well.

In the decade that has followed its first appearance, *The Talisman* has emerged to be ranked as one of King's (and Straub's) stronger novels. The young Jack Sawyer, "twelve years old and tall for his age," is an ideal protagonist for a coming-of-age novel that has as its core King's persistent dichotomies of "NIGHT and DAY, MOON and SUN, DARK and LIGHT." He undergoes trials that test his physical and mental endurance; along the way to California and the Black Hotel, he passes through a crucible that tempers him, strengthens and hardens him, and makes him an analogue to Roland of Gilead. The plot is complex, at times almost tangled as characters pass back and forth between worlds. That movement allows readers new and often startling perspectives on familiar themes; we see order dissolving into chaos both here and there, and the single act of a single individual may be all that can forestall disaster in both (perhaps in *all*) worlds. In this sense, *The Talisman* leaves behind the antiheroic naturalism of much modern fiction and returns to the same roots that underlie Tolkien and Lewis and even, in its own way, the Mark Twain of *Tom Sawyer* and *Huckleberry Finn*—to the prose-epic impulse that King had already evoked in *The Stand* and *The Dark Tower*.

The Talisman's length adds to this sense. At almost 650 pages it is one of King's weightier tomes (and Straub's). But the story attempted requires scope and length and time. It is a quest voyage covering days and weeks and months. Its heroes travel tens and hundreds and thousands of miles through psychically and physically draining landscapes. And even as it stands, it represents roughly only half of what King and Straub might have done with the tale. At the end, Jack returns home in a matter of days (in a Cadillac chauffeured by a werewolf, no less)—the original conception had him taking almost as long to return to the Alhambra Hotel as it did to get him to California. The scope of the story is ambitious; the themes it attempts are wide-ranging; the narrative mode, a seamless blend of King's energetic imagination and Straub's literary polish, requires length.

Seen in the larger context of the *Dark Tower* saga, we discover, as with *The Eyes of the Dragon, The Wastelands,* and *Insomnia,* that the story has not ended; this part of the tale has merely stopped. Mark Twain's words from *Tom Sawyer* are an appropriate epilogue to the kind of story *The Talisman* attempts:

> So endeth this chronicle. It being strictly the history of a *boy,* it must stop here; the story could not go much further without becoming the history of a *man.* When one writes a novel about grown people, he knows exactly where to stop—that is, with a marriage; but when he writes of juveniles, he must stop where he best can.

The tale King and Straub have chosen to tell must end with a flood of light; with the redemption and healing of Jack Sawyer's cancer-ridden mother and her

Territories analogue, Queen Laura DeLoessian; and with the transformation of the Talisman from thing to symbol and then to nothingness. Jack Sawyer will appear for a brief scene in King's subsequent novel, *The Tommyknockers*—and it is a welcomed and memorable return. But at the end of *The Talisman,* his task completed and his quest safely over, he is restored, for a short time at least, to the world of children balanced precariously on the verge of adulthood.

50
Thinner
(1984)

The fifth "Bachman" novel is also the closest to what readers have come to expect from Stephen King. The first four contained implicit clues (particularly when we read with the gift of superior hindsight) as to who Richard Bachman really was. Place names connect, as when one notes that Ray Garraty's mailing address is apparently the same as Johnny Smith's father's in *The Dead Zone* (1979)—rural delivery, Pownal, Maine. Brand names connect, especially the Blue Ribbon Laundry in *Roadwork,* in a branch of which Margaret White worked in *Carrie.* Dedications to Jim Bishop, Burt Hatlen, and others already familiar to King's readership add to these connections, along with a gritty, tough-talk tone that King had already mastered when *Carrie* appeared, and stories that were consistent with King's recurrent themes. But, as more than one reader noted, only Stephen King could have written the opening paragraphs of *Thinner:*

> And before Halleck can jerk away, the old Gypsy reaches out and caresses his cheek with one twisted finger. His lips spread open like a wound, showing a few tombstone stumps poking out of his gums. They are black and green. His tongue squirms between them and then slides out to slick his grinning, bitter lips.

As if to throw any questioning readers offtrack—but perhaps even more as a covert signature—Billy Halleck's doctor warns him that his tale of a curse had begun to "sound a little like a Stephen King novel . . . ." Halleck responds that "if you add Cary Rossington with his alligator skin and William J. Halleck with his case of involuntary anorexia nervosa into the equation, it starts to sound a little like Stephen King again."

King has noted that *Thinner* was originally intended as a King novel, and *Cujo* as a Bachman. This initial evaluation seems sound, since without the overlay of supernatural horror provided by the Frank Dodd references and the sporadic monster-in-the-closet episodes (which remain curiously unconnected to the main story itself), *Cujo* does in fact resemble the earlier Bachman works more integrally than does *Thinner*. King's tale of a Gypsy curse and its physical and psychological toll on Billy Halleck, and its final countering by Halleck's own "curse of the white man from town" opens the novel to dark fantasy in ways that would have been digressive, if not damaging, to *Rage, The Long Walk, Road-work,* and *The Running Man.* Grossly pulsating strawberry pies that may or may not contain all of humanity's hurts would be out of place in the earlier tales of interior obsession and exterior (but "realistic") threat, yet seem oddly appropriate in a novel about the apocalyptic effects of Gypsy curses.

In *Thinner,* something that is potentially obsessive and life-threatening in the "real" world—weight loss that goes well beyond simple anorexia nervosa—is treated to the full "master of horror" treatment as King envisions walking skeletons, alligator men, and zits-gone-wild in a story of manic revenge. Throughout King gives full rein to his assertive style of horror, in which not only horrific images appear directly in the story, but also the *language* of horror is richly and deeply embedded in even the most neutral descriptions or dialogue. Words such as *agony, terror, horror, blood,* and *scream* are woven throughout the text, giving virtually every page a verbal undercurrent of fear, pain, and threat to counterpoint the surface narrative.

The story is ostensibly about justice and about "pushes"—those moments when the give-and-take in the struggle to find a moral balance must dissolve or the horror of retribution will continue forever. King's Billy Halleck is not an entirely admirable person, but his punishment far outweighs his guilt, as least in his eyes. The old Gypsy woman he struck with his car was not entirely innocent, but her father will not rest until the man who killed her is hounded to death. Billy Halleck's wife is not truly guilty, any more than are the old woman's grandchildren, yet the struggle between the dual curses enmesh them all in horrible consequences. And still the curse spreads, to embrace and destroy a marginally corrupt judge and an overzealous small-town cop, and to damage all around them as well. Finally, Halleck's own urge for revenge grows so great that he inadvertently destroys possibly the only true innocent in the story . . . and brings us full circle, to the beginning point, and the simultaneous realization that all of the struggle in the novel, all of the painful quest for justice and mercy, all of the death and suffering have been for nothing. Billy Halleck will *still* die "thinner."

Thinner is the first Bachman novel to approach the intensity, complexity, horrific texturing, and wide market appeal that the King books had long since demonstrated. Had the truth about King's authorship not been revealed through Steve Brown's investigations of copyright papers on file in the Library of Congress, Richard Bachman might eventually have become as competitive an author as Dean R. Koontz's highly successful pseudonym, Leigh Nichols, whose books at one point were almost as popular as Koontz's own. King's private hope was that "Dicky" might gradually build his own faithful audience, unhindered by the expectations and hoopla that automatically attached to a novel under King's name; King notes that *Misery* might have been Bachman's breakthrough novel. By February 1985, when King was forced to acknowledge the pseudonym, the hardcover edition of Richard Bachman's *Thinner* had in fact sold some 28,000 copies—certainly a respectable number, and as King points out in *The Bachman Books,* substantially more than *Night Shift* had sold initially.

Less than a month after King's announcement, however, on March 3, 1985, *Stephen King's Thinner* was in a second edition (with first-edition prices spiraling) and had already appeared on the hardcover best-seller lists. By September 1985 there were in excess of 2,500,000 hardcover and paperback copies of *Thinner* in print; two months later, the number had topped 3,050,000. Between the paperback and the hardcover editions, the novel spent a total of forty-one weeks on the best-seller lists—not an unusual feat for a Stephen King novel, but a long stretch from the modest popularity of Richard Bachman.

Along the way, *Thinner* became the focus for a storm of publicity and media attention, extending from early 1985 through much of 1986, that made King himself a center of national interest. If he had not yet become a "brand name," following the Bachman revelations and King's record-breaking weeks of having first three, then four, and finally five titles appearing simultaneously on the national best-seller lists, he definitely became one. The succeeding months represent one of the most productive bursts in his career, with King publishing *Cycle of the Werewolf* (trade paper), *Skeleton Crew* (hardcover and mass market paperback), *The Bachman Books* (hardcover, trade paper, and mass market paperback), and finally, in late 1986, *It*. At the same time, the film or television versions of *Cycle of the Werewolf* (as *Silver Bullet,* 1985), "Word Processor of the Gods" (November 1985), and "Gramma" (February 1986) were released, with *Maximum Overdrive, Stand by Me,* and *Pet Sematary* in various stages of production.

If *Thinner* marked the end of Richard Bachman's career, it just as certainly signaled a public explosion of interest in Things-King that is still continuing nearly a decade later.

King's first true collection of short fiction since *Night Shift* (as opposed to the linked stories in the *Dark Tower* volumes or the four novellas that composed *Different Seasons*), *Skeleton Crew* was eagerly anticipated and well received. It remained on the hardcover best-seller lists from mid-June 1985 through the end of January 1986, logging nine weeks of successive appearances at number one—a feat almost unprecedented for a collection of short stories. When the paperback edition appeared in early May 1986, it repeated in small the success of the hardcover: eleven weeks on the lists, the first seven in the number-one position.

The sales records reflect many readers' opinion that *Skeleton Crew* contains some of King's best work. From its opening novel-length story to its concluding foray into a remarkably gentle ghost tale, *Skeleton Crew* surprises again and again with evidences of King's evolving skills.

Chronologically, the stories span nearly eighteen years, from the first published versions of "Cain Rose Up," "Here There Be Tygers," and "The Raft," in 1968, to "Beachworld," in 1985. Several of them were extensively revised for inclusion in *Skeleton Crew;* "The Raft," for example, has grown beyond King's original, narrower conception in "The Float" and ends differently, developing a motif that will become more and more important as the collection progresses and that crowns the final story, "The Reach." Additionally, a number of the stories had been available only in difficult-to-locate publications; now, for the first time, all of King's readership had access to some of his most intriguing tales.

Skeleton Crew begins with "The Mist." The length of a short novel, this story of unknown horrors suddenly descending on an unsuspecting humanity contains in miniature the distilled essence of King's storytelling. It showcases virtually every technique, device, theme, twist of characterization and plotting, landscape, and atmosphere that King's readers respond to so strongly. Its story is simple: one day, out of nowhere, a mist settles over a small town. A number of people, including the narrator and his son, are trapped in a supermarket when the first monsters arrive. From then on, the trapped handful of people battle for survival against the mist and the shadowy horrors it hides . . . and, in some ways more frighteningly, against themselves. Finally, a small group leaves the market to try to drive to safety, or at least to discover if there is an end to the mist. The story concludes with their holing up for the night in the lobby of a Howard Johnson's. The mist is still out there; and so are the monsters. Worse, instead of becoming familiar with continued exposure, the monsters seem to be even more alien, larger, more threatening. But, as the final lines indicate, there is also Hope. Out of darkness and death emerges optimism, a thin thread of hope that keeps the survivors struggling to survive. With its microcosmic scope, its emphasis on human types as well as on individuals, and its constantly transmuting monsters that take on the force of allegories for psychological states, "The Mist" taps into archetypal patterns of fear and strength, horror and hope. It is one of King's most tightly focused stories, presenting the illusion of vast human experience in an unusually compressed format.

Following this remarkable story are other stories that are narrow in ambition but that taken as a series examine a wide range of horror, from psychological to physical, from the internal to the external: "Here There Be Tygers," "The Monkey," "Cain Rose Up," "Mrs. Todd's Shortcut," and "The Jaunt." Almost all of the central tales deserve to be discussed individually; certainly "The Raft" and "Word Processor of the Gods" are hallmark stories that remain with the readers as potent images. "Beachworld" shows what happens when King immerses himself in a science-fictional universe; "Nona" owes its power to Lovecraftian horror and the directness of Poe. "The Reaper's Image" similarly suggests Poe, while "Survivor Type" hinges on a grisly (and gristly) pun when the unsympathetic and exploitative survivor of a shipwreck realizes that he now has to depend only upon himself. "Uncle Otto's Truck" tells about a similarly irascible exploiter whose demise has all of the mechanical, symmetrical justice of a classical tragedy. The semiautobiographical "Gramma" returns to Lovecraftian horror in the story of a monstrous woman willing herself to come back from the grave—and on a psychic level, at least, to devour her own grandson as she has figuratively devoured her daughter. "Morning Deliveries (Milkman #1)" and "Big Wheels: A Tale of the Laundry Game (Milkman #2)" are strange tales (even in a volume whose stated purpose is to present strangenesses) that depend for their effectiveness more upon a particularly chilling tone than upon complete narratives. Interspersed in the stories are rare but welcome examples of King's poetry: "Paranoid: A Chant" and "For Owen."

In the final story, however, King exceeds all expectations. "The Reach" is nothing less than one of the finest stories King has ever told, regardless of length. First published as "Do the Dead Sing?" and reprinted here under King's original title, this is a ghost story that does not frighten, a story about death that bursts with life, a tale of loss and sorrow that merges seamlessly with joy and restoration. Stella Flanders is the oldest resident of Goat Island. At ninety-five, she has decided to cross the reach (a strip of ocean separating island from mainland) for the first time and visit the mainland. Setting out in a violent snowstorm, she sees the dead of Goat Island coming to greet her. Later, when searchers find her body on a rock on the mainland, they realize that she is wearing her dead husband's hat.

A blunt plot summary is inadequate to the tone, texture, and feeling King gives this tale of life and death and the delicate line that separates them. His landscape functions perfectly on literal and symbolic levels (a technique he will exploit later in *Dolores Claiborne* as well). Island and mainland represent themselves, as well as a wealth of possibilities: life and death, experience and innocence, the physical and the spiritual, the ordinary and the extraordinary. Both as a story and as the capstone to a remarkably consistent collection of strong stories, "The Reach" ties up a number of the themes and motifs scattered throughout the book and makes *Skeleton Crew* King's most effective short-fiction collection to date.

52
Silver Bullet
(1985)

Silver Bullet appeared in October of 1985, in conjunction with the release of Dino de Laurentiis's production of King's screen adaptation of *Cycle of the Werewolf*. This NAL trade paperback of *Silver Bullet* appeared within six months of the trade publication of *Cycle of the Werewolf,* and not only reproduces both the text and the Berni Wrightson illustrations for *Cycle,* but also includes King's screenplay and a foreword by King outlining the development of the story from Christopher Zavisa's initial proposal for a story-calendar based on King's vignettes, to the gradual transformation of vignettes into novella, and the final manifestation of the werewolf tale as a major film (at moments, as during Megan Follow's opening and closing *To Kill a Mockingbird*–style voice-overs, startlingly effective). The value of *Silver Bullet,* then, lies not so much in its presentation of a King text as in its clear demonstration of the ways King develops ideas, the process by which his images shift from verbal to visual presentations, and the relationships between his novels and his screenplays. Since the final film version differs in some particulars from the screenplay published in *Silver Bullet,* the levels of transformation become even more extensive.

Perhaps the most telling indication that King's imagination continued to work with the basic story is implicit in the change of titles. "Cycle of the Werewolf" has two principal effects: first, it concentrates on the yearly cycle, on the unending sequences of light and dark, of good and evil, of life and death, of winter and summer that characterize human existence. And second, it places the werewolf at the center of the tale. In *Cycle,* for example, Marty Coslaw does not even appear until the July segment—halfway through the cycle. Only the werewolf is a consistent, persistent presence.

Silver Bullet as a title introduces important ambiguities. Now the emphasis lies less on the monster than on the means of its death—traditional, conventional, but in the end effective. The sense of cycle disappears; in fact, in the film version, far less is made of the passage of time. And, since Marty's hot-rod wheelchair is named "Silver Bullet" for reasons wholly outside strict werewolf lore, the title simultaneously focuses attention more on Marty. The film begins in summer and ends in fall, substantially truncating the yearly "cycle"; more critically, the film's first key scenes concentrate on Marty Coslaw as hero. The werewolf has been displaced by its destroyer.

While many of the changes might be accounted for pragmatically, given the complications inherent in cutting any story down to film length, many of them equally suggest that King was still working through the implications of his tale. What emerges in *Silver Bullet* is an intriguing glimpse of a mind at work, fashioning, refashioning, and polishing the essentials of a story.

53

The Bachman Books
(1985)

In October 1985, only months after King had formally acknowledged his authorship of the five Richard Bachman novels—*Rage, The Long Walk, Roadwork, The Running Man,* and *Thinner*—New American Library published an omnibus volume containing the first four, which until then had been available only in paperback editions with relatively limited print runs. The pressure simply for reading copies—to say nothing of collector's quality first editions—had become enormous, with asking prices ranging from $5 to well over $100, depending upon which novel, which printing, and what condition the books might be in.

On October 13, 1985, *The Bachman Books* appeared on the trade paperback best-seller list, reaching number-one position the next week and holding that slot for nearly another month, when it was joined by the hardcover edition. The extent of King's enormous popularity became increasingly apparent during the late winter of 1985 and early spring of 1986, as the near mania associated with his novels increased. With the first appearance on the best-seller lists of *The Bachman Books,* along with the hardcover *Skeleton Crew* and the paperback *Thinner,* in October 1985, King joined the highly selective ranks of American writers with three titles on the lists simultaneously. Less than a month later, when the paperback edition of *The Talisman* reached best-seller status, he broke his own record by having four titles on the lists.

Then, during the week of November 17, 1985, and November 24, 1985—and once again in January 1986—King made publishing history with *five* titles on the best-seller lists simultaneously: the hardcover *Skeleton Crew* and *Bachman Books;* and the mass-market or paperback editions of *The Talisman* (in the number-one slot for mass market paperbacks during November 1985), *The Bachman Books* (in the number-one slot for trade paper), and *Thinner.*

If nothing else, the publication of *The Bachman Books* demonstrated that a writer of King's stature and popularity would lose little by publishing more than one book a year; his readers were demonstrably willing to buy whenever he could publish . . . skeptical observers also suggested that they would buy *whatever* he chose to publish, his laundry list not excluded.

But more important, *The Bachman Books* made available some of King's earlier writing, notably portions of *Rage* completed when he was in high school, and *The Long Walk,* written during his first year in college. In his introductory essay, "Why I Was Bachman," King provides not only backgrounds to the four novels but also some bits of his own history and development, as well as his assessment of these early works. "Both *The Long Walk* and *Rage,*" he says, "are full of windy psychological preachments (both textual and subtextual), but there's still a lot of story in those novels"—accurate descriptions, in fact, of all four Bachman novels.

But in spite of the preachments, in spite of occasional overwriting, infelicitous word choice, or strained rhythms in the individual novels, *The Bachman Books* provides enlightening reading as it moves rapidly through a period of tremendous growth in King as writer. To be able to read uninterruptedly from *Rage* through *The Running Man* (not in one sitting, perhaps, but at least in one book) is to see King experimenting with genre and form; to see him examining modes of characterization and narrative ranging from mainstream to science fiction, from first person (one of his rare outings in first-person narrative, in fact, along with portions of *Christine*) to omniscient, submerged narrator; to see him develop setting and theme and symbol and style—and to see him engaging in nonhorror writing that illustrates his remarkable adaptability at a time when he was already being stereotyped as merely the King of Horror.

The Bachman Books makes it easier for readers to notice similarities among the four novels, including the straight-line, compressed narratives, characterized by a "countdown" effect as the moments tick by in *Rage,* the miles plod by in *The Long Walk,* the days drift by in *Roadwork,* and the chapter numbers in *The Running Man* run down from "100" to the cataclysm at "0"—an appropriate conclusion not only to the novel but to a collection of novels that all deal with discoveries, endings, conclusions, and ultimate closure.

54
It
(1986)

It is difficult to know where to begin a short assessment of *It*, if only for the simple reason that the novel is one of King's longest and most complex. At 1,138 pages, exceeded only marginally by the hardcover edition of the unexpurgated *The Stand*, *It* is an immense undertaking to read . . . and was, by King's own admission, an immense undertaking to write. In a letter discussing the novel's composition, he remarked that if he had learned one thing from the experience it would be never again to attempt to write a novel the manuscript for which was larger than his own head.

But beyond sheer length (always a sticking point for mainstream, establishment readers), *It* presents reviewers and critics with a complication of plot beyond anything King had yet attempted or has attempted to date. Interweaving seven characters at two critical junctures in their lives twenty-seven years apart, moving back and forth from childhood to adulthood for each narrator, controlling the pace at which each remembers key elements of the childhood experience and can relate them to what happens to the fellowship as adults, with frequent forays into earlier, deadly twenty-seven-year cycles that have haunted Derry, Maine, throughout its history—all of this is enough to keep writer and reader constantly at attention. Adding the typographical convention of shifting from italics to roman typeface to indicate a parallel shift from narrator as child to narrator as adult helps control the temporal sequences, but even so, *It* requires intense concentration as it spins its sometimes perplexing tale of a Lovecraftian Great Old One–style monster that emerges periodically to glut itself on the physical and psychic suffering of Derry's children.

To be fair, however, both the length and the complexity are justified by what King is attempting in *It*. He has frequently referred to the novel as an act of closure, as the summation of all of his preceding children-under-threat novels. This story would, he notes, resolve the continuing themes present in most of his early novels and stories: explorations of childhood and emerging maturity, as in "The Raft" and "The Body"; analyses of the difficult boundaries between adolescence and adulthood, as in *Rage, The Long Walk,* "Here There Be Tygers," and others; the sometimes life-threatening relationships between parents and children, as in *Carrie, The Shining, Cujo, Christine,* and *Pet Sematary;* and the utter "reality" of children's beliefs in monsters, as in *'Salem's Lot* and *Cycle of the Werewolf.* The importance of nearly forgotten incidents in childhood suggested in *The Dead Zone* (and repeated in *The Dark Half*) here becomes a central structural element. And the overriding theme of the sacrificial child implicit but largely unresolved in *Carrie, Rage, The Long Walk, The Shining, Firestarter, Cujo, Christine, The Dark Tower: The Gunslinger, Pet Sematary, The Eyes of the Dragon,* and *The Talisman* is here closed—these children are allowed to grow into adulthood, and they do so willingly. In ways not possible in earlier stories, their sacrifices are validated by their subsequent actions twenty-seven years later, when they save not only their own lives (or most of them, at least) but succeeding generations of Derry's children. After all, the deaths of Carrie White and Tad Trenton or Gage Creed have no positive consequences commensurate with the grueling pain they cause; the death of Eddie Kaspbrak, on the contrary, completes a choice he made as a child and has confirmed as an adult, and consequently gives a mythic resonance to the final pages of *It.* In King's own words, his eight years of effort in writing *It* climaxes in a "final summing up of everything I've tried to say in the last twelve years on the two central subjects of my fiction: monsters and children."

That King also intends *It* as a virtual encyclopedia of horror is equally implicit in the novel. Almost every variation on the monster is present at one level or another, if not physically as one of It's many manifestations, then imagistically in the form of metaphor or simile, or verbally as King embeds the language of horror into his text. As key figures in the story, we become reacquainted with the werewolf, the Mummy, the walking dead, ghosts, things that (quite literally) go bump in the night (and in the drains and sewers), Rodan-monsters, the crawling eye, gigantic beasties, haunted places and haunted people, *glamours* and shape-shifters, the unnamed creatures that haunt dark cellars and abandoned houses, and equally unnamed things that laugh as their teeth shred human flesh. The fact that all of these monsters are one monster that frequently presents itself initially as a clown, conventionally a figure at the the furthest remove from horror, only adds to It's ultimate effectiveness.

Most of the monsters in *It* are not King's original creations. Among the authors *It* evokes are masters of horror and terror: Shirley Jackson, H. P. Lovecraft, Poe, H. G. Wells, Joseph Brennan, and others. And where King does not draw on literary monsters, he falls back on cinematic ones: *I was a Teenage Werewolf, The Crawling Eye, An American Werewolf in London.*

Acknowledging his own status as a master within the genre, King also alludes to his own works. Settings as diverse as Hemingford Home, Nebraska,

Los Angeles, New York, Atlanta, and London are sufficient to evoke *The Stand, Firestarter,* and *The Talisman.* In a key episode, we are reintroduced to Dick Hallorann from *The Shining;* later, when another character meets a ghost, we are not surprised that the ghost drives a red and white Plymouth Fury.

In addition, *It* touches on King's own life in ways already familiar from "The Woman in the Room," "Gramma," and elsewhere. King is roughly the same age as his characters—ten or eleven in 1958, thirty-seven or thirty-eight in 1985. One minor character, Eddie King, resembles King physically: bearded, wearing bottle-bottom glasses. Derry is based on King's childhood home of Stratford, Connecticut, and many of the settings and events recall his own childhood. (Parenthetically, it is fascinating to return to Derry in *Insomnia,* to see an older Mike Hanlon still ensconced in the city library, to hear about the new city hall designed by world-famous architect Ben Hanscom, and to revisit the scenes of the devastating spring floods of 1985 when much of the city collapsed into the sewers beneath the streets. Since *Insomnia* links to the *Dark Tower* novels, and since Castle Rock burned in *Needful Things,* perhaps King has even more excitement in store for Derry.)

All of this is to say that *It* does in fact climax a stage in King's development as a novelist. For the first time, he successfully and completely combines children and adults, innocence and experience, naive energy and studied maturity. His monster is as multifaceted as the fears that face all children *and* all adults. It may be defeated in one form, but returns in another. Some monsters are non-human, the stuff of myths and legends and stories told at midnight. Others, and often the most dangerous, bear the guises of other children whose disturbed impulses lead to viciousness and violence, especially against the loners, the outsiders—the losers. Or they may appear as fathers of preadolescent girls who "worry a lot" about their daughters. Or as mothers of frail young boys, whose sole purpose in life seems to be to keep those sons frail and dependent. Or otherwise goodhearted parents whose grief over the loss of one son almost causes them to lose another. Repeatedly, *It* moves from one level of fear and horror to another, from the physical to the psychological, from the material to the spiritual, from the external to the emotional.

Throughout all of this complex maneuvering, however, King does not lose sight of his primary objective: storytelling. Complicated as *It* becomes, each of its parts is involving, drawing readers ever deeper into King's imagined world. Small episodes merge to create larger movements of characters and events. Past memories link with present events to create tapestries of understanding. The children who fought and almost defeated a faceless monster deep in the sewers beneath Derry in 1958—and who are inextricably linked during that experience by their initiation into adult sexuality (one of the few times in a King story when teenage sex does not lead inevitably to death)—grow up to be adults, almost without exception capable and willing to risk all a second time to complete what they hoped was finished twenty-seven years before. The fact that all the adults enter the story childless is significant, since only by retracing the paths of their own childhood, and remaking the decisions that brought them to where they are, can they take the final steps into adulthood and become parents themselves.

Monsters—both symbolic and real—have been met and, finally, convincingly, defeated.

55
Misery
(1987)

This is the book that made the phrase "I'm your number-one fan" resonate with horror. It is also the first in a series of post-*It* stories in which King explores the perils of being a writer: *The Tommyknockers, The Dark Half,* and "Secret Window, Secret Garden." The later stories move increasingly inward, to look at creativity and its impact on the psyche of the writer. In *The Tommyknockers,* Jim Gardener is as much destroyed by the demons of alcoholism and insecurity as Bobbi Anderson is destroyed by aliens from outer space. In *The Dark Half,* a pseudonym returns from the grave and demands that an author resume their collaboration. In "Secret Window, Secret Garden," a writer is destroyed by his own vividly drawn character.

But in *Misery,* the initial threat seems external. Paul Sheldon is first saved, then imprisoned and drugged, and finally terrorized by his "number-one fan," a woman who, in spite of her patent insanity, wants nothing more than to read one more novel about Misery Chastain (the fact that she may bind the only existing manuscript copy with human skin—Paul's—is only one evidence of her obsession).

After having decided to break with his own best-selling genre fiction and tackle something more "meaningful," more "relevant," Sheldon is injured in an accident and rescued by a nurse living alone in the mountains. At first she is solicitous, then flattering, and finally—after she has read the draft of Sheldon's new novel—furious. And a furious Annie Wilkes is not someone to trifle with. She forces him to burn the manuscript and then to resurrect Misery, and if his story does not correspond perfectly to the world Annie Wilkes expects when she enters a Misery Chastain novel, well, she has quite effective ways of making her displeasure known.

As the surface relationship and underlying codependency of these two characters intensify, the novel takes on an eerily claustrophobic atmosphere. Most of the story is set in Sheldon's bedroom; yet at the same time, his imagination becomes increasingly freed, largely due to Annie Wilkes's demands as reader. He goes along with her at first; his motive is simple survival. But as the new novel takes shape, as he revises and reimagines it, it takes on a power and a purpose of its own, overshadowing at times Sheldon's own precarious circumstances. As *Misery* progresses, Sheldon's story vies for space with Sheldon's *story,* until at the end whole pages are taken up with the continuing soap opera of Misery Chastain, reproduced in broken courier font to suggest that this is just the way the story looks as Sheldon types it. When first the "e" key and then other keys give out, the missing letters are painstakingly hand-written into the text.

The effect is almost schizophrenic. Two stories are superimposed, two identities undergo radical alteration, and for a long while, it is hard to tell which of the two stories—his own or Misery's—is more important to Paul Sheldon. With unusual wit, the paperback edition capitalized on this sense of split identity. The first cover illustration is typical King—black background, blood-red title in dripping letters set against King's name in stark white; the figure of a man in a wheelchair, the dull brown walls of his room highlighted by a fragment glimpse of the snow-bright world outside; and looming over all, the shadow of a woman bearing an ax.

When readers opened the first cover, however, they were presented with a second. This one is done in vivid blues and greens, with smoothly elegant white letters spelling out the title *Misery's Return.* The author's name, Paul Sheldon, is subordinated to the title—his persona is less important than his character's. The illustration itself is classic genre romance: ecstatic woman barely covered by diaphanous drapery; exotic background suggesting an untouched tropical paradise; dark-haired, dark-eyed man of mystery and erotic power, his eighteenth-century–style, full-sleeved shirt open to reveal well-muscled shoulder and chest. And the man's face is Stephen King's.

The extended joke presented by the dual covers is more than a publicity stunt, however. It focuses readers' attention on questions of identity that become increasingly important in *Misery.* King, like his avatar Paul Sheldon, has been typed as a genre writer. Like Sheldon, King had reached the stage where the demands of his fans threatened to impinge upon his career (because of the crowds that gathered, he had virtually to stop attending signings and conferences). But unlike Sheldon, King sees himself as more than just a horror writer; he has had the courage again and again to break through the barriers of genre horror and attempt novels that touch upon important issues in contemporary society. The *Dark Tower* series, the technological and social elements of *The Stand,* and more recently the social awareness in *Dolores Claiborne* show King's sure sense of his own identity. Even when readers (and perhaps critics) feel disappointed in a novel, King's comments are invariably that at the time he wrote a particular book, it was a *true* book.

Sheldon, on the other hand, is the creature of his imagination. As Tabitha

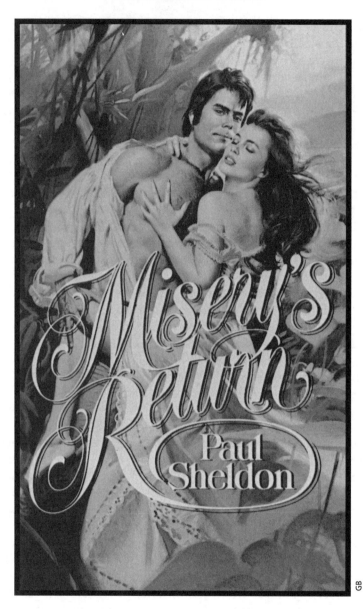

Interior double-cover to the paperback edition of *Misery*, published by
NAL. (This is the fake cover, *Misery's Return* by Paul Sheldon, the protagonist of *Misery*.)

King points out in an article in the August 1987 issue of *Castle Rock: The Stephen King Newsletter,* readers of *Misery* should not mistake creator for creation. King is not Sheldon; but in several important senses, Sheldon *is* Misery, figuratively and literally. And Annie Wilkes is not merely a representative fan. She is instead an amalgam of King's recurrent monstrous women (Mrs. Carmody of "The Mist," the grandmother of "Gramma," etc.). She consumes more than she gives; she destroys what she dislikes; and, more important, she serves as a stimulus for Sheldon's own captivity within himself. True, she forces him to begin "Misery's Return," but after a while, Sheldon himself becomes obsessed with the novel. Wilkes becomes, in Tabitha King's words, "a metaphor for the creative drive itself." Beyond merely a tale of torture and murder, *Misery* is "far more concerned with the way in which a creative person can be tortured by his own powers, addicted to the act of creation, damaged by it. At the end, Paul Sheldon has not freed himself of Annie Wilkes; she holds him captive still, emotionally and creatively."

In light of this reading of the novel, it seems less surprising that *Misery* provided the source for one of the few films to take King's work seriously. Kathy Bates's performance as Annie Wilkes justifiably earned an Academy Award (the first such award for a film adaptation of a King novel). But beyond that, she brought a sense of power to the portrayal that represented perfectly the dark force that Annie Wilkes embodies.

The fact that the novel could be filmed so forcibly, and that the film could be so well received, even by relatively conservative audiences, suggests that King has done in this novel what the novel talks about doing; he has acknowledged his position within a specific genre, and in the process of doing so has transcended the boundaries of that genre. In both novel and film, audiences realize with shudders of horror that the character King has created and Bates has portrayed is a human monster. But in a larger sense, she is terrifyingly *realistic,* in ways that King's earlier vampires or werewolves or shapeshifters cannot be. Monstrous as she is, Annie Wilkes merely reflects similar monsters that *really* exist out there. After reading a novel like *'Salem's Lot* or *The Shining* or *Pet Sematary,* one can look out the window and breathe a sigh of relief that, difficult as the real world might be, King's fictive world is worse. But with *Misery,* audiences inured to the never-ending horrors of the six o'clock news might feel almost the opposite sense: for once, Stephen King has made no attempt to move beyond the darkest possibilities of the world in which we live.

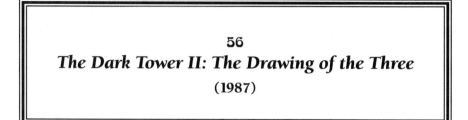

56
The Dark Tower II: The Drawing of the Three
(1987)

The Drawing of the Three begins some seven hours after the concluding action of *The Dark Tower: The Gunslinger*. Alone on a desolate beach, maimed by monstrous lobster-things that emerge from the sea at night, infected and ill and probably dying yet still desperate to find the clues that will lead him to the three who are to accompany him on his quest for the Dark Tower, Roland struggles northward. Almost at the end of his strength, he discovers a mystical doorway on the beach. Opening it, he discovers an entrance into another world and the first of his fated companions, aptly named by the dark man's tarot cards as The Prisoner. This second volume in King's ambitious epic-fantasy-Western-romance-quest series details Roland's interactions with our world in bringing back to his own the three: The Prisoner, The Lady of Shadows, and The Pusher.

Longer than *The Gunslinger, The Drawing of the Three* is also closer in tone, development, plot, characterization, and theme to King's other major works. Much of the action takes place in New York of the 1960s, 1970s, and 1980s as Roland enters those time periods first to rescue, then to recruit (or at least exploit) his companions in his quest. The central portions of *The Drawing of the Three* concentrate on images of physical corruption, psychic fragmentation, and mindless violence. The Prisoner, Eddie Dean, is a drug addict as dependent physically upon heroin as he is emotionally upon his diseased love for his weak and wasted older brother, Henry. He is also a sometimes messenger for one of King's frequent Italian-American mobsters (King provides a squinting reference to *Thinner,* in fact, when Eddie spots a delivery van advertising "Ginelli's Pizza"). In his own way, Eddie is as fatally infected as Roland, and Roland's intervention in Eddie's life offers the promise not only of healing but of honor and nobility through the quest—both attributes distinctly absent in Eddie's home-world New York of the 1980s.

The Lady of Shadows is a perfect schizophrenic living in the shadows of her own life, each personality totally unaware of the other's existence. King appropriately places her in one of America's most schizophrenic historical periods, the beginning of the civil rights movement in the early 1960s, when questions of personal integrity and identity became increasingly problematical. Odetta Holmes and Detta Walker are, like Roland, physically maimed; also like Roland and Eddie, they are desperately ill, but this time the illness is psychological, spiritual, and emotional rather than physical. Each half of Odetta/Detta represents an extreme that must somehow be integrated with its other half in order for a truly healthy personality to emerge.

The Pusher, the last of the three, is simply a horror. Even more gravely disturbed than Odetta/Detta, Jack Mort kills people for the sheer pleasure of it. His victims are arbitrarily selected, his plans carefully laid, and his acts of violence terrifyingly real—and, as Roland discovers when Mort comes within seconds of pushing Jake (so recently dead in *The Gunslinger*) into the flow of traffic, inextricably linked to the quest for the Dark Tower itself. King gives The Pusher one of his few obviously symbolic names; Jack *Mort is* death, and only death can provide Roland with the means of joining Odetta/Detta's fragmented psyche and uniting the gunslinger and his unwilling recruits into a single-minded entity.

Roland's encounters with each of the three, his own complications resulting from the initial attack by the lobstrosities, and his incremental discovery that Eddie and Odetta/Detta are potential gunslingers themselves provide most of the surface action of the novel. Embedded within those episodes, however, are stories of unknown heroism unmasked, of loyalty and love disastrously misplaced, of ineffective families disrupted by secrets and by perverted love (including one of King's easily recognizable monstrous mothers). King demonstrates the tragedy of drug abuse without letting any particular political or social agenda steal the scene. He forces empathy with Odetta Holmes's concern for civil rights in ways that highlight the fundamental premise of full human rights for all but that do not overshadow the story and turn it into mere polemic. And even when the monstrosity that is Jack Mort is destroyed, death is to fulfill a larger purpose—the redemption of Odetta/Detta and the completion of the three.

Although much of the epic sweep of *The Gunslinger* is missing in *The Drawing of the Three,* this volume is clearly necessary to the forward momentum of the saga. It provides the hero with a period of retrenchment and growth that enables Roland to emerge not merely as single-minded Champion of the Dark Tower, but as a true Gunslinger, passing on his skill and knowledge to those who just might have to take over the quest should he fail somewhere along the road ahead. The novel continues King's intricate intertwining of imagery in our world and in Roland's; it is not coincidence that Balazar builds towers of cards, or that his bar is called *The Leaning Tower,* or that Roland saves one of Jack Mort's chosen victims, only to have the boy Jake die a few days later at the hands of the dark man, Walter. By the time readers enter *The Wastelands,* it becomes clear that such intertwinings—figurative and literal exchanges of the stuff worlds are made of—are part of the matrix of the universe . . . and of the quest for the Dark Tower. Longer, more complicated, and more intimately connected to this world than *The Gunslinger, The Drawing of the Three* provides necessary transitions from Roland's world to ours and back again to the landscape of the Dark Tower and *The Wastelands.*

57

The Tommyknockers

(1987)

During the latter half of 1987, King's fans were concerned by rumors that he intended to retire. Certainly the pace King has set over the past two or three years had been strenuous and exhausting. From early 1985 through October 1987 he had published seven books: *Skeleton Crew, Silver Bullet, The Bachman Books, It,* the revised version of *The Eyes of the Dragon, Misery,* and *The Dark Tower II: The Drawing of the Three.* Almost all of them were long, sophisticated narratives; any one of them might justifiably have been considered the task of a year to see through publication. In addition, he had written and published scores of short stories and nonfiction articles ranging from the politics of publication to baseball, along with completing screenplays or teleplays for *Cat's Eye, Silver Bullet, Maximum Overdrive,* "Word Processor of the Gods," "Gramma," and "Sorry, Wrong Number." During that time, he had appeared on the best-seller lists with a record-breaking five titles simultaneously, and more than once settled in with three. By the end of 1987, his titles appeared at #1 (*The Tommyknockers*), #4 (*Misery*), and #10 (*The Eyes of the Dragon*) on the *annual* hardcover best-seller list.

That he might need a break seemed obvious—but *retire?*

In the September 1987 issue of *Castle Rock: The Stephen King Newsletter,* Stephanie Leonard noted that while King was not retiring, he did intend to slow down (he later indicated in "Straight Up Midnight" that the stories in *Four Past Midnight* were substantially written during the two years when he had presumably "retired"). Even so, when the final novel of 1987, *The Tommyknockers,* appeared, it was greeted as a summation of some kind; when the major publication of 1988 proved to be *Nightmares in the Sky,* it seemed to many of his readers that King might indeed have decided to publish less frequently.

The sense of *The Tommyknockers* as an ending was fostered by King's own comments about the book. As early as 1986 he had referred to it in precisely those terms. In a letter in March of that year, he noted that *It* would be his last monster-centered novel. *Misery* (then nearing publication) would have no monsters other than those that exist in the world around us—and for that reason, its horrors would be of an entirely different (but not necessarily lesser) order from those of his earlier novels. In *The Tommyknockers,* he continued, the monsters would have already been dead for millions of years.

When it appeared, *The Tommyknockers* confirmed the fact that King's perennial concern for children had largely been resolved. Both *Misery* and *The Tommyknockers* are about adults, and it is not coincidental that key adults in both novels are writers at crux points in their respective careers. Or that whatever happens in the narrative challenges their perceptions of themselves and their art. But the central point is that they *are* adults.

In addition, *The Tommyknockers* refurbishes the dark fantasy of earlier novels with a science-fictional overlay. King almost immediately thrusts his readers into a world where alien spacecraft might lie hidden under tons of soil . . . but still reach out to disrupt hundreds of lives. Equally rapidly, however, it becomes clear that this fundamentally science-fictional premise merely becomes the vehicle for quintessential horror. Aliens may influence humans, but after a while, it is difficult to tell whether the motivation for horrific acts is *truly* to be blamed on the aliens, or more properly on unacknowledged pools of darkness within us (a theme expanded upon in *Needful Things*). And on a more fundamental level, the novel has more in common with *Cycle of the Werewolf* than with stories about flying saucers and alien technology providing almost unlimited power sources; in *The Tommyknockers,* an unexpected evil simply materializes. As with the abrupt appearance of the werewolf in *Cycle,* there is no reason why Bobbi Anderson should stumble onto an exposed piece of the ship and thus set in motion the destruction of everything she loves.

The Tommyknockers not only seems to shift genres, but also incorporates more self-referential allusions than any other of King's major works. The frequent mention of previous novels and previous characters can be read either as part of the summation he intends *The Tommyknockers* to provide, or as merely self-inflating. Critics who see the novel as overly long, underedited, and careless in its particulars are especially savage about the intrusion of Jack Sawyer from *The Talisman*; Pennywise the Clown from *It,* appropriately enough as a hallucination; David Bright, John Smith, and the dead zone itself from *The Dead Zone;* the Shop from *Firestarter;* and more generalized but nevertheless recognizable allusions to *Silver Bullet, Thinner, Pet Sematary, Cujo, Roadwork,* and *'Salem's Lot,* as well as echoes of several short stories. At one point, in fact, King even includes *himself* as an allusion, when one character refers to stories "all full of make-believe monsters and a bunch of dirty words, like the ones that fellow who lived up in Bangor wrote." If *It* suggested an encyclopedia of horror and monsters, *The Tommyknockers* equally suggests an encyclopedia of Things-King.

The charge of self-indulgence these references elicited, coupled with the sense that the novel was wordy even by the standard set by King's other novels, has given *The Tommyknockers* the general reputation of being among his weakest works. Certainly its bleak ending keeps readers from any sort of deep empathy; by the end, only two major characters remain alive, and they are children who have no understanding of what has gone on. As with *'Salem's Lot,* an entire town (and the area for miles around) has been destroyed. There has been more than a full measure of grief and suffering and death (and a living form of death that is even more horrifying, since it is inflicted not by aliens but by humans in the process of transforming).

In spite of this, it is not as unreservedly dark as *Pet Sematary.* Bobbi Anderson and Jim Gardener learn what Louis Creed refuses to acknowledge: that there are things worse than death. While probably not among King's most effective works, *The Tommyknockers* nevertheless repays the five years King spent working through its themes, tying together disparate strands that had accumulated in over fifteen years of storytelling and end-bracketing one segment of his progress as a writer that began with the appearance of *Carrie.*

58

Nightmares in the Sky: Gargoyles and Grotesques
(photographs by f-stop Fitzgerald; 1988)

Although not strictly a "Stephen King" book in the sense that *Danse Macabre* is, *Nightmares in the Sky* deserves mention here because King's contribution to this photographic coffee-table book is a long (thirty-five-page) introduction that does far more than merely introduce the subject. Instead, King takes the subject matter—gargoyles and grotesques found on public buildings in New York City—and gives it his signature twist, transforming the book from an academic study of a small subdivision of sculpture into an exploration of horror that surrounds millions of people daily.

As part of the essay, King first gives a fairly straightforward account of how the book came to be, including the moment when Marc Glimcher pointed out a window at a stone carving in an archway across the street. King's response— "not a gasp, but close"—signaled a moment of transformation for him, when the carving ceased to be a simple piece of art embedded in an otherwise nondescript building. It became instead an icon for horror.

Later in the essay, King re-creates that moment, compressing and focusing to emphasize its emotional value—transforming it, as it were, to something approaching fictive, horrific intensity:

> He takes me to the window, small, dirty, crisscrossed with old chicken-wire, and points across the street to something which seems to be a monster being born not of a living creature but of a building. Seeing this obscene thing is a shock; what is worse is seeing the people passing to and fro beneath it, intent on either plotting their day's business or planning their evening's pleasure; they pass to and fro and do not look up.
>
> None of them look up.
>
> I hear him say it again: We don't see them . . . but they see us.

King continues with his trademark blend of personal reminiscence and writer's perception. He discusses films such as Cornel Wilde's 1972 made-for-TV release, *Gargoyles,* a "ninety-minute turkey" by any estimation but for

276

King a "genuinely disturbing" film because of the horror implicit in the idea of gargoyles—stone-eyed monsters staring down at passersby, watching and waiting.

And, King asserts, our fears of them stem not simply from their hideous countenances, carved into stone, but from something more fundamental: "That a really close examination will prove our worst nightmares to be reality . . . *That those monstrosities are alive.*"

Alive, as all art is alive.

The essay provides insights not only into King's aesthetics but also into his imagination. It shows him working from objective *things* within the real world—visages cut into dead stone—and transforming them into objects of fear, icons for horror. He connects stonemasonry with mythology, and argues that gargoyles and grotesques ultimately provide the same sort of emotional adjustment as the myth of Medea . . . or as *Oedipus Rex* and *Hamlet.* Seeing them stirs deep emotions of pity and fear; seeing them also purges those powerful emotions, a process Aristotle calls *catharsis:* "It is a painful meeting in which a human being is emotionally overwhelmed by some sort of art—brutalized by it, almost raped (and that is why the most cathartic art is almost always the most primitive)—but who emerges better for that invasion."

Nightmares in the Sky is not one of King's major works, but is an interesting and enlightening one. And thumbing through it, watching the parade of stone faces glaring out from its pages, goes a long way toward justifying King's assertions about art, about human nature, and about fear.

59
My Pretty Pony
(1989)

My Pretty Pony is a distinct oddity—and rarity—among King's books. King's text is little more than short-story length (roughly nine thousand words, and reprinted, in fact, on less than thirty pages in *Nightmares & Dreamscapes* (1993). Yet in market price, publishing hype, and peculiarities of presentation, the original hardcover edition of the story ranks with the asbestos-bound *Firestarter* and the Bible-paper, zipper-closed Scream Press edition of *Skeleton Crew* as suggesting the extremes to which King completists are forced to go.

For some time before its release, rumors had been active of a project involving King and the Whitney Museum of Art. A King story was to be given full museum-quality artistic treatment, with a special binding and lithographic illustrations by Barbara Kruger. The resulting book would have an extremely limited print run of 280 copies, only 150 of which would be for general sale . . . at a list price of $2,200, the highest price ever asked for a King publication. Long before the book was published, however, traders were advertising it in the $2,600–$3,000 range (while, according to the museum officials, there were still unsold copies at the list price). When the volume appeared, the binding turned out to be a stainless-steel and leather jacket with an inset digital clock, a bow to the story's concern with the passage of time. Even so, at only sixty-four pages, and in spite of the unique binding (which one dealer compared to an industrial-strength aluminum kitchen sink), most responses were incredulity at the price.

More to the point, however, was a sense that the edition did not come close to justifying the price tag, even as a work of art. One collector's response was reprinted in *Castle Rock: The Stephen King Newsletter* for September/October 1989:

> I personally found it a most impractical and poorly designed volume, containing the worst excuses for artwork I can think of. While I am an SK completist, I unloaded my copy within three weeks after receiving it. If this woman [illustrator Barbara Kruger] thinks enlarging halftone photographs is art, it is no wonder the rest of the book was so poorly designed.

The limited edition of *My Pretty Pony*, published by the Whitney Museum—$2,200. (Note the *functioning* clock on the cover.)

Photo courtesy of the Public Relations Department, the Whitney Museum of Art, New York, NY

If anything, the museum edition served primarily to spur criticism of King as opening himself to increasing commercialization, particularly in the limited editions.

The subsequent Knopf edition—fifteen thousand copies at $50 each—made the story a little more accessible. An oversize book, complete with slipcase, this edition of *My Pretty Pony* also ran sixty-four pages, but this time the story was bound in vibrant red and white covers. Even so, however, the cost seemed high for what was being offered; and after several months, copies were still occasionally available on bookstore shelves at list price.

Readers interested in "My Pretty Pony" now would be more effectively served by buying a copy of *Nightmares & Dreamscapes,* in hardcover or paper. While the story has a certain charm, and benefits from King's keen eye for character and setting, it is not among his strongest efforts. Not a horror story, it is more a gentle slice-of-life episode that defines the fluid nature of time and life. As part of a longer collection, such as *Nightmares & Dreamscapes,* however, it finds an appropriate niche.

60
The Dark Half
(1989)

Following the publication of *It* (1986), readers were intrigued as to what new directions King might choose to follow, since he had indicated that *It* would be his last exploration of the children-under-threat-from-monsters motif that characterized a large portion of his novels to date. With *Misery* (1987), it became apparent that for the moment at least, King's attention would focus not on children but on writers under threat; and that the monsters in these novels would be internal and external monsters that haunt creative minds. Later in 1987, *The Tommyknockers* examined the inner turmoil of two writers whose lives were shattered by the intrusion of the uncanny and the alien; while the story is largely science fiction, it is not accidental that the introduction of long-dead aliens alters the level of creativity experienced by both Jim Gardener, a poet, and Bobbi Anderson, a novelist. A few months later yet, King's introductory essay in *Nightmares in the Sky* (1988) extrapolated from fiction into reality, defining the purgative, almost healing effects of those creative arts relating to horror.

With *The Dark Half,* he continues his journey through the darkness of creativity, centering his attention on a writer whose pseudonym has recently been publicly unmasked—very like King's experiences in 1985 with "Richard Bachman," to whom *The Dark Half* refers in the introductory Author's Note, an exercise in tongue-in-cheek humor and irony: "I'm indebted to the late Richard Bachman for his help and inspiration. This book could not have been written without him." That writing *The Dark Half* was difficult for King is suggested by Stephanie Leonard's editorial comments in the November 1988 issue of *Castle Rock: The Stephen King Newsletter*: ". . . it is true that Stephen King has written a book by this title. But at this time he has no plans to publish it."

Completed, but no plans to publish it—the situation is reminiscent of the prepublication rumors that surrounded *Pet Sematary,* which King did admit was a painful story to write.

In spite of Leonard's comments, however, the novel appeared within the year, to generally strong responses from readers. In this marginally autobiographically inspired horror tale, King touches on inner fears that are intimately related to the external horrors his readers have come to expect, if not demand. Almost obscured by the creatures (supernatural, science fictional, and other) populating the pages of *It, The Tommyknockers,* and *Misery* is yet another species of "creature" that finally emerges in *The Dark Half* to command full attention.

The Dark Half anatomizes the complexity of creative imagination, merging King's experiences with his own pseudonym-run-wild (as witnessed by the continuing collecting mania for Bachman books) with thoughtful discussions of creativity and responsibility, of artistic integrity, of the destructive and regenerative powers of fiction . . . all without losing the essential sense of *story.*

Thad Beaumont's relationship to "George Stark" begins simply enough, as a matter of convenience. The novels published under Beaumont's name garner him a solid reputation among the literati, as well as ensure him his university teaching position. But "George Stark" and Stark's amoral killer Alexis Machine have paid for Beaumont's lifestyle, while keeping Thad Beaumont's personal and public identities distanced from commercialized, critically disparaged, genre-oriented best-sellers (not coincidentally the kinds of stories King is often assumed to write). Thus Beaumont can keep his unsullied reputation as one of America's promising young writers and National Book Award nominees (but whose books cannot command a reading audience sufficiently large to support him), and still enjoy the immense profits accruing from George Stark's bloody pulp-style thrillers. Now, with Beaumont's secret pseudonym revealed and George Stark officially interred in Castle Rock's Homeland Cemetery, Beaumont decides he can move on with his life.

George Stark, on the other hand, has distinctly different ideas about their writing partnership.

As Stark systematically eliminates everyone involved with revealing Beaumont's pseudonym, Beaumont finds himself under suspicion of murder. After all, *his* finger prints are conspicuous at all of the death scenes, and all of the victims are related to the *People* story about his pseudonym. And even though he can provide airtight alibis for several of the murders, the fact remains that he is the primary suspect. As even he realizes, he is the only *logical* suspect. After Beaumont discovers the truth, however, his situation is only peripherally better. Understandably, he has difficulty convincing the authorities that the true murderer is his *pseudonym* come to life.

As the story progresses, Beaumont and Stark merge more fully into a single identity inhabiting two bodies, one of which is rapidly disintegrating. As Beaumont and Stark face each other across a partners' writing desk, and as the new story they must tell progresses, the physical transformation shifts. Stark's rotting features heal, and Beaumont begins to disintegrate. As his own creation controls him more and more, he loses his sense of identity and self. Imagistically and symbolically, then, *The Dark Half* is more than just a horror story about a walking pseudonym; it becomes an allegory for the dangers of the creative act to selfhood, psychic integrity, and sense of identity.

Since this is a King story, and a horror story, there are alternate levels as well. The prologue focuses on a half-forgotten episode in the young Thad Beaumont's life, at almost precisely the point that he began thinking of himself as a writer. The discovery of the remnants of an embryonic twin, embedded in Thad's brain and threatening to kill him as they begin to grow after years of quiescence, triggers the novel. Then, once *The Dark Half* begins, that same pattern is repeated on a larger, even more threatening scale—a half-ingested remnant of his alter-ego challenges Beaumont's conception of self, identity, and reality. Ultimately, in spite of the horror trappings, however, *The Dark Half* is about art and creativity and their often contradictory relationship with reality.

As allusively suggestive as *The Shining,* more focused than *It,* more outward-oriented than the purposefully claustrophobic *Misery, The Dark Half* transforms the Frankenstein mythos to create a strong novel and an important artistic statement.

61
Four Past Midnight
(1990)

Writing about, not to mention struggling to assess, Stephen King's works sometimes seems an exercise in futility. Negative essays don't alter the sometimes astounding fact of his record-shattering sales, nor do they have any appreciable effect on his legions of dedicated readers and fans. Positive articles, on the other hand, often have almost as little impact, since they frequently serve only to confirm what that same legion of readers already intuit—that King is a master storyteller in whatever style he chooses to couch his words. In effect, the act of evaluating becomes an exercise in personal responses by a single reader to a writer who has long since attained the status of legitimate literary phenomenon.

To talk about a collection of novellas such as *Four Past Midnight*—and the earlier *Different Seasons*—seems even more problematical. As with *Different Seasons,* which shares the overriding time metaphor both in its title and in the arrangement of its stories, each of the four tales in *Four Past Midnight* is virtually novel length, each approaches the art of writing from different directions, each seems to belong to slightly different genres, and ultimately each varies in quality and evocative power.

"The Langoliers," for example, shows the quintessential King at his best, spinning a tale of fantasy and horror. In what readers will recognize as vintage *Twilight Zone* fashion, characters discover that *something* has happened . . . and worse, that something unknown and indefinable is coming, threatening the eventual disintegration of everything (perhaps including time itself). King's images of diminishing solidity, of worn-out matter, and of the encroaching nothingness that is the Langoliers remain long after the story is over.

"Secret Window, Secret Garden," on the other hand, belongs to a sequence of stories that anatomize the writer's imagination and that includes *Misery, The Tommyknockers,* and *The Dark Half.* If Thad Beaumont is haunted by a murderous pseudonym, Morton Rainey is pursued by the specter of plagiarism personified in "his greatest creation—a character so vivid that he actually *did* become real."

"The Library Policeman," like so many of King's finer shorter works, parallels psychic horrors with the deeper, darker horrors of "real life." And, simply put, any horror story that depends for its climax on combining a variation on Heinleinian puppet masters with a wad of Bull's Eye red licorice squashed on railroad tracks deserves to be read.

"The Sun Dog" provides a narrative link between *The Dark Half* and *Needful Things,* King's final Castle Rock story. In spite of the fact that the "sun" in question is a Polaroid camera—a "needful thing," as it were, for young Kevin Delevan—King quickly connects that common, everyday object with an encroaching supernatural horror. In this story, King's penchant for detail at times overwhelms his storytelling, so several pages, for example, are devoted to the relatively insignificant task of buying a roll of film. Similarly, when the Polaroid begins to develop and show something—the sun dog—moving inexorably closer to the barrier separating its world and ours, the story slows almost to a halt. One of the few tales that seem longer than required, it nevertheless prepared readers for what is to come in *Needful Things*.

Responses to the stories will vary with each reader, or course. Arguments as to which of the stories is the "best" will likely depend as much on the readers as on the stories. Of the four, however, "The Sun Dog" seems the weakest, particularly because it illustrates King's occasional need for careful, stringent editing. "Secret Window, Secret Garden," on the other hand, with its probing of diseased psychological states, resonates well with the earlier novels. Although none of the stories carries the weight and focus of "The Body" or the consistency of atmosphere and narrative voice of "Rita Hayworth and Shawshank Redemption" in King's earlier quartet of tales (and arguably among his better performances), *Four Past Midnight* nevertheless demonstrates once again King's unusual versatility and range of vision.

62
The Stand
("complete and uncut" version; 1990)

After years of rumors, promises, and tantalizing hints, in 1990 King's monumental prose epic, *The Stand,* finally appeared as King originally intended it. Its publication climaxed complicated negotiations with Doubleday, which allowed King to restore some four hundred pages of manuscript text excised for the novel's 1978 appearance and to update the setting to 1990. In addition, King has appended an explanation of some of the more substantive changes between the two editions, as well as an account of how and why the book was originally cut.

As King notes, a number of readers, reviewers, and critics attacked the first version for being too long. Confronted by the unexpurgated 1990 *The Stand,* exceeding 1,150 pages in the hardcover edition, such readers must be approaching apoplexy. But there are also those who see *The Stand,* even in its earlier truncated form, as ranking among King's most ambitious, coherent, involving, and ultimately successful novels.

The 1990 restoration substantiates those claims.

Most of the restorations appear in large blocks of narrative. Returning them to the text intensifies the novel, particularly in defining characters' motivations, backgrounds, and personalities. The new opening chapter thrusts us directly into the panic of the superflu as Charlie, Sally, and Baby La Von desperately flee a secret military base. The next chapter (Chapter 1 in the 1978 version) brings us back to familiar grounds as Stu Redman discovers that he and his friends have abruptly been immersed in a real-world horror. Beginning with panic, then moving to Redman's more phlegmatic calm, King alters the movement of the novel, creating an uneven texture designed to keep readers slightly off balance. Thus, something as direct as beginning the story one stage earlier than in the 1978 version introduces intricate variations of pacing and narration that King will exploit further as the story continues.

Other restorations substantively alter the novel's atmosphere. When Frannie Goldsmith confronts her mother in the family's formal parlor, she introduces much earlier than in the 1978 version the central theme of past versus future and the possible sterility of both. Frannie's obsession with keeping her child actually begins here, and thus intensifies her terrors for the child's life in her subsequent dark dreams, and again in the final pages.

The 1990 version also incorporates far more detail concerning the spread and the devastation of the superflu. The alterations range from single-paragraph vignettes, frightening in their simplicity and in King's ability to sketch plausible characters in a minimum of space, to near chapters designed to enrich the novel's portraits of social dissociation. These restorations establish more plausibly the survivors' reactions to the new world the superflu has created. In one instance, a devout Catholic has lost his entire family and can find no peace or purpose in his survival. Being a Catholic, however, he cannot commit suicide; somehow, he must reconcile the two. In a matter of a handful of sentences, King encapsulates the man's suffering, his grief and loss, and his fatal resolution. In another episode, a more extended passage covering several pages, King shows a contingent of black soldiers exorcising their frustrations with the white military hierarchy by shooting randomly chosen victims and televising the entire process. In his introduction not only of racial but of only barely subliminal sexual themes, King creates a segment compelling in its violence and frightening in its implications—for 1978 as well as for 1990. An episode detailing Trashcan's flight westward and his meeting with an embodied madness even deeper and more terrifying than his own—the Kid—highlights Trashcan and his devotion to the Dark Man; simultaneously it again explores the darker possibilities of sexuality, symbolically linking orgasm with death. In the latter two cases, it seems evident why King might have chosen to delete, in spite of his assurances in the introduction that censorship was not the key element in the 1978 cuts.

For critically in terms of *The Stand's* relationship to other works, a new final chapter emphasizes the Dark Man's centrality as theme and image in the entire range of King's fictions, from an early poem through the continuing narratives of *The Dark Tower.* In *The Eyes of the Dragon* and the *Dark Tower* episodes, Randall Flagg emerges as a mystical personification of evil, moving at will through alternate worlds. In the 1978 version, the Dark Man simply disappears when Trashcan arrives in Las Vegas with an armed nuclear bomb. In the 1990 restoration, he disappears, precisely as before. But now, he also reappears, this time on a white beach in a tropical, innocent world (the imagistic connections with the end of *The Dark Tower: The Gunslinger* and the beginning of *The Drawing of the Three* seem significant). His insidious introduction of evil into what appears as an untouched paradise emphasizes King's theme of Eden Lost and makes even more poignant the fragile hopes for life and peace that Stuart and Frannie express in their final dialogue.

Each of the restorations and changes strengthens the novel. King was not satisfied merely to reconstruct the novel as he had originally envisioned it;. he also carefully revised the entire manuscript to bring it up to date for 1990's readers. This often includes changing or adding such details as the names of songs and singing groups, fleeting political and social allusions, and brand-name references more immediately recognizable to later audiences. The fantasy elements intrude into the science-fictional framework much sooner, diminishing the sense that the novel begins as postapocalypse science fiction and then, about halfway through, abruptly introduces the fantastical elements of dreams and portents, prophets and prophecy. The greater emphasis on the superflu and its consequences makes the transition from extrapolation to mysticism more believable. In this respect, it is significant that most of the changes—especially those relating to characterization, setting, backgrounds, and atmosphere—occur early in the book.

The conclusion seems tighter as well. The bomb scene still occurs with about fifty pages to go, but since so much more has happened earlier it seems (subjectively at least) much closer to the end of the novel than in the earlier book. In the 1978 version, the bomb itself seems subordinated to Glenn Bateman's laughter when he finally sees the Dark Man and understands what a *little* thing they have all been afraid of. Stu Redman's long trek home almost displaces the explosion in Las Vegas as a focal point for the conclusion. Now, laughter, bomb, and trek are more balanced, especially against Flagg's appearance in the last chapter. We understand forcibly that one story of good versus evil, light versus dark, has concluded . . . but another has just begun.

The Stand in either of its manifestations is one of King's strongest novels. It is a consistent, readable, teachable response to life in a frighteningly technology-oriented world; it also reminds us that there we may sometimes be forced to find a place for the spiritual and the supernatural within that world. The restored novel confirms King's position as a master storyteller; and at the same time, it provides even readers familiar with all of his works to date increasing insight into the growth and transformation over more than a decade of his abilities, his themes, and his narrative power.

What would happen if a twentieth-century reincarnation of Mark Twain's Mysterious Stranger or his equally discomforting Man That Corrupted Hadleyburg decided to open a modest shop called "Needful Things" in the small New England town of Castle Rock, and began selling dreams? Or at least what *seemed* to be the answers to dreams?

In *Needful Things*, the result is a chain of initially superficial pranks that escalate into an unbroken and irrevocable sequence of interlocking horrors. By design, the actions in *Needful Things* culminate in King's starkest, most powerful confrontation to date of the Dark powers and the White. Along the way King touches upon and brings to final resolution the terrors and secrets revealed in earlier Castle Rock stories—*The Dead Zone, Cujo,* "The Body," *The Dark Half* (with echoes of *Christine, The Talisman,* and *The Tommyknockers*)—and opens his readers' imaginations to a place where love, belief, and magic tricks can fight evil to a draw. And by the end of *Needful Things,* he has also destroyed his most recognizable landscape, the haunted city of Castle Rock.

Needful Things begins slowly with a prologue, "You've Been Here Before," narrated in King's most colloquial, homespun voice, in which he introduces some of his major characters. Through these opening pages we enter the novel as if hearing the voice of an old and trusted uncle rocking on his porch telling us a tale . . . one of King's most effective narrative stances. The main movement of the novel is as carefully paced, with the people of Castle Rock systematically drawn by their curiosity into the new shop, Needful Things. A day before the store officially opens, a boy named Brian Rusk becomes Leland Gaunt's first customer when he buys a rare baseball card for eighty-five cents . . . and the promise to play a trick on someone later. One by one, townspeople drop by and unwittingly fall into the same pattern for buying at Leland Gaunt's emporium. Each finds the answer to what seems his or her heart's deepest desire, and each is allowed to purchase it at an unbelievable bargain . . . and the promise wrung from each that each will provide a small, really quite trivial, service for Gaunt.

Eventually, King lets us see how the interlocking circles of purchases and promises combine to release the worst in the people of Castle Rock. Greed, superstition, selfishness, self-centeredness, cruelty, and madness replace friendship, love, loyalty, marital trust. Of course, since this is a Stephen King novel, some of the apparent victims are less victims of Gaunt's persuasive manner than willing conspirators in their own destruction; several, in fact, are well on the way to damnation by themselves and need only a final push from Gaunt to lose their balance and spiral into madness and rage and death. Others, Gaunt realizes with preternatural acuity, must be handled more carefully; their needs and their secrets must be revealed only incrementally. Small, painless decisions make it easier for him to "sell" the larger, more destructive ones when his purposes call for them. But all of the sequences of purchases and promises progress at Gaunt's pace, timed so that Castle Rock's fears and frustrations and furies can be unleashed in a single, cataclysmic day of mayhem and violence that not only destroys human lives and ultimately the town of Castle Rock itself, but even more critically places in jeopardy the immortal souls of those who have bought dreams from Leland Gaunt.

To accomplish this, King engages in one of his most complex, multifaceted narratives, reminiscent of his achievements in *The Stand, The Tommyknockers,* and *It.* Townspeople are paired in Gaunt's vicious imagination, then others are set to work on that pair, and still others on the second set, until the tensions between the sets of victims reach the explosion point. King's narrative shifts back and forth from set to set, until even those who have never visited Gaunt's shop are enmeshed in the cycle of destruction.

The two focal characters—Sheriff Alan Pangborn and the woman he loves, Polly Chalmers—begin on the periphery of the spiral but are rapidly drawn into it. Polly's "need" is the most external and the most warranted of all the purchasers at Needful Things. She suffers from severely painful, debilitating arthritis in her hands; her only desire is for the pain to be bearable. When Gaunt's amulet somehow makes the pain go away entirely, she is on the edge of regaining physical comfort but of losing something far more precious. Pangborn's "needful thing" is deeper, fundamentally psychological and spiritual rather than physical. In order to proceed with his life, he needs to discover how and why his wife and son died. Neither his desire nor Polly's is itself vicious or evil, but in the skillful hands of Leland Gaunt, even such understandable motives become as distorted and perverted as a lonely housewife's need for surrogate sex with Elvis or a power-grabbing Head Selectman's to feed his hunger for racing, betting, and "borrowing" from the city treasury—even he cannot quite bring himself to admit to embezzling.

Eventually, King strips Castle Rock naked—metaphorically and literally. The fragile bonds of friendship and simple civility disappear under Gaunt's manipulations. Husbands turn against wives; mothers ignore and abandon children; lifelong friends fall prey to jealousy and envy. Hermitlike characters withdraw even further from society, and children put gun barrels in their mouths and pull the triggers. The larger groups whose basic function it is to create a sense of community, already polarized by prejudice and narrow-mindedness before Gaunt arrives, degenerate into violent, bloodthirsty, unthinking mobs. No one remains untouched by Gaunt's evil. In addition, King adroitly augments this maelstrom plot with highly appropriate references to Lovecraftian horrors ("The plains of Leng" and "Yog-sothoth," for example) and literary allusions, often twisted as in King's "Play me/Snort me" parody of *Alice in Wonderland.*

The result is a powerful tale of potential sin and possible redemption—sins past, long thought hidden and safe, as well as sins present; and redemption through trial and suffering and forgiveness. King uses horror, terror, fantasy, and magic to define elemental human states, leading to an unequivocal confrontation of the White against the Black, a motif he has worked with in a number of his novels, including *The Stand* and the *Dark Tower* series. Set against the apocalyptic physical destruction of Castle Rock, King's climax nevertheless relies on something as simple and as commonplace as Stanley Uris's bird book in *It* or the wad of red licorice in "The Library Policeman." At the same time, the moment of confrontation is equally apocalyptic in the true sense of the word—King offers an "uncovering" of fundamental truth that alters his characters' perceptions of themselves, their neighbors, and the world around them.

If *Needful Things* is the last Castle Rock story, it is a powerful one. It details a collision between a potentially good humanity and pure evil. Some characters survive, but no one escapes untouched by that evil, just as King's readers—whether they come to his books for the gross-out or for the force of his narrative or for the inventiveness of his imagination—leave the experience altered in fundamental ways. And in spite of the fact that Leland Gaunt's initials are not "RF," his connections with Randall Flagg and King's other invidious Dark Men are clear and conscious. In its own way, Castle Rock has entered onto the perilous journey that may—or may not—eventually culminate at the Dark Tower.

If *Needful Things,* with its destruction of Castle Rock, represents a capstone to one specific segment of King's career, it is an appropriate one. The novel concludes with a sense of farewell, as readers take leave of a familiar landscape through a forceful, complex, and ultimately uplifting parable of good and evil . . . and the triumph of the good.

64
The Dark Tower III: The Wastelands
(1991)

In 1991 the third of King's promised seven volumes composing the *Dark Tower* series appeared. Even longer than *The Drawing of the Three, The Wastelands* is narratively the most difficult of the novels thus far, as well as the springboard for the imaginative leap that will take King into the territory of the Dark Tower itself. At times abstract and philosophical in dealing with the nature of *Khef, Ka,* and *Ka-tet,* while at the same time requiring that readers juggle multiple pseudohistories, false memories, premonitory dream-visions, and rapidly developing characters, *and* become familiar with the terrain of an alien land, *The Wastelands* propels King's epic into unexplored lands and a good way along the path to the Dark Tower.

Again the action begins shortly after the close of the previous volume; in this case, about three months later. Roland has recovered from the effects of the lobstrosities attack and his subsequent fight against infection and death. His right hand has healed physically, but he is still not used to being left-handed. Eddie Dean has kicked his physical addiction to heroin but is still emotionally addicted to the drug and to a lifetime of idealized memories of his brother. Odetta Holmes/Detta Walker have merged into the fully integrated personality of Susannah Dean, now Eddie's wife. During the three-month respite, each has developed the skills of a gunslinger as far as possible, and now it is time for the three to begin the quest in earnest.

Unfortunately, while Roland has recovered physically, mentally he is in serious difficulty. While in Jack Mort's mind in New York, he saved Jake from being pushed in front of a car; as a result, he is increasingly afflicted with two sets of memories, one consistent with what we know happened in *The Gunslinger* (including Jake's appearance in the way station and eventual death), and another in which Jake does *not* die in New York, hence is not transported to Roland's world, and thus Roland cannot possibly be experiencing the situations he is. Simultaneously, Jake begins having similar dual memories, one set in which he is living a normal life in New York City, another in which he died a month earlier. The first half of *The Wastelands* shifts back and forth between worlds as

Roland and Jake struggle to balance their dual memories—they become almost as divided as Odetta/Detta, and certainly as obsessed with answers as Eddie Dean was with his heroin. Through the mediation of dreams, visions, and signs, however, Jake's world opens to Roland and Roland's opens to Jake's.

In the episodes detailing Jake's struggle to return to Roland's world—the world he increasingly thinks of as "home"—King expands the interplay between worlds, allowing Eddie and Jake to interact through dreams and memories, allowing Jake to "discover" books and phrases and signs (literal and symbolic) that will not only help him to penetrate the boundaries of Roland's world but also help the entire company understand critical elements of their quest.

The worlds finally intersect in one of King's archetypal Bad Places, a physical structure that embodies psychic evil. The Marsten House in *'Salem's Lot,* the Overlook Hotel in *The Shining,* the Black Hotel in *The Talisman,* the house on Niebolt Street in *It,* and the Mansion on Dutch Hill—all provide a nexus for evil, but in this case, the emanations become literalized as the Mansion reveals itself as the Gatekeeper to another dimension. The house does not simply contain evil, it *is* evil, and in one of King's most effective horror passages, Jake must move through the bowels of evil itself to reach the door that will take him to Roland.

Once borne into the other world, Jake takes his place as part of the company. At this point, *The Wastelands* effectively turns its back on contemporary America (although bits and pieces of that world will still be critical in the story) and finally sets out on the first true stage of the quest for the Dark Tower itself. Roland, Jake, Eddie, Susannah, and a native Billy-Bumbler named Oy move across an alien landscape, discovering new wonders and new horrors with almost each step. In traditional epic fashion, each episode accelerates their growth as individuals and as a company. They uncover clues as to the devastating past, the static present, and the dismal future of Roland's world . . . and by implication, of all worlds. In the once-great city of Lud, the company is separated, and again King uses a narrative shift to emphasize the tremendous changes that have occurred in all four of the questers since the tale began. Roland learns to love and to sacrifice to more than just the Tower; Eddie and Susannah learn not simply to put the past behind them but to use past sufferings positively and creatively. Jake learns faith and forgiveness.

While the episodes in Lud are as much action-adventure as anything else resembling bits of postapocalyptic SF films, complete with *Bladerunner*-toned sets in a ruined city afflicted with terminal squabbling between decadent tribes, King never loses the focus of his story. Every episode, every scene teaches about what it means when the world "moves on" and makes more critical the need to reach the Tower and perform whatever act of redemption, restitution, or revivification is necessary to keep this from happening in other worlds.

There are touches of humor as well, especially in the riddle play that takes up much of the final pages. As much like Tolkien's questers as like the Anglo-Saxons of *Beowulf*'s time, King's epic characters are entranced by riddles—by changes rung on reality by the illusions of language. When the most committed riddler turns out to be a sentient Monorail—which is also insane—all of the threads King has been preparing since the beginning of *The Wastelands* come together. The final image in the volume is of Roland and company, enclosed in Blain the Mono's metal body, hurtling over the Wastelands toward the Dark Tower, literally riddling for their very lives.

Here the story breaks off again. The fourth volume, *Wizard and Glass* is promised in King's afterword. It tells dually of "a seduction" and, in traditional epic manner, a recounting of things that have gone on before. In this sense, *The Gunslinger* begins in medias res ("in the middle of things"), with Roland suddenly appearing in the midst of his quest; *The Wastelands* moves the story forward, with only occasional glimpses backward into Roland's history. But Roland has promised Eddie that he will tell that story—only once, and when the time is right—but that he *will* tell it. *Wizard and Glass*, then, promises the central explication of conventional epic, and an appropriate direction to take at this point in the *Dark Tower* series.

One early review of *Gerald's Game* seemed to utter a sigh of relief as it said, in effect, that at last Stephen King has written the novel we all knew he could write as soon as he gave up his ridiculous obsession with monsters and the super-natural, and turned his talents to something realistic and socially relevant.

This comment recalled another reviewer's assessment that Richard Bachman's *Thinner* was the kind of novel that Stephen King would write . . . if Stephen King *could* write.

Both reviewers, it seems, were writing from positions of ignorance.

The second was, of course, mistaken in his assumption that *Thinner* was not by Stephen King.

And the first was mistaken in his assumption that everything King had written up to *Gerald's Game* was ephemeral horror.

Such an assumption, of course, consciously ignores a strong thread of real-istic, socially aware fiction that began even before King's first "horror" novels appeared. *Rage,* written in large part while King was in high school, begins a series of novels that include three other Bachman novels, *The Long Walk, The Running Man,* and *Roadwork,* as well as novels published under King's own name, most obviously *Misery.* The horror overlays in *Cujo* are more distractive than effective; and while *The Stand* does have elements of the supernatural, episodes centering on Mother Abagail do not necessarily include monsters.

In that sense, then, the review of *Gerald's Game* admires the novel for the wrong reasons. It is not that the story eschews horror, but that for the first time Stephen King subordinates his story to a specific political or social agenda. Rather than making *Gerald's Game* King's first true masterpiece, however, the decision to do so undercuts his primary strength—that of storyteller who along the way reveals important truths about human nature and social con-ventions.

The plot of *Gerald's Game* is straightforward, almost blunt. Gerald Burlingame enjoys (if not requires) kinky sex games, including bondage. When he handcuffs his wife, Jessie, to the headboard of their bed in an isolated cabin near an equally isolated lake (compare this set-up with "The Raft," a stronger story in spite of its narrower focus), she decides in a moment of feminist consciousness that she doesn't have to put up with such humiliation any longer. She demands to be released; Gerald assumes that she is responding to the game and comes on anyway; she kicks him in two strategic places; and Gerald dies of a heart attack.

Leaving Jessie handcuffed to the bed.

For almost 250 pages, she tries to get loose. Then for the remaining eighty pages, she tries to adjust to post-Gerald life.

Along the way, King struggles to transform a static situation into drama by allowing readers to overhear several voices—several partial identities—that co-exist in Jessie's mind. One is a prim and proper housekeeper, duly trained in societal responsibility; another is an energetic rebel, undercutting all of Jessie's assumptions about herself and her life. Yet another demands that Jessie remember what happened to her on the day of the eclipse in 1963—and, it turns out, this voice is one of the most important, since the events of that day, the novel repeats insistently, have inevitably brought Jessie to her current dilemma.

The difficulty with *Gerald's Game* is that it is too bluntly programmatic. King has a message to deliver about women and men and abuse of one by the other, and he delivers it directly. This is certainly his privilege; but readers have already intuited his message from passages in earlier novels that communicated it more memorably. It seems clear in *Carrie,* for example, that Margaret White behaves as she does because of various forms of abuse inflicted by her father and her husband. Barton Dawes's wife in *Roadwork* blossoms in unexpected ways as soon as the burden of her marriage is lifted. Abagail Freemantle suffered under a heavier load of discimination and abuse than Jessie Burlingame could ever imagine, yet her inner strength was sufficient to overcome the past and allow her to focus on the present and the future; she is strong because of herself, not because of her relationship to anyone else.

The difference was, however, that those "messages" were integral to a story being told. In *Gerald's Game* the story seems secondary to the message. The fact that there is not a single strong male character in the novel only adds to the feeling that King is not playing fair. When he goes out of his way to connect *Gerald's Game* with *Dolores Claiborne* through an apparently supernatural event (which, according to the first reviewer, this novel is not supposed to fall back on), the weaknesses of the first novel become even more apparent. *Dolores Claiborne* bears a similar message; but here, King's narrator is a strong-willed woman who refuses to bend or to be bent. Her story engages the readers' attention and imagination in ways that Jessie Burlingame's cannot. And in spite of King's attempts to present them as companion pieces, the two novels work in radically different directions, to radically different ends.

In the end, *Gerald's Game* seems more single-dimensional that one expects from King. Everything is neatly explained away, including Jessie's hallucinatory awareness that someone has been in the house with her (also initially described monsters and the supernatural). There seems little growth, little change. In important ways, she is still as handcuffed to herself and her past as she was handcuffed to her bed for most of the story.

66
Dolores Claiborne
(1993)

Of all King's recent novels, perhaps none so successfully echoes the feel of the "Bachman" King as *Dolores Claiborne*. This remarkable story of an old woman's life, loves, omissions, and sins showcases King's undeniable storytelling powers—not the least because the entire novel consists of a single, unbroken monologue. There are no chapter divisions, no bits of dialogue from other characters to break Dolores's spell. The entire story is told from a single point of view, through the mouth of Dolores Claiborne, with only momentary pauses as she listens to her questioners (although readers are never allowed to do so) and responds. The result is a work that depends for its overriding success upon an undeviating sense of character . . . and upon a character interesting enough to repay the readers' investment of time.

Dolores Claiborne is that interesting. Her story is a double tale of life and death, each portion twining about the other, each intensifying the other, and each ultimately explaining the other. In order to avoid being arrested for the murder of Vera Donovan, her employer of more than thirty years, Dolores presents herself to the chief of police and over the course of one long evening confesses to her one *true* murder, that of her husband over twenty years before. As Dolores explains herself, her life, and her motivations, readers are invited into the mind and imagination of a strong, sturdy, survival-oriented woman whose experience forced her to endure more than many might have endured.

In telling Dolores's story, King also touches upon issues of feminism, child and spouse abuse, marital relations and realities, and the crushing social restrictions inflicted upon women during the past several decades. To his credit, and to the story's eventual strength, however, these are not the central concerns of the book. Instead, at every point, King focuses on Dolores Claiborne and Vera Donovan, two independent women who make painful decisions, act on those decisions, and then live out long and difficult lives distorted by the consequences of their choices. Instead of asserting, as he did in *Gerald's Game,* King here demonstrates, and the results are a believable, remarkable story.

Told with almost no supernatural overlay, Dolores's history is as taut and gritty as the island that is her home (here one is reminded of King's other pro-totype of the woman strong in the face of life and of death, Stella Flanders in "The Reach"). In one of King's rare excursions into obvious symbolic value in names, *Dolores Claiborne* suggests what the novel declares is the foundation of human experience: *Dolores* is an English proper-name variant of the Latin *dolor,* "to suffer"; and *Claiborne* reminds readers that they, like Dolores, are "born from clay"—or in the case of women, are also fated to "bear the clay" of new lives. The impact of parents on children and of children on parents controls the novel. Everything Dolores did, she says, was done "for love . . . the love a natural mother feels for her children. That's the strongest love there is in the world, and it's the deadliest. There's no birth on earth like a mother frightened for her kids." The paradoxical strength and ferocity of mother's love are developed through the parallel stories of Dolores and Joe St. George and their three children; of the implied story of Vera and Michael Donovan and their two doomed children; and finally of Dolores and Vera, welded together in old age in an inverted mother-child relationship that both diminishes and supports each of them and finally threatens the secret Dolores has harbored for decades.

The greatest weakness of the novel, ironically, is the intrusion of something approaching the supernatural. For the paperback edition, King wrote a fore-word explicitly linking *Dolores Claiborne* with the previous novel, *Gerald's Game.* Key actions in both occur during a total eclipse of the sun on the late afternoon of July 29, 1963; both novels include maps showing Dark Score Lake and Little Tall Island as Maine's western and eastern extremes in the path of the eclipse; and both novels allude to their characters' peripheral awareness of each other. To the extent that Dolores Claiborne and Jessie Mahout Burlingame live lives that are "eclipsed," that they live in the shadow of actions and decisions long buried in the past, the connections are valid. But the interconnections be-tween the two novels suggest that King sees them as in some way bracketing the same experience, and that the semi-mystical voices and dreams the two women share make their individual plights one. To do so is to underestimate the power of Dolores Claiborne's voice as she speaks up to defend her choices. By the end of her monologue, she is convincing, even without the *Cujo*-like as-sertion of the supernatural or the fantastic.

Like *Rage, Roadwork,* and *Misery,* King very nearly steps completely out of his "horrormeister" persona to present a compelling portrait of a believable char-acter. His story is bolstered by underlying wells of anger and frustration, not consumed by it. And his point comes through clearly and directly in the character and speech of Dolores Claiborne, without any obscuring layers of overt agenda or political correctness.

67

Nightmares & Dreamscapes

(1993)

King's third collection of short stories is arranged much like the first two; after a strong opening piece, the stories are placed more for effect than for strict chronology. Like *Night Shift* (1978) and *Skeleton Crew* (1985), *Nightmares & Dreamscapes* represents a cross-section of King's interests over a dozen years or so. One of the earliest, "Suffer the Little Children," appears third in the collection, even though it had appeared in print over thirteen years before—one of many early stories published in men's magazines such as *Cavalier*. One of the most recent, a nonfiction piece on baseball called "Head Down," appeared in the *New Yorker* in 1990 and suggests that King's reputation has in fact moved in new directions since the days when his primary markets were *Cavalier, Gallery,* and other outlets of that sort.

The opening story, "Dolan's Cadillac," is almost as interesting for its history as for the tale it tells. The story is a Poe pastiche, borrowing plot, touches of characterization, even bits of dialogue from "The Cask of Amontillado." The primary difference is that while Poe's unnamed narrator never explicitly defines the "thousand injuries of Fortunato," King's narrator lets readers know precisely why Dolan must die, and how, and when. While Poe's story becomes a free-form exercise in insane retribution extracted by an insane narrator, King's is set more firmly in reality and its narrator is carefully and coldly sane. Much of its strength comes from the meticulous detail with which Robinson (Robertson in the original version) carries out his revenge. The first version suffered by comparison with Poe's story, perhaps because it was too close to the original. (The story was serialized in issues 2 through 6 of *Castle Rock: The Stephen King Newsletter*.) In 1989, however, as a mark of King's increasing stature, Lord John Press (Northridge, Calif.) released the story as a limited edition of roughly 1,250 copies, in slipcases and signed by King. The edition was relatively costly at $250 for the deluxe and $100 for the limited (although less so by far than the Whitney Museum's $2,200 *My Pretty Pony*), perhaps more so than the story warranted. "Dolan's Cadillac," revised and tightened, nevertheless provides a strong opening for *Nightmares & Dreamscapes*. With none of the trappings of supernatural horror one might expect from King, it places its horror firmly in the real world; the retribution meted out is rough, perhaps, but just.

The second story, "The End of the Whole Mess," suggests *The Stand* as it touches on the disaster that follows humanity's meddling with nature. In this instance, Bobby Fornoy discovers a way to negate the aggressive human impulses that lead to war, violence, and crime—only too late does he realize that his "cure" has wholly unexpected and undesirable side effects. In a time of AIDS and Alzheimer's, this story about a self-generated plague that wipes out humanity seems a bit less far-fetched than it might have even half a dozen years ago.

"Suffer the Little Children" and "It Grows on You" are revisions of earlier stories, the first from 1972, the second from a year later. Again, King has revised and tightened for this appearance, with "It Grow on You" in particular substantially changed. In between these stories of indirection and psychological ambivalence, he has placed two indisputably "monster" stories. The twin vampire tales "Night Flier" and "Popsy" (1988 and 1987, respectively) each appeared in specialized hardcover collections of horror fiction featuring a handful of best-known, and best-selling, writers.

Again, it is a mark of King's increasing stature that he was invited to write for a number of such collections. Several stories collected in this volume first appeared, not in magazines, but in relatively ambitious collections. In 1980, "Crouch End," one of King's more strictly Lovecraftian tales, appeared in *New Tales of the Chthulhu Mythos,* edited by one of the brightest stars in 1980s horror, Ramsey Campbell. The first story in Campbell's anthology, "Crouch End" is unremarkable except as an homage to one of King's most pervasive influences, and as one of his few stories not set in America, and more specifically, in New England.

"Sneakers" and "Dedication" (along with the as yet uncollected "The Reploids") were the opening tales in Douglas E. Winter's *The Skin Trade* (1988, 1990), showcasing stories by King, Dan Simmons, and George R. R. Martin. In the same year Winter's *Prime Evil* opened with "The Night Flier." The next year John Skipp and Craig Specter published a particularly gruesome selection of tales set in the world of George A. Romero's walking dead; King's "Home Delivery," while not the lead-off story, provides a moment of something approaching sanity and normality in the context of cannibalistic zombies. Three years later Jeff Gelb's *Shock Rock* followed up an introduction by Alice Cooper with King's "You Know They Got a Hell of a Band," the longest story in the book and one of the central tales in *Nightmares & Dreamscapes.*

King's stories were not only in demand for horror anthologies, however. In 1987, another pastiche, "The Doctor's Case," appeared in the *New Adventures of Sherlock Holmes,* edited by the indefatigable anthologist Martin H. Greenberg

King signs *Nightmares & Dreamscapes* at a Bangor bookstore.

in conjunction with Carol-Lynn Rössel-Waugh. Immediately following in *Nightmares & Dreamscapes*, King gives us a second mystery pastiche, "Umney's Last Case," which capitalizes on the distinctive tone and atmosphere of the hard-bitten detective novel. A third story, distinctive by its similar treatment and tone, is much older: "The Fifth Quarter" first appeared in *Cavalier* in 1972 under the pen name John Swithen—the only other case of a King pseudonym besides Richard Bachman.

One final story that deserves attention here is "My Pretty Pony." King notes in his comments at the end of *Nightmares & Dreamscapes* that this is a remnant excised from an abortive Bachman novel, and that it was previously published in "an overpriced (and overdesigned, in my humble opinion)" edition by the Whitney Museum, then again in "an overpriced (and overdesigned, in my humble opinion)" edition by Alfred A. Knopf. Its appearance in this collection presents "My Pretty Pony" in a more appropriate format—as one of several interesting King stories that range from outright horror to strict mainstream, from the deadly serious to the comic, from the inexplicable to the logical.

If there is a single flaw in *Nightmares & Dreamscapes,* it would be the lack of distinctive strength in the opening and closing selections. "Dolan's Cadillac" is a worthwhile story, but not on the same level, among King's works, as *Skeleton Crew*'s "The Mist." And putting "Head Down," a prose piece on baseball, in the final position only underscores the lack of a powerhouse conclusion such as that provided by "The Woman in the Room" in *Night Shift* and to an even greater extent by "The Reach" in *Skeleton Crew.*

On the whole, *Nightmares & Dreamscapes* offers King's readers a great deal to sample and enjoy; in the last analysis, however, is does not meet, let alone exceed, the remarkable strength of *Skeleton Crew.*

68
Insomnia
(1994)

Insomnia is probably not to every reader's taste. A long novel that threatens an odd kind of stasis in its opening chapters, it has as its hero an old man of seventy, recently widowed and increasingly suffering from an unnerving kind of insomnia. It is not that he can't *get* to sleep but that he awakens a minute or so earlier every day until eventually he is living on two or three hours of sleep, constantly fatigued, almost hoping for death. This is a relatively long process, and King allows the novel to move slowly over the course of months, detailing the consequences of the affliction on Ralph Roberts's life and on his relationship with old friends and neighbors—some of whom simultaneously begin acting strangely, even threateningly.

King's pacing is unlike the movement readers have come to expect in his more action-oriented novels, more nearly suggesting the drugged semidream state of Paul Sheldon in *Misery,* the unbroken monologue of *Dolores Claiborne,* but lacking the distinctive character's narrative voice. Instead, readers are immersed in a world of sleeplessness, of debilitating fatigue, and of heightened disconnection with events in Derry, Maine—a place readers already know from *It* and have learned to distrust. As Roberts's insomnia cuts further and further into his energies, Derry itself is caught up in a spiral of controversy centering on a clinic that provides medical services and counseling for battered women . . . and abortions. A leading abortion-rights activist, Susan Day, is scheduled to speak in the Derry Civic Center (designed by local-boy-made-good Ben Hanscom to replace the original structure destroyed in the devastating spring floods of 1985). As happened in Castle Rock when the Catholics decided to hold a bingo night in *Needful Things,* Day's plans divide the town, with confrontation escalating to violence and beyond.

Through it all Ralph Roberts finds himself waking earlier and earlier each day.

Only when he begins seeing little men that remind him of nothing so much as Whitley Strieber's aliens in *Communion,* or the aliens featured in newspapers such as the *National Enquirer,* does he begin to fear for his sanity . . . and soon for his life.

To this stage, King has allowed his narrative to move slowly, creating intricate word pictures of key characters, allowing them in turn to speak directly about social, political, and philosophical issues, including both prochoice and prolife arguments, analyses of wife and child abuse, and discussions of appropriate modes of political activism and protest. Unlike *Gerald's Game,* however, *Insomnia* balances information with narration, embedding both sides of key arguments into the movement of the story itself. If King has been struggling since *It* to find an appropriate alternative focus for his stories to the children-under-threat-from-monsters motif prevalent in almost every novel from *Carrie* through *It,* he may have found a structural paradigm in *Insomnia.* His primary characters are adults, their concerns are adult concerns (and none of them is a novelist obsessed with pseudonyms or number-one fans or a drying wellspring of creativity), and yet they still allow King to do what he does best—to tell stories, and in the process to analyze and assess what it means to live in this society and this time. To paraphrase the Latin poet Horace, he both entertains *and* instructs—key elements in what is essentially a highly moral form of literature.

Then, at the point when readers may begin to complain that King's characters are interesting, that their concerns are valid, and that their actions are appropriate, but that they don't seem to be going anywhere, King suddenly expands the horizons of the novel.

Ralph Roberts discovers that he is not the only one who sees mysteriously energizing auras and little bald men carrying odd implements, or even the only one who can look on someone's aura and abruptly know everything there is to know about that person, including whether he or she (or it, in the case of Rosalie the dog) is about to die. With that discovery comes the concomitant discovery that he is *not* insane, that his insomnia has a larger purpose beyond anything he can truly comprehend, and that he and his newfound love Lois Chasse have been involved in actions on the cosmic scale approached in *It* and *The Talisman.* Confronting one of the little "docs" (who willingly go by the names Ralph suggests for them—Lachesis, Clotho, and Atropos, after the Greek Fates that spin, measure, and cut the thread of life), Roberts demands an explanation for their intrusion into human affairs.

He gets one.

There are, Clotho explains, four constants in existence: Life, Death, the Purpose, and the Random. Ralph and Lois have been recruited on the side of the Purpose against the Random. When one of the docs attempts to explain their relationship to humanity through the metaphor of a skyscraper, in which humans occupy only the first two floors, unaware of level after level above, Roberts does not so much hear as *see,* and what he sees is . . . the DARK

TOWER, described in precisely the terms the boy Jake dreams it in *The Wastelands*.

This moment of true apocalypse is as startling as the equivalent revelation of the vampire in *'Salem's Lot*. After almost three hundred pages of text—interesting and engaging in its own way but not as focused as one usually finds in King—*Insomnia* asserts itself in one short paragraph as a linchpin in King's quest-vision, linking itself with *The Stand, The Talisman, The Eyes of the Dragon,* and the *Dark Tower* novels as explorations of that mystic nexus of all existence whose own existence is threatened by a single action about to take place in Derry, Maine.

From this point the pace intensifies. Ralph Roberts and Lois Chasse become warriors of their own sort, whose task is as critical in the long run to the survival of the Tower as that of Roland of Gilead himself (although none of them fully understands how, nor do King's readers . . . yet). Their complacent, largely self-involved, mundane world is shattered as they open themselves to new perceptions, new understanding, new levels of *being*. And as so often happens in high fantasy, in epic, in heroic quests and sagas, they find within themselves wells of strength and power they could never have imagined—sufficient, in fact, to forestall the destructive forces of the Crimson King himself.

Insomnia is slow-paced at the beginning; but the pacing has the stolidity, solemnity, and inevitability of something approaching epic, appropriate to the incremental power of revelation and truth. As King makes connection after connection in the second half of this novel to other works and other worlds, the story takes its place as one of King's most ambitious works, attempting with *It, The Talisman,* and the *Dark Tower* series to penetrate the underpinnings of reality itself. And with an adroitness that demonstrates the intensity of his vision, King links the novel's earlier (mundane and therefore transitory) social and political concerns with the heightened sense of a cosmic game between the unseen forces of Light and Dark—between the Purpose and the Random. Susan Day's appearance at the Civic Center, as well as the disruption it causes in thousands of lives, also becomes the focus for this episode in the struggle for the Dark Tower and the scene of a key victory for the Purpose in the war that may have no end.

But as with other such victories, this one is not complete. The Random is forestalled; thousands of lives are saved. But scores are also lost. And Ralph Roberts himself—very like Frodo the Nine-Fingered (whose story provides an important source text for *Insomnia*)—enjoys his victory only for a short while. Then like Frodo, and in a scene that echoes the enormous sense of loss and of paradoxical rightness that accompanies Frodo's passing to the Grey Havens, Ralph Roberts too must pass. He must act more on intuition than on memory, since he and Lois (like the child-adults who once saved Derry's children from the monster in the sewers) have forgotten much of what they had done to save not only Derry but larger levels of existence beyond their own.

In his final sacrifice, and in its final moments—and Ralph Roberts's—*Insomnia* attains a dignity, grace, and even grandeur that place Death firmly in the pantheon of immutable cosmic forces, along with Life, the Random, and the Purpose.

The master of the macabre hams it up for his appearance in an American Express television ad. "Do you know me?" he asks. "I carry the American Express card."

Copyright Continuation

Acknowledgments

I am especially grateful to Dr. Michael R. Collings, who on very short notice reread King's books and wrote a unified book-by-book examination of the King canon, from *Carrie* to *Insomnia*. His insights shed new light on well-trod territory.

Similarly, I am grateful to my many friends at Andrews and McMeel who, for the second time on this book, rolled up their shirtsleeves and put their shoulders to the stone to bring this project to fruition. *This* is the book I had hoped to write back in 1989 when the first edition of *The Stephen King Companion* was published. *This* book—visually, textually—is to my mind a leap forward, a new and improved version of the original. And for that I especially want to thank: Donna Martin, my book editor, who helped shaped the manuscript into a book; her majordomo, JuJu Johnson, who kept the lines of communication open; and Katie Mace, who shepherded this book through the editorial process.

I am also grateful to the following people who lent their invaluable assistance: at the *Bangor Daily News,* Charles Campo and Jill Marston, for sending photos and faxes; Barry R. Levin, for bibliographic assistance; Clive Barker and David Lowell for contributing to the project; Stuart Tinker at Betts Bookstore; Lori Zuccaro, Charles Fried, and David Hinchberger for much needed information and updates; and Rusty and Maria Wornom, Stephen Spignesi, and Colleen Doran for much needed, and always welcomed, moral support.

And, as always, I am indebted to my wife, Mary, who provided suggestions and support in equal measure.

Stephen King writing a book at his office in his home.

Q: How would you like to be remembered?

A: As a good storyteller.

—Stephen King, in interview for *Cosmopolitan* magazine

King attends a Little League ballgame in Maine.